FACES of Salsa

A SPOKEN HISTORY OF THE MUSIC

LEONARDO PADURA FUENTES

Translated by Stephen J. Clark

Smithsonian Books • Washington and London

Photographs of Mario Bauzá, Willie Colón, Johnny Ventura, Johnny Pacheco, Rubén Blades, Cachao, Wilfrido Vargas, and Papo Lucca courtesy Izzy Sanabria's Latin NY Magazine archives (SalsaMagazine.com).

Photographs of Juan Luis Guerra and Nelson Rodríguez courtesy Leonardo Padura Fuentes.

Photographs of Juan Formell and Adalberto Álvarez courtesy Ange G. Baldrich.

Photograph of Radamés Giro courtesy Radamés Giro.

Copy editor: Gregory McNamee
Production editor: Robert A. Poarch
Designer: Janice Wheeler

Library of Congress Cataloging-in-Publication Data

Padura, Leonardo.
    [Rostros de la salsa. English]
    Faces of salsa : a spoken history of the music / Leonardo Padura Fuentes ; translated by Stephen J. Clark.
       p.   cm.
    ISBN 1-58834-080-5 (alk. paper)
    1. Salsa musicians—Interviews. 2. Salsa (Music)—History and criticism.
I. Clark, Stephen John, 1965– trl II. Title.
    ML398.P2613 2003
    781.64—dc21   2003041539

British Library Cataloguing-in-Publication Data is available

Manufactured in the United States of America
09 08 07 06 05 04 03 5 4 3 2 1

⊗ The paper used in this publication meets the minimum requirements of the American National Standard for Information Sciences—Permanence of Paper for Printed Library Materials ANSI Z39.48-1984.

This project has been supported by federal funds for Latino programming, administered by the Smithsonian Center for Latino Initiatives.

Yo soy el cantante porque lo mío es cantar
Y el público paga para poderme escuchar...
Yo soy el cantante muy popular dondequiera
Pero cuando el show se acaba soy otro humano cualquiera
Y sigo mi vida con risas y penas,
Con ratos amargos y con cosas buenas
Yo soy el cantante y mi negocio es cantar
Y a los que me siguen mi canción les voy a brindar...
  —El Cantante

I'm the singer because singing is my thing
And all the people pay just to hear me sing . . .
I'm a popular singer wherever I go
But I'm just another guy at the end of the show
My life goes on with laughter and tears,
With bitter times and joys throughout the years
I'm the singer and singing's what I do
And to those who follow me I offer them my tune . . .
  —The Singer

Lyrics: Rubén Blades
Arrangement: Willie Colón
Performed by: Héctor Lavoe

Contents

Among Friends . . .

I would like to express my gratitude to the following individuals for the invaluable assistance they provided in the preparation of this book. First of all, to the thirteen interviewees who gave generously of their time and intelligence during our conversations. Likewise, to good friends already familiar with this story, such as the Cuban musicologist Helio Orovio; the New York "salsaologist" Professor Vernon W. Boggs; and the maestros César Miguel Rondón and Domingo Álvarez, friends whose hands I have yet to shake. Also, of course, to my Mexican friends Paco Ignacio Taibo II and, especially, Paloma Saénz, without whom I would not have been able to conduct several of these interviews. To Freddy Ginebra and Thimo Pimentel, who assumed as a matter of Dominican honor the need to interview Juan Luis Guerra. To my many friends who recorded salsa music, most of all to *el gordo* Peyi. To my "New York guide," my old friend Pancho Miguens. To my colleague Scott Mahler, thanks to whose persistence this North American edition exists. And, of course, and as always, to you, Lucía.

Prologue

The *Salsero:* Music and Conscience

Legend has it that one night in the 1950s Benny Moré arrived at the Alí Bar after a long day of performing on the radio and later playing at a dance along with his famous Banda Gigante. The Alí Bar, a run-down, third-rate nightclub on the outskirts of Havana, owed all its notoriety to the concerts given there by Benny Moré, who had cut his professional teeth as a unique vocalist in that very establishment. Benny lived near the old cabaret; he had built himself a house in a rather pastoral borough known as The Summit. This explains why on many an evening Benny would do a closing number or two at the Alí Bar, hunkered down behind a glass of Bacardi on the rocks and hounded by the friends and admirers who had become ever-present since his conversion into "El Benny"—with all the significance that the definite article bestows upon proper nouns in Cuban Spanish. As on any other night, there were many requests for him to sing something that evening, and because Benny wasn't the type whose arm had to be twisted, he forgot about his fatigue, approached the piano armed with his rum, and proposed a melody. I can almost see him removing the wide-brimmed hat that he wore on the big stage and gently placing the enormous weight of his immortality on a stool. He sang an opening number, surely one of those inimitable boleros that only he dared imitate, and, lubricated by a second drink, he decided that he did, in fact, feel like doing what he did best in life: singing. Music had taken him to Mexico, where he became famous interpreting mambos by Pérez Prado and where he shared stage and screen with Ton-

1

golele and Ninón Sevilla; music had made him famous in Venezuela, in Santo Domingo, in Panama, in Colombia, and all throughout the Caribbean, where his voice and rhythm had allowed him to establish a veritable musical dictatorship. Music had made him an idol, and Benny never stopped singing. But, as the story goes, that night, on precisely that night, Benny sang as he had never sung before—free, ethereal, splendid. Eager to outdo himself even further, he removed his dentures quite nonchalantly and flashed an empty smile. "Now I'm really comfortable," he said, and then he truly sang.

This anecdote, told a thousand different ways by a thousand different spectators who quite possibly were not present that night at the Alí Bar, has always seemed to me the perfect portrait of the essence of Benny's personality. The image of that outrageous, toothless idol seated next to the piano and singing as never before, as if satisfying a visceral urge, says it all about the man who around that time would confess, "Look, brother, I don't know a thing about music . . . even though I've written the lyrics and music of most everything I sing. I've never studied music. What I do have is a great ear. I recall that on one occasion I was a bit worried about this, and so I decided to study music. Maestro González Mantici told me it was the worst thing I could do, and he was right, because my success owes to the fact that I sing by ear, using the rhythm that runs through my veins."[1]

Several years later, in 1963, when El Benny succumbed to the hepatic cirrhosis that destroyed his liver but never his voice, music lovers throughout Latin America bemoaned his passing as they had done only twenty years earlier upon the death of Carlos Gardel. The mourning blanketed the entire continent: after all, *El Bárbaro del Ritmo* had died, that farmhand from Lajas (his beloved hometown) who had managed to conquer all the bastions of popularity, success, fame, and even of sentiment.

As with Benny Moré, a direct son of Cuba, Puerto Rico produced Ismael Rivera, who was decorated with the magnificent title of *Sonero Mayor* [the greatest singer of *son*]. His story, however, began as a lead singer of *bombas y plenas* for Rafael Cortijo's combo, ever since the day when Cortijo went to get him at the construction yard where Rivera was working as a master bricklayer. As the story goes, Cortijo said to him, "Get rid of your tools, tomorrow you start singing with me," and the mulatto Ismael, who consid-

---

1. Amín E. Naser, *Benny Moré* (Havana: Ediciones Unión, 1985), p. 53.

ered himself one hell of a mason but who, like Moré, confessed to knowing "not a thing about music," soon was transformed into Maelo, now a master of rhythm and for years the leading voice of joyful Caribbean song, belting out the *son montuno* as only he could do. (There's another story—would that it were true—that it was El Benny himself who baptized Maelo as the *sonero mayor*.)

Like Benny Moré and Ismael "Maelo" Rivera, the history of Caribbean music comprises a hundred similar biographies (such as that of Arsenio Rodríguez, blind from birth, virtuoso of the *tres*, who forever transformed *son* by "inventing" the ensemble without knowing anything about music). These monstrous talents, motivated by pangs of hunger and later transformed into the idols of an entire musical and cultural region, forged a mythology that is one of the most significant components of—how else to call it?—the Latin American identity. Because while the United States was creating stars that glittered brightly, far away, on the silver screen and the enviable stages of Broadway (although they were perhaps not so bright when one looked at the light they shone), and the European cult was producing political or cultural figures, languid or rebellious but always conscious of their status as figures, the people of Latin America, listening each evening to another episode of *El derecho de nacer* and living lives of melodrama, were incapable of giving birth to anything but idols, simply because, as our novelist friend Luis Britto García observes, "the idol does not traverse the paths of metaphysics, of the epic, of science, of politics or riches, but rather those of sentiment, the only space from which the masses have yet to be evicted. The only homeland free from invasions, the only place where I am still the king. The free territory of sentiment. And for Latin Americans, sentiment is sensuality. Although this homeland, just like all others, can only be founded on the pain of its martyrs."[2]

Thus, the Latin American Olympus received in life and sustained in death the idolatry of Pedro Infante and Jorge Negrete, of Daniel Santos and Cortijo, of the eternal Celia Cruz and the evasive Dámaso Pérez Prado, of Iris Chacón and Chabuca Granda. And it was a strangely democratic Olympus that could be governed by a toothless black farmhand like El Benny or a master bricklayer, also black, like Maelo, all because, as Luis Britto once again tells us, "An idol is the compendium of all that we lack. The popular

---

2. Luis Britto García, "Daniel Santos in Memoriam," *La Gaceta de Cuba* (Havana), Jan.–Feb. 1993, p. 37.

Latin American singer helped to cure the immense misery of the collective soul (alone, always alone) by pointing out its place in the cultural universe and its role in the order of things. The popular singer crooned for the masses while the intellectual wrote for a bourgeoisie that had eyes only for English memoranda or French etiquette."[3]

So, once we had idols, a cult was born. But the cult draped itself in glamour nevertheless. An eternally unsatisfied need for beauty, for success, for bright colors, for overwhelming perfumes—the more beauty the better—allowed a profane altar to be built to those idols molded from the earth. But if the idols were made in our image and likeness, if their voices were our voice, if they sang our same misery, then their greatness was our (dreamed) greatness, and their beauty was also our (much needed) beauty. That cult thus became the dogma of the image industry (the merchants always end up invading the temple), which insisted on forgetting about farmhands and proletariat pasts, on putting dentures in toothless mouths, on using sequins to intensify the limelight, only to end up inventing kitsch many years before the cultural critics would patent the term. They made Tito Rodríguez jump into the ring, singing boleros, so he could compete with Frank Sinatra and his ballads. But the ring had to be glamorous, and the Tropicana cabaret, the symbol par excellence of the Latin American dream, our Scala, shone beneath the stars as if those few square meters of stage (more lights, more splendor, more tinsel) were reality. As if patent leather were real cowhide.

This is how the stars came to be: mined from the quarry of idols or simply mass-produced, they were sculpted out of necessity and distributed on a massive scale. Unlike true idols, these lacked authenticity—and at times, of course, talent—but they filled the chosen stages while a fellow like El Benny lavished his talents upon the Alí Bar because he and his Banda Gigante (too many blacks together in one place) were unwelcome in certain venues. Benny, like Maelo and Arsenio and so many other true idols, never learned (or refused to learn) to be a star. His hands always smelled of the earth, which perhaps is why his greatness was invincible and his idolatry eternal, irreversible. Glamour barely touched these essential artists, and this lack of contamination spared them for mythology. A rare consciousness alerted them to their proper place and destiny, and they resigned themselves

---

3. García, "Daniel Santos in Memoriam," p. 37

to singing and playing, wherever, until the end. They knew they had been born to do as much, and that certainty was more than enough.

That starry and apparently evanescent yet perfect universe of Latin American music of the 1940s and 1950s, which exploited the idols (be they real, popular, or populist), burst like a bubble in the 1960s. Too many political, social, and economic upheavals decreed the end of the spell, and the entire world, including Latin America and the Caribbean, would never be the same. While Cuba was proclaiming a socialist revolution and the United States was responding with an economic embargo (which included music), the Mexican film industry was entering a long period of crisis. Music was losing its splendor as cities were growing exponentially, overflowing with people. New images were needed for the existential altars.

In Liverpool, for example, in a dark and dingy club completely devoid of glamour, a new type of music was being played by a group of rather rebellious teenagers who would soon be transformed into The Beatles, icons of a counterculture. In New York, meanwhile, the great dancehalls where Tito Puente, Tito Rodríguez, and Machito and His Afrocubans once reigned supreme in their shiny tuxes and tails began to close their doors for an undeniable reason: people were no longer coming.

The masses had begun to think in a new way—politically, economically, and musically—and this new worldview would engender new idols. Shaken at its very foundations, music (just like its parasite, movie musicals) could no longer sustain the image of the winner, of sensual beauty, of the Latin lover with the slicked-back hair, and less still that of insouciance: one now had to be aware. The era of the "mambo kings playing songs of love" was long gone: it now made no sense to dedicate bucolic and idealized songs to an ever more remote countryside, to a joie de vivre that was no longer very joyful, or, even less, to impossible loves simply because they were loves and were impossible. A new quarry of idols was about to be mined, and the changing of the guard brought a streetwise perspective rather than a glamorous one. This was the modern urban milieu, which a new group of artists attempted to put to music with unrefined rhythms and aggressive lyrics that, while not always reaching a high aesthetic quality, did at least manage to set the standard for a project that implied rebellion and revision. This project expressed a new, raw, and aggressive relationship between people and their surroundings: the urban Caribbean barrio, that beloved place that was not always (actually, never) peaceful and romantic, but really quite the contrary.

It's not coincidental that the first indisputable idol of the new developing consciousness (this time in the Caribbean heart of New York) was a boy of Puerto Rican descent, barely fifteen years old, who had been baptized in the South Bronx as William Anthony Colón Román and who made his debut in the music world in 1967 with an album significantly titled *Willie Colón, El Malo [Willie Colón, The Bad Boy]*. That young man and his bandmates, completely unknown in musical circles and hailing from one of New York's most undesirable districts (as well as from other places in the Caribbean), burst upon the scene with an imperfect sound, full of shrill trombones like car horns, raspy voices, and with no stage presence whatsoever. Theirs was a new type of music that would become the foundation of an entire genre: songs about the barrio sung from the barrio, songs about robbery, drugs, prostitution, nostalgia, the loss of cultural values, and, in sum, about everyday life in Latin American and Caribbean cities. This "bad boy" was unlike many others during those years in that he had the talent and the wherewithal to become a true idol, the very first of those who would practice what would later come to be known as salsa music. Willie Colón easily reached one of the most difficult spots on that rough-hewn wooden altar because in his music he maintained a rare connection to his birthplace along with an incorrigible rebelliousness. All his later work would do nothing but perfect those tendencies to guarantee his artistic authenticity.

It's worth recalling that Willie Colón was not an isolated case in the new musical community of New York. Soon there began to appear alongside him a group of diverse personalities of prime importance for the launching of what would become a true movement. The singer who at the time accompanied Willie and was quite adept at interpreting those new sentiments was a man by the name of Héctor Pérez, who would become Héctor Lavoe for posterity. Together with these two, perhaps the most irreverent character of all was the pianist and director Eddie Palmieri, who began playing trombones before Willie did and who proposed a new, avant-garde, experimental sound based on the old Caribbean models of *son, bomba,* and *plena.* Also part of the movement were figures who were already enjoying success at the time, such as Pete Rodríguez, one of the prophets of Latin boogaloo, a hybrid genre made up of equal parts Caribbean sounds and pop; Ricardo Gay, creator of the ephemeral jala-jala; Ray Barreto, with his mixture of *son* and rock christened as Watusi '65; or José Calderón, better known as Joe Cuba, also a native of the New York barrio, who with his sextet (in which Cheo Feliciano sang during the 1960s) produced a daring, streetwise *son,* filled with meaningful phrases (sometimes in English) for barrio folks, and who warned in one of his memorable pieces, *"la calle está durísima"* ["the street is really tough"].

It should not surprise us that this cultural transformation, another true counterculture accompanied by a certain rejoicing in the demolition of the old false idols, had its origins in Latin New York, or to be more precise, in Caribbean New York. In his exhaustive study *El libro de la salsa,* the Venezuelan researcher César Miguel Rondón analyzes the sociological and cultural factors that fostered the birth of this enlightenment on the most distant shore of the Caribbean. Among the reasons he cites are the following: the existence of a vast Caribbean community in which people of all the islands of this cultural universe intermingled, sharing their specific regional traditions; the essentially marginal character of these communities, subjected to all types of discrimination and therefore clinging even more strongly to their cultural origins; the demise of a preponderant Cuban influence, now blockaded (and in crisis, I might add), that was characterized until 1959 not only by the music of Benny Moré or Félix Chapotín but also by the glamour and the brilliance of its big stars; and finally, the existence of a need to express, through music and poetry, a sense of uprootedness, a state of being and a vision of the present-day world that would find in the barrios of New York the perfect laboratory conditions for the gestation and birth of a new musical vision of reality.

Regardless of the musical origins of salsa (all the interviewees in this book offer their take on the old dispute regarding the relationship of salsa to Cuban *son*), no one can deny that the new aesthetic filled a cultural void in the popular dance music of the Caribbean and a good portion of Latin America, and that its best-known faces would soon enjoy the status of idols usually reserved for religious deities. But unlike the gods of old, many of which were still in vogue at the outset of the rebellion, salsa would propose, and later establish, a new model: the *salsero,* an artist who, whether or not he shared origins similar to those of his predecessors, would embark upon something that his forbearers never did: a project. A conscious project. Salsa and consciousness.

Undoubtedly one of the most important characteristics of salsa music is this new image of the artist projected through the figure of the bandleader. Often a singer, generally the director of the group; almost always a composer and arranger; white, black or mulatto; a trained musician or a spontaneous creator, the band leader acquires an intellectual dimension and an artistic projection that the popular musicians of our continent never enjoyed, thanks to the aesthetic program that, in most cases, underlies his works. Despite being an inherently festive music, almost always made for dancing and meant to be heard by large groups, salsa encompasses an aesthetic attitude absent in the music of the wild old idols of the 1940s and 1950s who, though full of talent (and often more talented), lacked the intentionality that during the last three decades has characterized the best salsa music.

In the beginning, the humble barrio origins of the majority of the soon-to-be salsa idols served as an umbilical cord connecting them to the complex circumstances that nurtured their music and songs. These irreverent personalities, "who are no longer artists or stars, emerge now as simple popular characters, common folk who move from the street to the stage, without pretense or poses,"[4] and who with their very presence and music manage to transform the tastes of an entire continent, which in the 1970s opens its arms to the salsa innovation that begins to touch the most distant points of the Latin American sentiment, from New York to the Caribbean.

An undeniable authenticity, a new projection—visible in characters like Willie Colón, still enveloped in his bad-boy image; the newcomer Rubén Blades with his long tunes about contemporary guerilla fighters and nineteenth-century outlaws; the almost unknown Juan Formell, who demolished the old, sickly sweet formula of the typical *charanga;* or the combative *merenguero* Johnny Ventura, singing with the Dominican rebels in 1965—was slowly establishing itself as a new hallmark of less dazzling but more conscious idols than those raised to the same status by the previous generation. (Many of these new characters had shady backgrounds, even including jail time in some cases.) The new attitude also begins to be seen in other characters related to the salsa wave, such as Roberto Roena, a totally intuitive musician; or Larry Harlow, the American who so greatly helped to define the new music by recomposing old *son* patterns; or even in the veterans rescued for salsa such as Celia Cruz or Ismael Rivera, who also contributed to the establishment of the new image as a result of an aesthetic break that nevertheless could not always overcome the inevitable schemes of an industry that soon began to exploit a new gold mine and introduced, since

---

4. César Miguel Rondón, *El libro de la salsa* (Caracas: Editorial Arte, 1980), p. 32.

we're talking about gold here, the indispensable costume jewelry, made from fool's gold.

This explains why, in its initial moments of explosion and authenticity, the new Caribbean dance music (which was now beginning to be called *salsa,* a name with a completely commercial origin, created for the obligatory industrial homogenization and marketing of the new artistic product) offers this entire gamut of characters that revolutionize the image of the musician and of music itself, expressing the needs of a new society. The industry begins to create other stars immediately, more pleasing and closer to the norms of "good taste," with which to round out the variety of products that the salsa labels would soon need to offer to the public, with Fania at the head of the list. By the mid-1970s there begins the inevitable fabrication of images and idols that come to represent a made-to-order salsa (more like a ketchup) wrapped in cellophane, which in large part curiously depended on the old Cuban repertoire of the 1930s, 1940s, and 1950s. And when no one was expecting it, these prefab idols once again started crooning bucolic evocations of the countryside, festive and light-hearted *guarachas,* and a full gamut of frivolities (that is, when judged from the perspective of the avant-garde work of the true artists), which nonetheless appeased the hunger of a good portion of the public.

The process of fabricating new stars was not particularly complicated, because "salsa, in some sense, had to assume part of that spirit, had to inherit something of the pomp [of the 1940s and 1950s]. It's true that the circumstances today are considerably different from those that gave rise to that placid and showy love: for salsa, aggressiveness always precedes sweetness, and ferocity is more important than gentleness. However, these binary opposites were not sufficient to obviate certain bridges. . . . After all, one had to make a formally sophisticated salsa that was capable of breeding with the old [romantic? dreamy? elegant? cinematographic? corny? refined? idealized?] spirit without betraying the new."[5] So the *fabricated* stars assumed that bridge role, which was not the only one (money was involved after all). Then another bridge was built, this time to the Anglo-American public, with a sort of salsa-disco music that did, in fact, completely betray the cultural propositions of the salsa phenomenon.

---

5. García, "Daniel Santos in Memoriam," p. 133.

Meanwhile, the experimentation in sound and music could not be halted. Toward the end of the 1970s, for example, one of the most transcendent and revolutionary fusions of the entire movement comes about when Rubén Blades, that young man who was a bit too intellectual (he had a law degree, of all things), who had never been accepted because of his "protest songs," joins Willie Colón, and the two take the salsa universe by storm with a pair of simply classic recordings, *Metiendo mano* (1977) and *Siembra* (1979). With these albums they founded a new tendency: salsa with a conscience, a project by means of which Willie Colón once again declared himself in complete opposition to standardization and transcended the image of the violent bad boy that he had assumed in *El malo, El juicio,* and *Lo mato.* Meanwhile, Rubén himself, convinced of his role as a critical conscience, pens in 1980 his impressive salsa opera *Maestra vida,* a challenge to the tastes imposed by the big labels. For their part, musicians such as Oscar D'León, Papo Lucca, Juan Formell, and Wilfrido Vargas experimented openly with Caribbean sounds and genres, continuing the necessary revitalization of *son, plena,* and *merengue,* and opening more space to crucial and much-needed influences from jazz and Brazilian music.

This unstoppable revolution, precisely at the moment when the commercial salsa boom was imposing a vulgarization of the genre, came to demonstrate the potential of the movement and proved that, alongside the festive *guaracha* or the immortal bolero, experimentation, searching, and even social and political criticism all enjoyed a privileged space in the musical project of the contemporary urban Caribbean. The *salseros* had set out on a mission, and they were accomplishing it.

The news that Rubén Blades was aspiring to the presidency of the Republic of Panama would perhaps have shocked an entire continent had it occurred on that day in 1970 when he was recording the story of the guerrilla Juan González for his album *From Panama to New York: Pete Rodríguez Presents Rubén Blades.* But more than twenty-three decisive years had passed in Latin American cultural history, to the point that a *salsero* could aspire to executive office or a *merenguero* to the mayorship of the most important city in the Dominican Republic, or that ever-exclusive Yale University might confer an honorary degree upon an orchestra leader who would present a speech titled "Salsa: A Sociopolitical Perspective."

Somehow salsa has managed to triumph in its revolution and, as a counterculture born as an expression of the barrio, has managed to reach the status of authentic culture by becoming an identifying characteristic of a large world region. This victory, of course, has been won in spite of an industry rather unconcerned with transcendence—the same industry that, after exhausting the "Cuban mode" and "salsa-disco music" (or "supermarket salsa," as Roberto Roena called it) in the 1970s, introduced "erotic salsa" in the 1980s, full of inconsistent and often desexed stars, as postmodernity demands. But genuineness was able to overcome flash this time.

The conscious project that motivated the authentic *salseros* in their drive for musical renovation and verbal expression of a new urban reality seems to have acquired its full-fledged citizenship in the musical world. And with it, the image of the musician reached another level, that which had heretofore been reserved for "intellectuals." This is, precisely, the conclusion that this book proposes: thirteen interviews (with one precursor of salsa; six first-rate *salseros;* a figure who bridged the gap between the Cuban tradition and the salsa wave; three *merengueros;* and a musicologist and a disc jockey-cum-commercial manager), conducted over a span of eight years and carried out more through chance encounters than intentional searching, revealed to me (along with the personalities of this new breed of idols) the depth of their individual projects in the midst of a larger, almost continental, undertaking. I should confess, therefore, that in many cases I myself was the first person to be taken aback by the intellectual commitment of these artists. That these distant men, devoted to singing and dancing, were sustained by such a well-defined intentionality slowly became clear to me and led me to this conclusion: those who make salsa do so with a conscience.

In these men—and in others whom perhaps I may be able to interview someday: Cheo Feliciano, Oscar D'León, Joe Arroyo, Eddie Palmieri, and so many other idols—it is not uncommon to find, therefore, clear political positions together with articulate social proposals that none of our former idols would have bothered themselves with. It seems as though nothing human is foreign to them, and they express this participative vocation more or less directly in their works: Willie Colón singing no to injustice or to celebration of the five hundredth anniversary of the Spanish conquest, a rebel in the face of Puerto Rican cultural castration[6]; Rubén carrying out the political expression of his program in records like *Amor y control;* Formell ex-

---

6. At the beginning of the 1990s, Willie Colón was the Secretary of the Association of Hispanic Arts, which assists Latino artists and raises funds for their projects. He also served on the board of directors of the New York Hispanic Caucus, which brings together congressmen and congresswomen of Latino origin.

pressing a picaresque vision of the hardships of everyday life for Cubans; and finally, all of them proposing a true cultural identity in which rage, pain, and indignation commingle with happiness, dance, and joy.

But along with these explicit postures in the musical texts, salsa and its major prophets have returned to their fans the pleasure of dancing, an indispensable pleasure in a zone of the world where it is impossible to conceive of a music not to be danced to: from *danzón* to mambo, all lasting Caribbean music has been dance music, and salsa, in the midst of the rock and pop invasion that began in the 1960s, waged a singular battle that has allowed it to preserve to this day an indispensable tradition. This explains the importance of figures such as Eddie Palmieri, Papo Lucca, Adalberto Álvarez, Joe Arroyo, and Wilfrido Vargas, revolutionaries of Caribbean rhythms that, in their most capable hands, underwent a notable transformation and, without betraying their origins, achieved the musical novelty demanded by our times.

Of course, at this stage of music history, salsa has managed to become one of the most impressive projects of Latin American cultural fusion ever undertaken: the consistent and necessary communion of many rhythms originating from the most diverse regions of the continent (from New Orleans to Brazil, from Cali to Santo Domingo), working from a common model and for a common purpose, has created an impressive musical amalgamation that has renovated Latin American music by uniting it, blending it, and identifying it.

The magnitude of the project, which began as the mere expressive necessity of the New York barrio where they lived—not quite in harmony, I might add—has culminated today in an artistic creation that has revealed its enduring nature. Those initial mixtures of Cuban *son* and other Caribbean rhythms is today, beyond all labels, a true salsa—much more than a watered-down ketchup—in which the conscience of its creators, cultivators, and sustainers (the dancing public) has for the first time played a decisive role in a musical project of our continent. The *salseros'* body of work validates this affirmation.

Let us listen, then, to those who make salsa with a conscience, some of the most recognizable faces of the new Caribbean dance music of our day.

1

Conversation in La Catedral with Mario Bauzá

La Catedral [The Cathedral] bar stands on the corner of Amsterdam and 106th (also known as Duke Ellington Boulevard), right on the border between Harlem and El Barrio. La Catedral is an old Irish pub, built perhaps in the 1920s, a dark and cavernous place despite its high glass windows, which face the street. It has a long bar made of black wood, the obligatory stools, and in the center of the room (which is longer than it is wide) stands a partition, also made of black wood, which separates the bar from a row of tables where, in addition to imbibing, one can enjoy the simple fare prepared by the kitchen. La Catedral smells as a good Irish pub should: like spilled beer, fiery whiskey, and pale, sweet cigarettes made from Virginia tobacco.

Being located in such a "strategic" spot, La Catedral is not exactly the type of place one finds recommended in New York tourist guides. Seated at one of its tables, you can observe the body language of the black and Latino residents of Harlem and El Barrio as they go about their business in their everyday clothes. Very few of these passersby, however, are interested in crossing the threshold of this unique watering hole, an Irish pub with a Spanish name frequented only by its habitual clientele: discreet and laconic drinkers who in the late afternoon hunch over the bar to watch a Mets or Yankees game, the local news, or a sitcom that seems quite entertaining, to judge by the laugh track playing in the background.

In a corner of the bar, downing the first of seven Budweisers that I would

MARIO BAUZÁ

see him consume, Mario Bauzá was watching TV on that cold November afternoon in 1992. At his side, nursing a whiskey on the rocks with plenty of ice, was Rudy Calzado. The two appear unenthusiastic and distant, even when conversing with the bartender, who is also enjoying the program. Mario Bauzá lives on Columbus Avenue, a few blocks from the bar, and he likes to schedule all his business appointments there, including chats with his band members. In some respects, the tavern has become his executive office, which is a rather advantageous setup given that he doesn't have to make the coffee (at his house it would be Cuban, of course) and that one of the tables has been permanently reserved for him.

Before this afternoon I had seen only a few photos of Mario Bauzá, pictures in which he was generally laughing with his crocodile mouth wide open. Nevertheless, every time I heard people talking about Caribbean music in New York, his image took on an ever more mythical stature. And now he's right here before my eyes, almost tiny in his grandeur, carrying his eighty-two years with an amazing ease. I recognize him immediately: in spite of his six decades in New York, this man has too Cuban a face to be anyone other than Mario Bauzá. And he recognizes me as soon as I approach him (no doubt from my own facial features, I think to myself). I greet him, addressing him as Maestro, and he introduces me to Rudy Calzado, his colleague and the principal vocalist of his orchestra, and I then introduce both to Pancho Miguens, my old friend from high school who's serving as my private New York guide.

Despite the cordial greeting, Mario Bauzá does not appear too excited by the idea of having to stop watching the hilarious TV show to talk with me. After a huge burst of prerecorded laughter fails to amuse him, he leaves the bar and leads us to his table beside the partition. He takes his Budweiser along for the ride as well as his "Rolando La Serie" cap, which he puts on as if he were about to embark on a long journey in either space or time.

Now he's seated before me, and I soon realize I don't know what to say: there's something in Mario Bauzá that demands respect, or perhaps it's just my nervousness in the face of an unbelievable encounter. After all, this is Mario Bauzá, and I'm in New York about to realize one of my most far-fetched and, until now, inconceivable desires: to interview this man who, instead of a corduroy cap, should be wearing a triple crown: that of the first Latin jazz king, that of the most resolute cultivator of Cuban *son* in the United States, and that of the first patriarch of the musical fusion that would later be known as salsa. From his throne, Mario is like a guru to be consulted by all who wish to learn the story of Caribbean music in the Big Apple.

Mario Bauzá—a figure in the same league as Benny Moré and Arsenio Rodríguez, Ignacio Piñeiro and Miguel Matamoros—has long been one of the most important names of Cuban popular music and jazz. . . . And the most forgotten of all.

NEWS FLASH

Washington—Mario Bauzá, the Cuban musician who created one of the most transcendent fusions in contemporary music—Afrocuban jazz—died in New York City at the age of 82. Since the 1920s, Bauzá had been a resident of the U.S., where he had relocated to perfect his musical experiments. He was the last great living pioneer of Afro-jazz, a genre also practiced by Chano Pozo, Frank Grillo "Machito," and the North American Dizzy Gillespie. "After all, we come from the same roots: it's a perfect marriage," Bauzá said in reference to the mixture of rhythms that immortalized him and that he always refused to call Latin Jazz.

—Prensa Latina (published in the cultural page of the Cuban newspaper *Granma* on Tuesday, March 13, 1993, two days after the death of Mario Bauzá; this was the only note on the death of the musician to appear in the Cuban press)

Son, Danzón, and Jazz: Everything Started Somewhere

LPF: Shall we start from the very beginning?

MB: Listen, *chico,* that was a ton of years ago. . . . I was born in the Cayo Hueso barrio, in Havana, in 1911, and I began playing at fourteen, when *danzón* was still all the rage in Cuban music. It was the era of the typical orchestra, and I played with Felipe Valdés, with Juanito Zequeira, with Raimundo Valenzuela, all of whom had very good *danzón* orchestras. At the same time, since I had done serious musical study, I played clarinet with the Havana Philharmonic. And later, when *charanga* came into vogue, I recorded with Arsenio María Romeu's band, the most prestigious in Cuba and the one with which I came to New York for the first time in 1926. Since I was still a kid, my parents had to give me permission to travel. But when I saw the atmosphere here, the orchestras of Paul Whiteman, Fletcher Henderson, and Tommy Dorsey, when I saw the parties and the theaters, the way the Negroes danced and played and enjoyed themselves, I said to myself, "This is the country for me." A man with my aspirations simply couldn't have stayed in Cuba. The problem was that I wasn't old enough to have a passport and so I had to go home, although I had already decided to come back. I waited in Havana until 1929, when I turned eighteen and was finally able to get my passport. In 1930 I returned to New York, on the SS *Oriente.* At that time I was playing at the Sans Souci and the Montmarte, which were the best cabarets in Havana, and I was earning $25 an hour, which was a fortune back then. But even so, I had my mind made up. I went to see my girlfriend, Estrella, and I told her: "I'm leaving tomorrow." Oh, how she cried, the poor thing.

LPF: What was happening at that time with Cuban music here in New York?

MB: When I arrived, the first orchestra that had brought Cuban music to this city was Don Azpiazu's. That was when "El manisero" ("The Peanut Vendor") took off in New York, and the Victor label signed him to record it. He formed a quartet to make the record with people from Azpiazu's orchestra, among them Daniel, who sang backup, and Remberto Lara, who played the trumpet. The quartet stayed together until Lara had to return to Cuba with Azpiazu. Then I bump into Machín at a party where he was playing and I discover he's having problems finding a trumpeter to accompany him and I say to him: "Listen, Machín, I can play the trumpet for you," and he tells me I'm not trumpet player, and then I tell him: "Buy me a trumpet and you'll see whether or not I can play it." And Machín buys me a $15 trumpet and I lock myself in a room with it for two weeks. . . . That was my first job in New York, as a trumpet player in Antonio Machín's quartet.

LPF: Were you and Machín good friends?

MB: I always respected and admired him, in addition to being grateful to him for buying me that trumpet, which changed my life. He was a great musician, and that's why in Spain, even today, Machín is still a god. He deserves every honor.

LPF: How did you get involved in the jazz world?

MB: A while later, as a trumpeter, I get a gig with the Noble Sissle band and I play a couple months with them, until they get a contract to go to Europe and I decide to stay here. Then I take my trumpet and join a little jazz group—called Hy Clark's Missourians—to play at the Savoy, and the people from Chick Webb's orchestra hear me play and ask me to join them, and a bit later I hook up with Don Redman's band and finally with Cab Calloway's, where I stay until 1941.

LPF: What did you learn about jazz? And from whom did you learn the most?

MB: I learned a lot about jazz, of course, most of all from a fellow named Chick Webb. When I started playing with him, around 1933, he called me after hearing my first rehearsals and said, "Look, Mario, you have something I need and I have something you need. Music is an international language, and you and I understand each other. . . . The day you really understand the phraseology of American black music, combined with what you know about Cuban music, you're going to be a respected musician." And I worked hard to understand it, and I think I did, because a year later Chick Webb called the group together and announced that I was the new musical director. He taught me what I never learned at any conservatory: how to enjoy the limitless freedom of jazz and, most of all, to combine Cuban rhythms with American ones, to combine them in one style, which was mine, and there you have the seeds of Afrocuban jazz.

LPF: And how did you make out with Cab Calloway?

MB: I played with him for several years, until 1941. But even before then I didn't feel right with the group because there were people who were envious of me ever since I had Dizzy Gillespie join the orchestra and tried to start my own style with him because we knew that jazz was something big, but the rhythms were monotonous and we were always trying to see how we could fix that. We finally solved it with bebop. But in Cab's orchestra they didn't understand me, and they even told me that my rhythms were horse music, and so I told them, "Any day now you fellas are going to hear an orchestra better than this one playing my music." And then I left to form Machito's Afrocubans and to do my experiments, which was what I wanted to do.

AN OPINION

With Mario Bauzá in the band, I really started to become interested in bringing Latin influences, especially Afrocuban ones, into my music. Or perhaps I should say only Afrocuban ones because there are no other influences in our music, there are no other influences in jazz. No one was playing that type of music at the time. . . . I was totally captivated by the possibilities of expansion and enrichment in jazz, both rhythmically and musically, through the use of Afrocuban rhythm and its melodic inventiveness. But I still wasn't prepared to create something so strong, nor was anyone in the jazz field.
—Dizzy Gillespie

A Perfect Marriage

Three days after my dialogue with Mario Bauzá, on November 13, I had the unexpected privilege of occupying a seat at "Mario's guest table" at the Terrace Room of Newark Symphony Hall, where a Latin Jazz Dance Party was taking place as part of the Newark Jazz Festival. Mario Bauzá's new orchestra was performing a recital that evening, and in addition to my conversation in La Catedral, I now had another unforeseen experience of watching him play and sharing his table during the intermissions. The show, more than two hours in length, allowed me to witness the vitality of that man who never stopped moving in front of his orchestra, and to hear with my own ears one of the protagonists of the history of Afrocuban jazz: Graciela Grillo, Machito's sister, an émigré from the female Anacona orchestra who had become the lead singer of the Afrocubans for some thirty years.

During one of the intermissions, Mario told me he was pleased by the resurgence that his music had enjoyed in recent months. He had recorded a new version of the Tanga suite with a twenty-five-member orchestra and he had prepared and edited the album *My Time Is Now*, with classic *sones, danzones,* and boleros from the golden days of the Afrocubans. He also told me, with his raspy and quintessentially Cuban voice, that lately those live performances were taking too much out of him, but he finished his Budweiser and returned to the stage, smiling at the crowd. . . . Neither Mario nor I imagined that the concert at Newark Symphony Hall would be one of his last performances in this world, which he inhabited for nearly eighty-three years.

LPF: Mario, why do you use Machito's name for the orchestra rather than your own?

MB: That was a gift I wanted to give him. When I traveled to Cuba in 1936 to marry his sister Estrella, he asked me to take him back with me. And since we had always been inseparable, I did the paperwork and he came along. I had known Machito from the time I was twelve years old and he was singing with the sextets, which was the start of a very long friendship. We founded the orchestra in 1940, but I didn't join until the following year.

LPF: What type of musician was Machito?

MB: A *sonero* with three pairs of *timbales.* I considered him the best maraca player in Cuban music. He had sung with Abelardo Barroso, with María Teresa Vera at the Rialto Academy, always in top orchestras, and he was the one who taught me the keys to Cuban music, the basics.

LPF: When you formed the orchestra, did you have the Afrocuban thing in mind?

MB: Of course. I wanted an orchestra that had the sound of the great American bands, but that played Cuban music. At that time it seemed crazy but that's the reason we founded Machito and His Afrocubans, and we debuted on December 3, 1940, in the Conga Club on 52d and Broadway, where we played for four years. Things worked out in such a way that I stayed with the group until 1975. I was musical director the entire time, and although all the arrangements weren't mine, I was the architect, so to speak, who gave shape to the music and I did a lot of experimenting, like on the album that I wrote all by myself titled *Kenya,* or the Tanga suite (*tanga* means marijuana in an African dialect), which later everybody played. And to achieve the best fusion with jazz, I invited a lot of people to play with us, including Charlie Parker, Stan Getz, Dexter Gordon, and Herbie Mann, or Tito Puente, who was the orchestra's first drum player, from 1940 to 1942, during the war, and then he got drafted. For all those reasons, we were always one of the five most popular Latin groups in New York.

LPF: Mario, what's your definition of Afrocuban jazz?

MB: Well, it's a perfect marriage: one goes up and the other goes down, it doesn't matter which one. Or like a tree that has the same root, the same trunk (which comes from Africa) and two distinct branches, which I united: *son* and jazz. It was a natural, loving union.

LPF: When people talk about Afrocuban jazz, they always mention four indispensable figures: Mario Bauzá, Machito, Gillespie, and Chano Pozo. What's the real story of how Chano got into jazz?

MB: You want the real story? Well, in 1947 I was once again playing at the Conga Club, where I was the musical and artistic director, along with playing in Machito's orchestra. And one day I hear a group from Cuba has arrived, some musicians and a pair of dancers, and they were looking for me to see if I could get them a gig at the club. So I went to see them where they were working and I introduced myself. That's where I met Chano Pozo and Cacha, who was his wife. That same night Miguelito Valdez, who was like Chano's father, came to the cabaret. Just imagine, when he spoke to him Chano even lowered his head, like a little boy. And Miguelito said to him, "Look, Chano, pretend this man is me; pay attention to everything he says."

LPF: Chano had a reputation of being rather treacherous, no?

MB: I never knew him to be that way. What I do believe is that a lot of people spoke badly of him out of envy. Remember that never in the history of the Casino Nacional in Havana had anyone had their image in lights, way up high, until Chano Pozo came along. You could see the lights all the way along Third Avenue. . . . And those things can be trouble in Cuba, you know, people are envious. I myself had problems there, when I was playing in the Tokio cabaret, where no black musicians performed at the time. That was when I was starting to form what would later become the Afrocubans with Machito, and with Miguelito Valdés on violin, Absalón Pérez on piano, and Ulacia on trumpet. And we sounded so good that a theater representative who traveled a lot in South America suggested we do a tour. Then word started to spread throughout Havana that I had an orchestra of blacks who wanted to play at white clubs, and I didn't like people saying that. That's one of the reasons I decided to leave Cuba.

But getting back to Chano. I had never seen him play, but you only had to see him once. That's why he had about about eight *"jil"* numbers: "Nagüe, Nagüe," "Pin, pin, cayó Berlín," "Boco-boco," "Ariñáñara Bocuere," and in 1947 they opened a Latin club, not far from the famous Palladium, that was named after a song of his: the Blem-blem. Everything he recorded took off, and the most amazing thing is that Chano didn't know a thing about music, but he was born with a gift. He played, sang, and danced like a genius. That's the truth. There's no other explanation.

Then one day Dizzy came to see me. He had also gone to play in Cab Calloway's orchestra, and he says, "Mario, I've gotten my big chance to play a concert at Carnegie Hall and I'd like your advice about what to do." And I tell him, "Don't give it a second thought, play Afrocuban jazz." And he looks astonished and tells me that without me he doesn't have a clue about Cuban rhythms. And I tell him, "Don't worry, I know a guy who's just your ticket." We hop in the car and come over here, to 111th and 7th Avenue, where Chano was living. And when we get there, without explaining a thing, I say to him, "Hey, get your drums and play something for my friend." And Chano played "Manteca" and Dizzy was spellbound. That was one of the seminal moments of Afrocuban jazz for Mario Bauzá because the version of "Manteca" that Mario Bauzá played with Chano and Dizzy during that recital at Carnegie Hall went down in the history of bebop and all of jazz.

LPF: Another story you know is the story of Chano's death. What happened on the night of December 3, 1948?

MB: On the evening of December 3, Chano, Miguelito Valdés, and I were supposed to debut at a bar and that afternoon I was cashing some traveler's checks. Since we had some time to kill, I stayed at home listening to Cuban baseball games on a little radio I had. All of a sudden I get a phone call telling me: "Mario, Chano's just been killed. On Lennox, between 111th and 112th. At the Rio Café bar."

So I went to find out what happened, and I discovered that someone else had arranged his death, out of the same envy that started up here because of his success and his money. But the person who arranged his murder is paying for it with his life today, and the one who killed him, who was known as El Cabito, a Puerto Rican who had come back from the war half-crazy, was only the instrument who carried it out. They even put the gun in his hand. And he paid for it, too. I remember seeing him one day, a while later, and he told me he was leaving New York because he couldn't stand the shame he felt for having done it. So he went to Miami, and one day he got into an argument and the other fellow told him, "You're not going kill me like you did Chano," and right there he stabbed him.

LPF: A half-century has passed since Chano's death. Can't you tell me the name of the person who arranged his murder?

MB: I can't.

LPF: What was Chano Pozo's legacy in Afrocuban jazz?

MB: I'm going to tell you a story. After his death I saw Dizzy and he told me, "Listen, I don't want another conga player," and I tell him there are other good ones out there and that without a drummer there's no Afrocuban jazz. So I send Marcelino Valdés to see him. But it doesn't work out and he says to me, "Listen, Mario, all those guys are like babes in the woods compared to Chano. On everything I played, he played something that transformed my rhythm, and none of these does that. It's not the same without Chano."

AN OPINION
In 1947 only one orchestra (of Latinos, and black Latinos at that) had managed to make it on Broadway: it was Machito and His Afrocubans, an orchestra that at the height of the bebop craze had managed to combine Cuban rhythms with the harmonies and twists of avant-garde jazz, the famous and ill-named Latin Jazz created by Mario Bauzá, musical director of the Afrocubans and, as he himself admits, the father of the baby.
—César Miguel Rondón, *El libro de la salsa*

Salsa: Yes or No?

But in reality this interview almost ended before it started, only because I had made the mistake of beginning my conversation at La Catedral with the word *salsa*. For many connoisseurs, the fusion experiments initiated by Mario

Bauzá in the 1940s are the most distant origins of the salsa phenomenon of the 1960s, when the mixture of Cuban music (son) with other Caribbean and North American rhythms (especially jazz) reaches a dimension that would soon overwhelm New York, where, once again, everything began.

LPF: Mario, what is salsa? (I naively asked.)

MB: Salsa? Salsa? Listen, son, this isn't a serious interview. Do you want to interview me or poison my blood talking about that? Who said salsa exists? Go ahead, show me a paper with salsa music, come on. The other day I saw a Cuban cassette titled *Mi salsa,* and I said to myself, "Now we're really screwed if they're talking about salsa over there, too." Who said salsa exists? Look, ask Tito Puente himself; he knows where all this started, and he'll tell you the same thing—that the only salsa he knows about is spaghetti sauce.

LPF: Well, even if salsa doesn't exist, the word "salsa" exists to identify a type of music, right? So where did this come from?

MB: The word comes from a very old Cuban song, that was inspired by the old saying *"Más salsa que pescao"* ["more sauce than fish"]. And here they took off the fish part. That was when the Fania label had a great deal of influence over the radio stations and the recording studios and people started talking about salsa, salsa, and the word began to stick as a way of identifying Cuban music here in New York.

LPF: So is what's known as salsa only Cuban music?

MB: I didn't say that, but look, has any building been built without a foundation? Of course not, because that's impossible. The foundation is Cuban music, with other arrangements and additions. What's known as salsa had the virtue, I don't deny it, of putting Cuban music on the map, especially when what was being made on the island wasn't being disseminated, nor was it very good, as it is now. But that's it. It's still about Cuba and this is just another process in a musical history which is longer and more important than that of any other Caribbean nation, because Cuban music has been spanning the globe for more than a century.

LPF: Another very important musician in the origins of what's known as salsa is Arsenio Rodríguez. What happened with him and his music in New York?

MB: What happened was what I warned him would happen: he was playing in a tempo that you had to be Cuban, black, and a good dancer to follow, because it was very slow. That's why in Cuba his band played only for blacks at the Tropical and places like that. But Arsenio refused to speed up the rhythm, and that's why he never enjoyed the success he deserved over here: his music was never understood. But in any respect, the rights to his works provided him a good living, and it's not true that he died poor and forgotten. Arsenio dressed like a prince, with fancy threads and a diamond on his fingers.

Musically, Arsenio's opposite was Fajardo, who did have a great deal of success in New York. When Fajardo y sus Estrellas come on the scene in Havana, the music changes a lot because he speeds up the rhythm and the Montmarte dance floor gets four separate orchestras because Fajardo created a style that appealed to all the white dancers. The people who danced with Arsenio and later with the Todos Estrellas de Chapotín didn't feel very comfortable because the music was too fast for them and I remember someone shouting to him, "Hey, where ya going in such a hurry?" That's what happened. But that was the key to his success here, where his style came into vogue, like the *charanga,* and he had a lot of influence on musicians like Eddie Palmieri and Johnny Pacheco.

LPF: The case of Fajardo and Arsenio means that the Cuban music boom in the United States preceded salsa, doesn't it?

MB: No one can imagine the amount of Cuban music that came to this country in the 1950s. It wasn't so much the number of musicians that were working here as the quantity of music that was arriving. There was a company, Musicabana, that handled a lot of this new music, and they gave a lot of it to me and I distributed it to the groups in New York who were always asking me for it. That was also the golden age of the Palladium, when Tommy Morton, the local manager, came to Machito's orchestra during a crisis and asked them to save him. The orchestra had a lot of influence with the Latin public and the white dancers—Italians and Jews were always our best supporters—and during the first season we were already able to incorporate Tito Puente, the Piccadilly Boys, and later we brought in Tito Rodríguez. So, there was plenty of Cuban and Caribbean music without anyone calling it salsa.

LPF: Which contemporary Latin American musicians do you consider the most influential right now?

MB: One that I like is Oscar D'León. For a Venezuelan, he does a great job, because Venezuela has never had a *sonero* like him. The first time I heard him, I said to myself, "This is incredible." He's a man who feels what he's doing and he's responsible, to a great extent, for the surge in popularity of Cuban music. Another one who I really admire is Johnny Pacheco. I recall that he began here in the Palladium carrying instruments because he liked music a lot, and when Gilberto Valdés, from the Tropicana, formed the first *charanga* here in New York, they gave Pacheco a wooden flute and he learned to play by copying the Cuban style, Fajardo's style, and nowadays he's the only one who knows how to play it with Cuban melodies.

LPF: And what about Celia Cruz? What's her role in Cuban music?

MB: Her role? *Chico,* she's one of the greatest Cuba has ever produced in this genre. She's the greatest woman, and I'd put her alongside Benny, way above the rest. The most important thing that Celia has is her voice. She's got some pipes. And she also has the charisma and inventiveness to create on stage, which is something you don't see today. Just like me, she's got Cuban music in her blood.

LAST OPINION

As a way of honoring Bauzá, then mayor of New York Ed Koch pronounced the following words: "When the maraca met the tenor sax, it was love at first sight. Call it Latino, call it Afrocuban, call it what you will; that marriage was made in jazz heaven. And it's a marriage that will last for centuries." As Gillespie confessed to a reporter, "Perhaps the press underestimates him, but musicians certainly don't. Mario is the one who knows it all about Afrocuban jazz."
—Carlos Galilea, "El legado de Mario Bauzá," a chronicle published upon the Cuban musician's death

Epilogue

LPF: Mario, you never cared that your name was hidden behind Machito's as the name of the band?

MB: I've been a lot of things in life, but pretentious isn't one of them. I told you I was the architect, but Macho was the leader, and he did that very well. It didn't bother me because what was his was his and what's mine is mine, and we complemented each other very well.

LPF: And at this stage of life, what are your hopes for the future?

MB: Not much. I just hope I enjoy good health to keep playing Cuban music and to drink beer, which helps you see things more clearly. I just hope Cuban musicians don't forget what we've done and that Afrocuban jazz survives, because I know I wasn't born to be a seed. That's not too much to ask, is it?

New York, 1992

2

Willie Colón: The Salsa Kings Don't Just Play Songs of Love

Willie Colón is one of the essential gods of salsa mythology, perhaps the most essential of the entire pantheon. Whether he's wearing a perfectly tailored formal suit, as on this morning in 1991, or looking like a true scoundrel on the cover of one of his albums (*Lo mato:* "I'll kill him if he doesn't buy this record"), his image, music, and temperament have served as the consummate manifestation of salsa since the days before it was called salsa, when Johnny Pacheco, with his bloodhound nose, signed him for the nascent Fania label. Willie Colón was fifteen years old at the time, and all he had was his trombone and his simple New York biography to transform himself into the first archetype of a music that was being born in the Big Apple: a music full of street odors, raspy trombones that sounded like car horns, barrio stories of aggressive rebels youths, like Willie himself or Héctor Pérez—soon to become Lavoe—who sang the lyrics on that initial record: *El Malo* (1967).

> El malo de aquí soy yo,
> porque tengo corazón . . .

> I'm the bad guy here,
> because I've got heart . . .

Since then, Willie Colón has been a protagonist of all the stages, waves, and important moments of salsa—a participant in the famous Estrellas de Fania

WILLIE COLÓN

recital at the Cheetah Club on 52d Street in 1971; a leader of the avant-garde and folkloric tendencies of the 1970s with records such as *Asaltos navideños, El bueno, el malo y el feo,* or the Latin ballet *Baquiné de los angelitos negros;* founder, along with Rubén Blades, of the "conscious salsa" movement; and even a beneficiary of the commercial boom that started in 1975 and that during its demise in the 1980s couldn't manage to knock Willie Colón off his firm pedestal.

Nevertheless, as the commercial "face" of salsa for many years and at the same time (according to more than one specialist) the "least accomplished musician of the salsa leaders," Willie Colón's consistency and artistic vitality throughout his twenty-five-year musical career cannot be the product of mere chance or novelty. There are no twenty-five-year novelties. What, then, is Willie Colón's secret? I've asked myself a thousand times, up to the day I finally met and, of course, interviewed him.

The interview began as a merciless interrogation by a nosy reporter who managed to outdo his colleagues at a press conference. We were attending the Third Festival of Caribbean Culture in Cancún, [Mexico,] and that night Willie's concert was to take place, which meant that he was supposed to meet with us reporters earlier that day. Later, tempting him with a Coca-Cola that he had desperately been requesting, I managed to drag him to a reserved room to continue our conversation and to prove to myself what I had long suspected: more than a musician affected by certain styles and commercial images, this band director is a consummate intellectual, full of political and social concerns that many people in the music world couldn't care less about: he does cares about the purpose of music, the destiny of his cultural homeland, musical experimentation, and poetic searching—for example, wanting to know what Rubén Blades had said to me about him, or how to respond to the Mexican audience that evening—which means that nothing human is foreign to him. Because after all, as he said at one point in our dialogue, "the salsa kings don't just play songs of love."

Conscious Dialogue with a Salsa King

LPF: Willie, if you look back at the 1960s and 1970s, would you say that the best days of salsa have come and gone?

WC: I don't know why you're asking me that, because from what I can see, salsa is still very much alive and well. Salsa is becoming more popular all the time: it's listened to in Latin America, it's winning over Europe, and it continues to involve. And that evolution provokes transformations, passing fashions, which by no means signify exhaustion, such as erotic salsa, which has been the most recent wave. The same thing happens with musicians: new stars are appearing all the time, and among the newest and the best are Juan Luis Guerra, Frankie Ruiz, and Eddie Santiago. So, I would describe salsa as a sort of Latin American rock because of its ability to evolve, but like rock, it's here to stay.

LPF: You were always a typical barrio guy. What's the significance of the barrio in the birth and character of salsa?

WC: Look, for many reasons Latinos in the United States don't assimilate well; they don't have confidence, and the barrio is a refuge, a ghetto for Latin Americans. In the United States, Latinos are a minority living in a context of discrimination, and only in the barrio are they able to reproduce their original environment. And that very environment creates a necessity: in the barrios a social formation takes place, which is the expression of a little piece of the homeland of each immigrant, and in that environment all things Latin American are valued as important and indispensable; without them one can't live (or one refuses to do so). I think that in those spiritual necessities and the lack of communication beyond the borders of the barrio, we can find the profound psychological and cultural factors that give rise to salsa precisely in the Latino neighborhoods of New York, where it emerges as a manifestation of cultural resistance. After all, if we know we're still not completely accepted by U.S. culture, why not follow the lead of rock and roll or another type of music? And salsa emerges as something of our own, which is why it's full of politics and stories from the street. It's a music of the city, and its melodies are essentially urban.

LPF: And for you personally, what has the barrio meant to your musical formation?

WC: I was born in the South Bronx, the son of two Latinos also born in New York and the grandson of a Puerto Rican woman who left the island in 1923 and who still doesn't speak English. The woman who took care of me as a child was Panamanian, and on our block there were also Cubans, Dominicans, Venezuelans, Chicanos, people from all over the Caribbean, and all you heard was music in Spanish. So you're formed in that social and musical environment, absorbing all the folklore, mannerisms, music—*son, cumbia, el aguinaldo*—and suddenly all those roots begin to meld very naturally inside of you, with no contradictions. . . . That's the story of salsa it-self: a harmonic blend of all the Latin music of New York, expressed in a new way through a completely mestizo type of music.

LPF: Whenever you talk about your roots, you mention your grandmother.

WC: That's because she's been an important person in my life: she's my blood link with Puerto Rico and was the person who bought me my first trumpet when I was ten years old. That's pretty important, don't you think?

LPF: And does your "bad boy" image, which was your calling card in the 1960s, come from that barrio where you were born?

WC: For a lot of people, I'm still the "bad boy," but at one time I really was. In my barrio, if I wanted to keep the trumpet my grandmother bought me, I had to defend it. . . . Even so, it was stolen twice. I think that's why I changed to the trombone: it's a lot bigger and more difficult to run off with.

LPF: One hears a lot of talk about certain limitations of Latin music in the United States. There's even talk of censorship. Is there any truth to all this?

WC: There's really no censorship per se. . . . It's just that within the com-mercial scheme of things, the creative space for working and experiment-ing is always shrinking, for the simple reason that one must obey the mar-ket forces, and that's a limitation. An example from my own perspective is the length of the songs, which are usually around four minutes, and for me it's very difficult to write an important work if I have to think about time constraints. Can you imagine if jazz were created in a similar format? Well, it's the same for us, and that's why many of my best pieces haven't been hits in the United States and Puerto Rico, even though they have been in Latin America. On the other hand, the control of the media by the large multi-nationals means that one cannot escape certain restrictions, and merely holding liberal views—especially when you're a Latino—is already danger-ous from a commercial standpoint.

And on the other hand, you have the lyrics of our songs. Lyrics that are a bit harsh can always scare off a sponsor. Luckily, the ultraright doesn't worry too much about our lyrics because, fortunately, they don't under-stand Spanish. But in any case, it's always easier for musicians who write softer lyrics and less complicated melodies that can easily penetrate the market, and this reality limits the artistic elaboration of our music.

LPF: But in your case, the lyrics seem as important as the music, because you're one of the founders of "conscious salsa."

WC: Yes, that's right. I've never stopped writing music with a message. At the beginning I did it with Héctor Lavoe, and later with Rubén Blades, and now I'm still doing it on my own because I think it's useful and necessary. And that type of composition caused us a lot of trouble, so much so that at one point when we were doing "Pedro Navaja" or "Tiburón" with Rubén, we had to perform in bulletproof vests.

But I also try to assure that my lyrics have positive messages for our people, and I complement my role as an artist by participating in lots of programs for youth. I go to schools and give speeches, I do ads on TV, I attend cultural events that help give Latinos pride and help raise their self-esteem because a good number of them, most of all the young people, suffer a cultural schizophrenia that makes them reject their values since they're not allowed to participate fully in the society in which they live. I think we should help them recover the pride in their roots and the idea that their culture is as valuable as any other. In the same vein, it's not a coincidence that I've just recorded an album titled *Honra y cultura [Honor and Culture]*.

LPF: Why do you feel that need to give salsa a social content?

WC: Salsa is like a newspaper, a chronicle of our lives in the big city, and that's why it talks about topics like crime, drugs, prostitution, pain, uprootedness, and even about our history of exploitation and under-development. We no longer talk about cutting sugarcane or the life of the *campesino*—although that's still possible—but rather about the social problems of Latinos living in the modern world and the causes of these problems.

LPF: But you also sing love songs.

WC: None of that means that songs about love, music, or happiness have to be excluded. But as a significant cultural movement, I don't believe salsa can renounce the possibility of exploring social themes. That's why, to paraphrase Oscar Hijuelos, "the salsa kings don't just play songs of love."

LPF: What's your definition of salsa?

WC: I don't believe salsa is a rhythm or a genre that can be identified or classified: salsa is an idea, a concept, the result of a way of approaching music from the Latin American cultural perspective.

LPF: Around 1975 the first great salsa boom occurred. To what extent did it help to consolidate this new music?

WC: The boom was a double-edged sword: it helped us get exposure, but it definitely introduced commercial interests. When salsa began to become popular among the Latin public of the United States and the Caribbean, it became part of a business, and soon the record labels started looking for formulas to take advantage of that success. One of those formulas was the most typical of all: to ride certain talented singers and create a repertoire for them, give them some arrangements, a band, and even a style, and then launch them. Another of the ideas was to dust off the old Cuban hits from the 1950s—the music of Benny Moré, Arsenio Rodríguez, and Celia Cruz and the Sonora Matancera—and "salsify" it a bit with new arrangements and melodies. These songs were sure to be hits all over again. So the boom became an obstacle for experimentation, and it has affected me personally quite a bit because I've always tried to improve with every new record. As far as I know, the only way to do so is to unleash your creativity, without worrying too much about whether or not you're going to sell a lot of records. That was a risk we took with Rubén, and you see, *Siembra* is still the best-selling salsa record of all time.

LPF: In my view, it's no coincidence that when the labels went back to the Cuban music of the 1950s they chose Benny Moré, Arsenio Rodríguez, and Celia Cruz and Sonora Matancera. What do you think of these artists?

WC: Without a shadow of a doubt, I think Cuban music has been my teacher and the teacher of many *salseros*. It's clear that salsa has its deepest roots in Cuban *son* and that due to the blockade and the political climate of the 1960s, less information started to come out of Cuba. That break was a decisive factor in the birth of salsa, which emerges as a grafting of the musical folklore of other Latin American countries onto *son*. And it's precisely this element that distinguishes *son* from salsa: while *son* has a specific structure, salsa is pure freedom, which means it can start with a *guaguancó* and finish with a Puerto Rican *aguinaldo,* with a dash of Brazilian *batucada* or a passage from Mozart.

But that root has names, and Benny, Arsenio, and Celia were the most important and the best known. Benny is freedom and talent, so much so that even today there are people making a good living singing his tunes the same way he did, or almost the same. So if he were alive today, he'd still be on top. I remember having seen Arsenio two or three times in New York; I was quite young, but I always listened to his records and he was our number-one teacher. We learned the feeling of Cuban music from him, orthodox *son,* so to speak. And Celia Cruz and Sonora Matancera were the models of fidelity to Cuban music. I always dreamed of working with Celia—she was the living image of the greatness that came from Cuba—and thank God I was able to do so. And we are also indebted to Celia because she always fought for Afro-Caribbean music, often in the face of great adversity. It's fair to say that without her and her determination, salsa might not have come to be in New York.

LPF: What do you know about the Cuban music of today?

WC: I've had the opportunity to share the stage with great orchestras like Los Van Van and Irakere, and I've heard a lot of what's being recorded in Cuba because fortunately we can get music from there now. And what makes me the happiest when I hear them is that the Cubans also prove we were right when we opposed the purists who refused to change a few things. They were trying to make music like putting on a Shakespearean play, which is staged time and again with the same text. And now, with the new Cuban groups that have started to emerge, the purists have seen that music cannot be reined in by a static model. The fact is that salsa also helped the Cubans to evolve; they nurtured their own music through salsa. There's no doubt about that.

Honor and Culture

He runs on stage smiling at the crowd that shouts his name. He picks up his trombone and approaches the microphone. He starts out with "El gran varón" and the applause is tremendous: *"No se puede corregir, a la naturaleza"* ["you can't correct nature"]. Because this concert on the evening of November 14, 1991, during the Third Festival of Caribbean Culture in Cancún, is a special concert: at the end of the performance, Willie Colón has an appointment with a notary public at the Cancún Country Club. He's decided to marry Julia Craig, his companion of the last ten years and the mother of his sons Diego, Antonio, and Miguel. The entire crowd knows this, and that's why they're applauding Willie Colón like never before.

I applaud him as well. I'm a diehard fan of his music and of his personality too, I think. But I also applaud him because I know that by clapping for him I'm also applauding an entire cultural project of which this man, dressed in a suit, once considered a New York scoundrel, has been the cornerstone from the days when salsa was only a barrio fad until now, when it enjoys the status of a universal cultural phenomenon.

LPF: Salsa has been enjoying a lot of success in Europe recently. How has this come about?

WC: Salsa has been winning over Europe in many ways. At the beginning, most of all, it was through our playing at dances for the Latino communities in Europe; we'd go play like we did in New York or San Juan. Later on, thanks to the jazz content of salsa rhythms and the polyrhythms, we've been able to play at the great jazz festivals like Paris or Newport. Then came the moment of the big concerts and the records. Looking back, it's been easy: the strength of salsa is an undeniable cultural fact.

LPF: So why has salsa been better received in Europe than in the United States?

WC: I think our acceptance in Europe is due to a cultural factor: Europeans, for the simple fact of being surrounded by so many cultures, are more open to the foreign, to the new. They're a more tolerant people, and although we've had a good reception in countries like Germany, this doesn't mean that Europe is our Garden of Eden. . . . But it's definitely easier than succeeding in the United States. I'm sure you've heard the joke: a person who speaks two languages is called a bilingual, if he speaks three, he's a trilingual, and if he speaks only one he's called an American. . . . Nevertheless, I think our success in Europe is more than just a passing fancy.

LPF: What about the increasing presence of Anglo musicians in salsa? Is this helping salsa commercially or culturally?

WC: I believe the exact opposite is happening: they've helped themselves because they're using salsa as a tool, not as a collaboration in its most profound sense. It's not feasible for a David Bowie or a Paul Simon to open doors for us to the world of rock and pop. Now, on the other hand, something like what Gloria Estefan has done with her fusion of rock and Cuban rhythms has greater chances for success because she's a Latina, but she'll have to do it playing by their rules. . . . From my perspective, we Latino musicians always end up getting the short end of the stick in those so-called collaborations; we get a lot less out of them culturally and economically. It's just another chapter in the same old story of cultural relations that are very problematic for us.

LPF: And, in your judgment, what's the explanation for the great influence and popularity of Caribbean music all over the world?

WC: The Caribbean is exactly where a confluence of three important cultures took place, and its history is as rich as the Mediterranean—from the Mayas, Aztecs, and Taínos who lived there to the Europeans and Africans who came and mingled in the Caribbean, bringing their longstanding cultural patrimony with them. And if the fundamental expression of that culture is music, it shouldn't surprise us that it's achieving success and being played all over the world.

LPF: In some sense you yourself have posed this question: are you for or against celebrating the five hundredth anniversary of the arrival of the Spanish to the New World?

WC: I can't have a negative opinion about the quincentennial of the Discovery or the Encounter of Two Cultures because I'm a product of that collision: I have white, black, and Indian blood, and to top it all off, my last name is Colón[1] . . . and that's why I believe we should use this celebration to find the things that unite us rather than those that divide us. I think, for example, that the quincentennial can still be a magnificent excuse for cementing the unity of the Spanish-speaking peoples, because we really need that unity. It would be absurd to claim that this is a purely festive celebration because many terrible things have happened over these five hundred years, but this is the best moment to attempt to unite us because Latin America desperately needs unity now for its cultural and economic survival.

LPF: As a Latino in the United States, what are your expectations and concerns?

WC: One of my great concerns during recent years has been the need to create a united Latino front in the United States. Recently I was awarded an honorary degree at Yale and I had to give a speech that I titled "Salsa: A Sociopolitical Perspective." I did a lot of research in preparing my talk and studied the Latino community in New York, which is more than one hundred years old, and I found out how it participated in the Cuban independence movement and the Dominican revolution. For example, the Puerto Rican flag was made in New York. . . . And when you observe the present-day conditions in this community, it's evident that for very obvious reasons we have not managed to carve out our own space as U.S. citizens. And I think it's fair to say that we bear a good deal of the blame for this situation because there's passivity among our people. But by the year 2000, we're going to be the largest minority in the United States, with more than thirty million people, and if we can create that united Latino front, along with an identity for the Latino vote, we can affect the political decisions of the country, as do the Jews, who seem to have a say in everything. I think that

---

1. "Colón" is the Spanish version of Columbus (translator's note).

united front could have avoided blockades, dirty wars, and interventions against our people.

LPF: Do you see that unity among Latinos as fitting into a larger Latin American unity?

WC: Of course. We all need to be united. The events of the Gulf War and other things that happened later have revealed how far the United States will go and have brought to the forefront the urgency of that unity, which is the only thing that can save us. Fortunately we're making strides toward this integration, and I reiterate that the example of how they crushed Iraq, one of the cradles of civilization, is a lesson we should learn. And that unity should concern itself above all with the blockade against Cuba, which is a punishment for disobedience, and with the case of Puerto Rico, which is a matter of life or death for our culture and our nationality.

LPF: Now that you've mentioned it, what do you think of Puerto Rico's political destiny?

WC: First of all, we have to get rid of the fears they've instilled in our people: the old fear of communism, of losing protection, of being totally independent. But I think that, in any case, we have to think about one day obtaining self-determination, but that has to come step by step, without scaring people, because there are a lot of people who fear a radical change. That's why I think the first thing is to establish the rights of Puerto Ricans under any status and create a strong and respected constitution. Becoming a republic, however, would have to be a long process, of between five and ten years, in order to avoid chaos and panic. In the meantime, I dream that perhaps by 2000 Puerto Rico will finally be an independent republic, in spite of the results of the most recent plebiscites.

LPF: And does this mean that Willie Colón will eventually move to Puerto Rico and participate in politics?

WC: Not for now. I have a lot of responsibilities in the Latino community of New York that are also important, such as serving on the board of directors of the Hispanic Arts Association or being active in the social programs of the community. We're determined to achieve excellence in education and economic power for our people. . . . But by no means do I plan to enter politics.

LPF: What about Rubén Blades? Is he going into politics?

WC: That remains to be seen. Rubén's been talking about retiring from music for many years, but he can't seem to make up his mind.

LPF: In the meantime, might a reunion of the two of you be possible?

WC: Although our relationship didn't end very well, a lot of water has passed under the bridge, and I don't rule out the possibility of our working together in the future. As I already mentioned, I like to be creative, to experiment, and if I were to work with Rubén again, it would be to do something different. Always something different.

Cancún, Mexico, 1991

3

Johnny Ventura: Merengue Can Be a Very Serious Thing, but Also Wonderful

Part One: Or, Everything You Always Wanted to Know about Merengue but Were Afraid to Ask

LPF: Well, I'm going to go ahead and ask: What is merengue and what's your approach to it?

JV: Look, *chico*—as you Cubans say—merengue has its origins in the farmland of my country, when we were trying to achieve our independence from Haiti, in the first half of the nineteenth century. During that war Colonel Fonseca, being a musician, decided to create a rhythm that would identify our troops and alert them to battle. A good idea, no? People really liked something about that rhythm, they identified with it, and soon it was much more than a battle cry. But at the end of the war it stayed there in the countryside, and it started to gain strength until it became the typical country music for a long time. But since people were moving around a lot and migrating to the cities, its influence keeps spreading and reaches the masses through the back door, that is, through the most humble barrios. Nevertheless, upon reaching the cities, that countryside merengue is reined in by the *tumba curasoleña*, which was the favorite rhythm of Dominicans at the end of the nineteenth century. By that time, one of the presidents of the republic, Francisco Ulises Espaillat, had prohibited the diffusion, dancing, or playing of merengue because he thought it wasn't very appropriate for polite society: it struck him as too crude and vulgar. But that decree arrived

38

JOHNNY VENTURA

too late: merengue was already too popular and couldn't be stopped even by legislation. Meanwhile, high society, which was used to the *tumba*—which was from other places in the Antilles, like the Dutch East Indies—remained uncontaminated by merengue. Finally the twentieth century arrives, and the credit goes to Luis Alberti Hernández (after the intervention of Juan Espinola and Pancho García, who were the first to go out to the countryside to collect the music) for modernizing merengue and popularizing it as a genre. Although those three (Alberti, Espinola, and García) were contemporaries, the difference was that while the latter two transcribed what they heard, Luis Alberti, who's still alive, worked from that material and made his own music, his own arrangements, and was the first to put it down on pentagrams.

That's how the urban history of merengue begins. At the end of the 1920s merengue is starting to become an urban music, although it remains limited to the humble barrios because high society still won't accept it. But Luis Alberti and his orchestra, which was the most important band in the 1930s, start to bring it into the big ballrooms, although they made the concession of not playing it on its typical instruments, like the *tambora*. This was a rustic instrument made from goatskin, still somewhat hairy, and it was embarrassing to take such a thing into the big ballrooms; so instead, merengue was played on international percussion drums. That's how merengue is preserved, somewhat modified, until the time of Trujillo, a dictator who governed the country with an iron fist for thirty-one years.

Trujillo, like all dictators, had his populist rhetoric and was looking for a way to win favor with the people. He did this through his nationalism, which helped to consolidate merengue. Even his political campaigns were conducted to the rhythm of merengue, and he began to make an issue of this to the point that merengue had to be played at all the parties he attended. So there's no way to disguise the fact that it was thanks to Trujillo that merengue began to break down the barriers that had been established by high society, while among the masses it was growing more popular all the time. Nevertheless, in my view a sort of stagnation then occurs: merengue, which originally had its rhythmic base in the *tambora* and the guiro (the only musical vestige of our aboriginal peoples in merengue), also had some chord influences from the guitar and the *tiple,* but when the German accordion arrived in the Dominican Republic, it took the place of the string instruments. And that format had many limitations, which caused

JOHNNY VENTURA

merengue to be played in a very monotonous way. As a result, the possibilities of diffusion and creation were reduced.

But let me get back to Trujillo, because the "generosity" of dictators is usually double-edged. In his time, composers didn't receive any compensation for their work, but when they wrote a piece exalting Trujillo and his regime, the Partido Dominicano, which was his party, gave the songwriters some money. Logically, this encouraged people to write a certain type of merengue, since that was the only way to get anything for writing music. But at the same time it stunted creativity, because almost every song was a tribute to *el Jefe*, as Trujillo was known, who was also an aficionado of a certain type of merengue, and the composers and the interpreters also stuck to this model in hopes of pleasing him.

Finally, Trujillo is assassinated in 1961 and the Dominican Republic euphorically launches into a search for democracy, and that's when my generation takes up merengue and we begin to play free from the constraints of the Trujillo regime. Almost spontaneously, out of a pure reflex reaction, we begin to sing epics, songs about love and life, humorous songs, songs for children, in sum, a very free kind of merengue. For example, we celebrated with merengue the attempted revolution in 1965, and we went to the barracks with merengue at the time of the U.S. intervention. With our generation a new musical landmark is established: a new freedom in dance emerges, a more creative interpretation, and we start doing things that fortunately have endured to this day and have served as a foundation for many of the new talents that emerged later.

When Johnny asked me, "So, you said this was the last question, right?" I had to nod and end the interview. My amazement had subsided a bit by now, and although I wanted to ask him a few more questions that had occurred to me during our conversation, I understood that it would have been too much. Johnny was only proposing that I turn off the tape recorder and that we continue talking over a drink, and besides, what I had captured on tape was much more than I'd hoped to obtain from the most celebrated Dominican *merenguero* of the last thirty years.

When I arrived at his hotel in Cancún, at 11:30 in the morning, I was hoping to do a bold and "gracefully penetrating" interview, like merengue itself. After all, what I had in my head was Johnny's performance from a couple days earlier: on stage, leading his group, the man was transformed into a singing and dancing machine for nearly two hours, overwhelming an adoring crowd, especially a group of women who nodded in agreement when Johnny would say, "he's a rather cute black man," or flattering them with the most convoluted and prolonged *piropo* I've ever heard, recited, by the way, at the speed demanded by merengue: "God bless the hands that carried the machete used to dig the hole where they sowed the seed from which grew the tree from which they cut the branch with which they made the handle of the hammer used to build the crib where you were born, *mami.*" And I asked myself, "Can this be the same musician who was aspiring to the mayorship of Santo Domingo?"

Part Two: Or, Everything You Wanted to Know about Johnny Ventura but Were Afraid to Ask

LPF: From what you've told me, I gather that, in some way, the history of merengue reflects the history of your country over the last 150 years. So, even though it doesn't seem so now, merengue at times has been a very politicized rhythm. What relationship do you, as a politician, have with merengue?

JV: Yes, you're right. Merengue is a music that was born politicized, on the battlefields, as I told you, and throughout the history of the Dominican Republic there have always been singers and composers who've used it to alert their followers. And I'm convinced that those of us who become artists and in some way are the voice of the people should use this voice to denounce wrongdoings, to show the way, to help us get along better. I believe one has to be very lazy, perhaps indifferent, not to take advantage of that possibility.

On the other hand, I've been a member of the Dominican Revolutionary Party since April 14, 1962, when the great political euphoria erupted in the country. I was a very young man then, just twenty-two years old, and as such I couldn't think abstractly about what was happening at the time. That's why I started participating in several liberation movements for our country, which is how I ended up holding positions within and outside the party. I'm a member of the executive committee, which is the highest level of the party, and have been vice president of the capital district. Later I went on to become president of one of the five regions into which the party divides the country—the one with the greatest density of population. In 1982 I was nominated by the party for a congressional seat, and I won it; in 1986 I ran for assistant mayor of Santo Domingo, and I also won that post. Later, in 1990, we lost the possibility of my becoming mayor of the capital because of a division in our party. There was a problem among the primary candidates, and we went to the elections divided and lost them. Now we're in a battle to strengthen the party, and I think we have a great shot at winning the next election. Our presidential candidate is a man of my own extraction, and if we win it will be the first time we'll have a president of the country born from the ranks of the people: Dr. Francisco Peña Gómez, who has a very wide political vision, with an enviable ability to form coalitions and very interesting and well-defined political and economic policies, and above all, with a concrete program to address the country's greatest problems.

But getting back to your question: I've been in politics for thirty years and in music for more than thirty-five, so these have been practically two simultaneous passions of mine. As a musician I've lived with the same expectations and struggles as I have as a politician, and I've directed my music toward that struggle to help improve my country's destiny.

During these thirty-five years, my music has gone through different stages, as happens with any artist. Around 1964 I began my career as an independent musician. Before then I played and sang in different orchestras, among them the Superorquesta San José, directed by Papa Molina, which was the most prestigious band in the country. But when I went my own way, I formed a group of only eleven members who at the beginning didn't have great expectations; we didn't think we'd earn the acceptance and success that we eventually did. The important thing was that we liked music and we began to make it. At that time our style of merengue differed from that of the earlier period because we used a reduced format, which was the only one possible after Trujillo's reign came to an end, along with the subventions for selected large orchestras. Things got really bad. . . .

By the end of the 1960s we had to start modifying our style of merengue. Without knowing it, we were initiating a musical revolution parallel to the one the *salseros* had begun in New York. In our case what happened was that American music began to dominate the country; it's the music that everyone was dancing to and that all the stations were playing, so we were forced to introduce some new ingredients to bring back the young kids to their musical habitat. First we started to use a Cuban instrument, *la tumbadora,* which was already part of merengue but had been put on the back burner. We rescued it because we understood that a great rhythmic richness was being lost, and when we combined it with the *tambora,* we managed to create a great fusion. As a result, the traditionalists accused us of destroying the classical form of merengue, and God knows how many other offenses, when what we were really doing was revitalizing the *tumbadora* to achieve a more solid rhythmic base. But at the same time we had to modify the role of the double bass because we were now playing at an international level. When we saw the dance styles of the different audiences, we realized that Cubans dance to the double bass but Puerto Ricans dance to the *tumba-dora,* so we started molding that structure to make sure our music would be well received by those diverse groups—so that they would feel the music and accept it as their own. Everything we did had a reason, and all these modifications served to modernize merengue, to move it forward.

But along with this, one day something very funny happened that re-vealed another key to the problem. I remember we were attending a party in Santo Domingo, and the music was being played by my group, by mae-stro Rafael Solano's group, and by a disk jockey with recorded music. It was a graduation party, around 1973 or 1974, and Solano's admirable orchestra went on stage and no one got up to dance, not even to watch. It was as if they weren't even playing. Then came my group, with the singers up front, a great show, and people barely batted an eye. Then the disk jockey started playing and the room overflowed with people. So Solano says to me, "Mae-stro Johnny, we're going to have to get rid of these disk jockeys," and I told him, "We can't even win by killing them: we've got to jump on the band-wagon or give it up." It was then that it occurred to me to bring down David Santiago from New York, the son of Puerto Ricans born there, who had a marvelous voice. At that time the Bee Gees were at the top of the charts, and we decided to cover all their songs, and every time we played one the people danced and applauded like crazy, although I felt very un-comfortable because I had been known up to that point for doing my own thing. Yes, I felt ridiculous, but I thought about what was happening with that music and I discovered that its strength was in the *tambora,* and I de-cided to introduce it. But since we didn't have a drum section, at the re-cording studios we'd improvise with by grabbing the two-inch tape box and with a towel in our hands we'd use it as a drum, until we finally incorpo-rated it for good into our orchestra, and the reaction was overwhelmingly positive. The kids went back to dancing merengue, as if by magic, and since then no group plays merengue without the drums.

We were also the first group in the country to put the show on center stage, with the singers acting as dancers, and we also incorporated some-

JOHNNY VENTURA

thing that wasn't very common at the time: talking to the audience, which established a direct communication with the people. So little by little we started to change the character of merengue, and for a long time we worked at that on our own until Wilfrido Vargas came along and created another variation of merengue with a great deal of success. And later came Wilfrido Manuel Tejada, who started to arrange different groupings with a different orchestration, so cleverly incorporating elements of jazz that his modifications of the genre remained intact until Juan Luis Guerra came along and sealed the merengue's success. In my own case, I've been able to carry merengue to different parts of the world for over thirty-five years, including places we've always dreamed of conquering, such as Mexico, Argentina, and Spain, where we'd never had success before. And now Juan Luis, with the talent he has and the platform that guides him, has finally been able to consolidate merengue internationally. Don't forget that in the past we had trouble finding good composers. Not a lot of songwriters wanted their lyrics put to merengue rhythms because of the political situation I talked about earlier. We had to wait for people to come along such as Mundito Espinal, Máximo Polanco Estrella, and, finally, Ramoncito Díaz and Uchi Lora, before our lyrics reached a competitive level on a par with the rest of salsa. And now, at just the right time, an artist like Juan Luis Guerra emerges, making melodies and writing lyrics that give our rhythm elegance, and winning over regions of the world that had previously not opened their doors to merengue. For me it's a matter of pride that a musician as talented as Juan Luis Guerra has emerged, and I hope he can keep it going for a long time. For the sake of merengue.

At one in the afternoon, when I turned off the recorder and, against my well-established custom, accepted his offer of Brugal rum—I never drink before six—I gained a glimpse of the Johnny Ventura that I hope each reader obtains upon reading this interview. This is a second Johnny Ventura (an image that before my eyes was superimposed upon that of the dynamic showman I had rightly expected to meet): an incredibly flexible, articulate, and profound man, capable of arousing the admiration that well-used intelligence always provokes. In addition to being an excellent creator of images, this man is an intellectual in the best sense of the word.

As we drank our farewell drink, he showed me the lyrics of the song he would soon record with Willie Colón: a long tune about friendship that would be part of the album he planned to record in honor of his thirty-five years as a musician and on which he shares the microphone with other figures of Latin American music such as Celia Cruz, Andy Montañez, Daniela Romo, the Colombian group Niche, Armando Manzanero, Wilfrido Vargas, Sergio Vargas, and other friends and colleagues. Then I wished him luck, because a man like him, who finished his show the previous evening at 4:00 A.M., truly deserves it. He then told me to come back at 11:00, "because I want to study a while in the morning," as evidenced by the tome of the Dominican penal code, lying wide open, that had been listening to our conversation from the bed.

End of Speech and Beginning of Dialogue:
Merenguero, Ballplayer, and Promoter

LPF: From what you've told me, it's evident that merengue, like all popular genres, is a rhythm open to external influences. Among these elements, what is the relationship between merengue and Cuban music? And with which Cuban musicians have you felt the closest connection since you started?

JV: No one doubts the importance of Cuban music in the Caribbean, and throughout all Latin music, for that matter. Its legacy, rhythms, and instruments—I've already talked about the *tumbadora*—have influenced all popular music in the region. And I, in particular, have said many times that I've been influenced by two great artists—one Dominican and the other Cuban—whom I have idolized and greatly admired: Joseíto Mateo, who for us is the king of merengue, and Benny Moré, who for Cubans in the king of *son.* I think both of them influenced my style and my way of making music, and I'm not ashamed to admit it. I've been a great admirer of both, and I think they've had a lot to do with my success.

LPF: As an observer and protagonist, to what do you attribute the international popularity that merengue has enjoyed in recent years?

JV: Honestly, I think that merengue, which is the music that represents us and portrays us in all our facets, is essentially a vital, happy music—a music that easily wins people over, as it were. And after liberating people's dancing style, allowing people to dance comfortably, with no inhibitions whatsoever, this explosion and massive acceptance was unavoidable, especially when you add to the mix the international diffusion merengue has been enjoying as well as the arrival of new figures who've been able to adapt it to the changing times (technologically as well as musically and lyrically). For all these reasons, I'm convinced that merengue is a rhythm that's here to stay.

LPF: As a musician, a politician, and a Latin American, what do you think of the celebration of the quincentennial of the Discovery, which made such an impact on your country?

JV: Rather than offer a reflection on a topic that's been so overdiscussed and imposed like a fashion—and that like all fashions will pass—I'd like to make an appeal to people to remember our history. There's a political maxim that warns, "A people that doesn't remember its history is forced to live on its knees." I say this because I see no reason to celebrate the anniversary of this event. For me, the arrival of the Spanish, the encounter of two worlds or two cultures, was actually the forced imposition of one culture on another. And from the human point of view, it was one of the most terrible genocides in human history. We cannot forget that a few years after the arrival of the Spaniards, the aborigines of our land had disappeared due to mistreatment and genocide. Then there was the imposition of slavery upon the black race, of which I am a direct descendant on both sides of my family. Our people were brought to this continent by force, and on the island of Santo Domingo they were received at an embarcadero where they were sold like cattle and welcomed with the branding iron. Is that what they mean to celebrate? If we take the theological point of view of evangelization, we need only recall Neruda's poem to Quisqueya, in which we read that the Spanish exchanged living Indians for dead Christians. Now, speaking in Christian terms, we can recall that the church celebrates Holy Week to commemorate Christ's Way of the Cross. I think we should do the same thing: commemorate our people's Way of the Cross—but as a memorial, a tribute, not a celebration.

Unfortunately, the government of the Dominican Republic invested a great amount of money in the quincentennial that should have gone to education, to healthcare, and to feeding our people. In my country education is one of the areas most neglected by the government, and when I look at the present-day world I wonder if Latin America is prepared for what's ahead. We are all eager to become developed, but the only way to get there is by educating our people. So I think a useful and lasting way to invest that money would have been exactly that: to invest it in educating our people.

LPF: Upon hearing you speak, its amazing to see how you split into two people: the reflexive Johnny Ventura with very well defined political positions, and the other Johnny Ventura who goes on stage and unleashes all that energy in song and dance. Which makes me wonder, how important is the spectacle in your performances?

JV: First of all, I don't think I split in two: that's how I really am. When I feel the music, I live it, I enjoy it, and I identify with it to a great extent. That's why it's easy for me to get into it and put on my show. As far as the spectacle is concerned, my group and I do a somewhat stylized performance because when we began listening to merengue in the Trujillo era, the big bands of thirty-some musicians were in vogue and they all played seated. It looked like they didn't feel what they were doing. I was always struck by that, and when I had the opportunity to make my own group, I broke that mold. First of all, I didn't have the means to create a big band, and we decided to play standing up and dancing to our own music in order to show people that we felt the music we were making. Naturally, that provoked the scorn of the traditionalists, but it really opened the doors for us to the masses.

LPF: How have you been affected personally by being such a celebrity and having achieved such success?

JV: I sometimes wonder if I'm really such a popular guy because I still consider myself—and I hope I'll always be—a man of the people, one who shares his life with his people and makes friendships and understands that music is a profession and that he's lucky to have succeeded. So, since for me success has been a long road along which my fan base has grown little by little, I haven't felt that sudden change from anonymity to stardom. I've had the good fortune—and the intention—of not letting fame go to my head.

LPF: Before I turned on the tape recorder, you mentioned something about the Dominicans playing in the big leagues. Did you ever play ball in addition to playing music?

JV: As a kid I played baseball, and I even had offers to play professionally because I was a good hitter. But I had one problem: I was a lousy fielder.

LPF: Who were your idols in baseball?

JV: That's a funny story. In the big leagues my favorite team was always the San Francisco Giants because when I was a kid they sold gum with baseball cards and the cards had pictures of the players, which is how I saw a black player in the major leagues for the first time. His name was Monty Irving, and since he played for the San Francisco Giants, I became a fan of theirs. And I remained their fan when Willie Mays replaced Monty Irving in center field. And although the Giants haven't won a championship for years, as luck would have it, the Dominicans who later started to make it to the big leagues worked their way up through the Giants organization. This was the case with Osvaldo Virgil, the Alou brothers, or Marichal, who all played for my team back home, the Leones, of which I became a member of the executive board and later vice president.

LPF: Now I'm aware of three of your great passions: music, politics, and baseball. Outside of these three, and with the time you have left over after your studies, what type of books do you like to read?

JV: I have a wide range of tastes. As a reader I'm very heterodox, and since I'm really self-taught (I had to abandon my studies as a young man, and at the time I should have started college it was impossible, so I had to take a commercial secretary course), I've always tried to continue reading to improve my education. That forced me to read all kinds of stuff, and this is still the case now that the so-called Senior Citizens University has arrived in the Dominican Republic, a university made especially for adults that is run through seminars and research, and that makes me read constantly.

LPF: Would you like to write a book someday?

JV: I have a lot of ideas I'd like to put down in black and white someday, but I don't know if I'll have the time, the ability, or the talent to do so. But yes, I'd like to write my memoirs, to tell my life story, even though I'd do so with all the limitations of a literary novice. I dream of starting it soon.

LPF: And as with ballplayers, do you have favorite authors?

JV: In Latin American literature there are two obligatory deities, Neruda and García Márquez, whom I read as much as I can.

LPF: And Juan Bosch?

JV: Although Professor Bosch and I are in different political camps now, after the division of the party, I've always admired him as a writer and I believe I have his complete bibliography at home, which is quite extensive, by the way. I think that even today, although in my opinion he doesn't represent the best option for Dominicans, he's still a figure who deserves our respect as a politician and a writer: after all, you have to render unto Caesar what's Caesar's, you've got to give a man his due.

LPF: Now I promise you we're almost finished. . . . You're also described as a merengue talent promoter. How do you approach that task?

JV: Look, my band has already recorded about ninety-three albums. . . . And that number, which you find astonishing, is the result of an effort in which I'm not the only one involved: many of those albums have been solo productions recorded by the new kids who've passed through the band. That's because I believe everyone deserves a shot in this world. I record them, promote them, and give them all the opportunities I can, and several of them have become stars precisely due to this type of assistance.

LPF: What's your view of Caribbean music today? What's the present state of salsa, and what does the future hold in store?

JV: I think the Cubans should feel very proud of having been the fountain and nurturing source of all that has become the salsa phenomenon. Although I should clarify that, for me, salsa is not a genre, but rather a name whose origins and purpose I'm well aware of: Afro-Caribbean and especially Afrocuban rhythms melded together and received that name out of coincidence. I remember Fideas Escalona, a Venezuelan radio host who had an afternoon program and whose slogan was *"Fideas Escalona, con más salsa que pescao"* ["Fideas Escalona, with more salsa than fish"]. At that moment, Venezuela was a great venue for all of us who cultivated Afro-Caribbean music, and to get in good with Escalona was the best way to break into the country. Johnny Pacheco realized this, because in addition to being a talented musician he's a visionary businessman, and he attracted Fideas Escalona with that movement he called salsa. But we know that every one of those rhythms has its first and last name and its birthplace, which doesn't prevent salsa, which serves as a global nomenclature for a whole series of rhythms, from being one of the most potent musical movements in the entire world today. And our Dominican merengue is part of that movement, and with all the pride in the world I tell you that it pleases me to have been—and to be—part of a music that is making so many people dance. You said that we were about to finish, right?

Postscript

At almost three in the afternoon, after two more drinks, I left Johnny Ventura's room totally convinced that this prince of merengue is one of the artists whose name will never be erased from the sentimental chronicle and the true story of Latin American music. Whoever doesn't believe me, let him tell me at the end.

Cancún, Mexico, 1991

4

Johnny Pacheco: From the New Tumbao to the Old Tumbao—The Great Chronicle of Salsa

If salsa exists (and at least I'm sure it does), there's a name without which one cannot even conceive of its existence. And that name is Johnny Pacheco. . . . (Since such affirmations are usually untrue, while transcribing this interview I took it upon myself to find parallels, and I discovered that, at least in the realm of popular music, such categorizations are in fact pertinent, because it is possible to affirm that Cuban *son* would not be the same without Arsenio Rodríguez, that tango would be an orphan without the voice of Carlos Gardel, or that the bolero would be lacking its best sighs without the contributions of Agustín Lara.)

The truth is that Johnny Pacheco is the spinal cord from which have sprung all—or almost all—the musical and artistic structures that form the basis of the contemporary urban music of the Caribbean, known today as salsa. From the days when he lead the fury of *charanga* orchestras that came into vogue in New York in the early 1960s to the creation of the *tumbao* that would come to identify his group of *son* musicians in 1964, or the recovery of Celia Cruz and the traditional style of Cuban *son* in the 1970s, his musical presence laid down the ground rules that later became models that ended up as untouchable arrangements. Pacheco always knew how to be one step ahead of fashions, always on top of the wave and often creating the wave himself, if need be. In addition, it was his work as a promoter and producer that not only spurred the romantic creation of a record label called Fania but also allowed Fania to become the most important label in

JOHNNY PACHECO

the origin, establishment, and popularization of salsa, from New York to the Caribbean to the rest of the world, thanks, most of all, to Johnny Pacheco's musical and commercial instincts and his innate charisma.

Even though Pacheco's music may not be salsa's most notable body of work (when compared to Willie Colon's, Rubén Blades's, or Juan Formell's), and despite the fact that his flute is not the most exquisite of the Caribbean (where Richard Egües and Antonio Arcaño reigned supreme), nor his *tumbao* the most revolutionary (which would have been difficult after Arsenio Rodríguez, Eddie Palmieri, and Larry Harlow), I believe Pacheco, along with his music, his flute, and his *tumbao*—and above all, with the zest that has always permeated his melodies—occupies a privileged place in the history of salsa, so much so that, as I said at the beginning, if this music exists, it's because of a man named Johnny Pacheco.

How a *Tumbao* Is Born

LPF: Where does your interest in music come from, especially your interest in Cuban dance music?

JP: I've been in music since birth. My father, who was a saxophonist, used to direct the Santa Cecilia Orchestra, which at the time was the best in the Dominican Republic. He and several of his brothers played in the orchestra. They played any type of music, but mainly *danzones,* because in those days merengue was played only at the end of dances, as a festive touch, since it was considered popular music, vernacular, but also a music of the poor people. At that time—I'm talking about the 1940s; I was born in 1935—the music I most enjoyed listening to, and that ended up having a lifelong influence on me, came through the radio, because it so happened that my mother would listen to the soap operas from Cuba every afternoon. And I listened along with her and became a fan of *Tamacún, el Vengador Errante [Tamacún, the Wandering Avenger],* for example. And after the soaps came the musical programs, with Arcaño y sus Maravillas, the Sexteto Habanero, the Conjunto Casino, Chapotín, and all those fabulous groups from that era, which marked my musical tastes forever.

LPF: And does your vocation for the flute also date from that time?

JP: Yes, of course. And it was Arcaño himself who inspired me to take up the flute. I recall that there was a good flutist in Santo Domingo by the name of Pepín Ferrer, who founded the first *charanguita* in my country, but I never got to hear much of his music because in 1946 my family came to the United States. By 1949, when I entered high school, my interests were completely musical and had been defined by the music I'd heard on the radio back home in the Dominican Republic. Furthermore, I had already learned enough with my father to be able to play in his orchestra. The first instrument I played was the violin, and then I learned the clarinet, the accordion, and the saxophone, although the flute was my favorite. Then, at the age of seventeen, I got a call from Gilberto Valdés, who had already created the first *charanga* in New York with Mongo Santamaría. He hired me as a *timbalero* to take over for Tito Puente, who had left the orchestra. Even so, it was Gilberto Valdés who gave me my first wooden flute, a very old model, one of those flutes with six keys. I played that flute until 1956, when José Fajardo arrived in New York with his orchestra. By that time I had acquired a better flute at a pawnshop, and Fajardo taught me the correct positions because here there was nowhere to learn the right way to play. And later, the other person who helped me a great deal was Richard Egües. He taught me two basic things about flute technique: he told me that since I had strong lips, I should open up the mouth-hole of the flute a bit more so the sound would carry better, and he taught me certain positions and tricks that he used to get more out of the instrument. So I can't complain because I feel I've had the best possible teachers: I learned vibrato from Arcaño, craftiness from Fajardo, and elegance from Richard Egües. And there you have the origin of Pacheco's patented technique.

LPF: After playing with Gilberto Valdés, what did you do until you created your own orchestra?

JP: I studied engineering, but when I graduated in 1954 and passed the city test to work in an engine plant, they wouldn't give me the job because I still wasn't an American citizen. So I started going around to several different companies, and what they offered me were jobs for $32 a week. To make ends meet, I played with my father and my brothers in a quartet that played merengue at a time when it was very popular here. That was when Luis Quintero called me to play for his quartet, offering to pay me $95 for the weekend alone, just three days, and so I said to hell with my degree and decided to stick with music. Soon I had the opportunity to play with important people, such as Tito Rodríguez and Tito Puente, and even to organize Pérez Prado's orchestra for several recordings they did here at the Manhattan Center and at a place called Western Home, which was later known as Casa Galicia. In addition, I directed several orchestras for NBC that recorded with a lot of important musicians, such as Pedro Vargas. And the reason I was offered so many recording jobs is not that I was great at it, but because I was the only percussionist at that time who could read music, and that made me very popular.

LPF: Is that around the time you entered Xavier Cugat's famous orchestra?

JP: Yes, I worked with Cugat's orchestra for about a year, and I earned a good deal of money, by the way. But I was very bored because he had a limited repertoire of eighteen pieces, all of them with very similar arrangements. Then something happened, and although he didn't fire me, he did ask me to leave, which is basically the same thing, no? It all happened because there was a number titled "Cuban Mambo" that was very boring, and so to have some fun I arranged the saxophones to spice it up a bit. One day, while Cugat was in Las Vegas signing some contracts, I got together with the pianist, who was a fellow from Holguín by the name of Enrique Avilés, and we played "Cuban Mambo" in our style and the orchestra sounded like a whole new band. But when Cugat came back, the party was over for Avilés and me. And he said something very interesting to me: he asked me how many people there were in the United States. I told him there were about 250 million and he responded: "Well, I've played for about 50 million Americans, so that means I've got 200 million to go. And I'm going to play my numbers, in my own way, because if a formula works, there's no reason to change it." And that was the best lesson I learned from Xavier Cugat.

LPF: And that's when you decide to create your own *charanga*?

JP: Toward the end of the 1950s I started to work with two brothers who were my neighbors in the Bronx: the Palmieri brothers. First I had a quintet with Charlie, and we played in a very exclusive club in New York, near the Palladium. We would always fill the joint, playing vocal numbers in the *filin* style, and also cha-cha-cha, which was in vogue. And then we created the Duboney orchestra, of which I was a member only briefly because we had artistic differences and we amicably decided to go our separate ways. Then I realized one of my life's dreams by creating Pacheco y su Charanga [Pacheco and His *Charanga*] in 1960. A year earlier, with my dear brother Louie Ramírez, I prepared a demo with his "El guiro de Macorina" and "Óyeme mulata," which was mine. But all the labels refused to record it because they said it was trash. Then, when I was really losing hope, I got the idea to go see a man named Rafael Fons, who had a radio show that played only Cuban music, with the best Cuban bands, and luckily he accepted my demo and played it on his station on a Friday, without my knowing it. The following Sunday I was playing with a band and got a visit from Al Santiago, who at the time was head of the Alegre label, and he said he had found out that people were asking for my record, and when he realized it didn't exist he offered to record it. So we did, and we sold 250,000 copies right away; it was a hit with Jews, Latinos, blacks, everybody. We went to the top of the Latino charts right away, even passing Tito Rodríguez, Tito Puente, and Vicentico Valdés. So I started recording with Alegre, and I ended up making five records with them.

LPF: Pacheco, at what point in your career did you meet Arsenio Rodríguez, El Ciego Maravilloso [The Marvelous Blind Man]?

JP: I met Arsenio when I was nineteen and spending every waking hour with Cuban musicians. I already told you, for example, what Fajardo and Richard Egües taught me. Well, I was always trying to get Arsenio to teach me, and finally one day he told me he'd show me how to play real Cuban music and he took me to a show in the Bronx. At that time he had Cuajarón on bass, one of the best Cuban bassists, and his orchestra sounded wonderful, but most of his musicians were really scary-looking black guys who said they had their own cemetery in Cuba. So I started playing the *timbal* and every time I got off beat, Arsenio would shout *"machete"* and all the black guys would give me the meanest look you could imagine, until I got back in tempo. But they were all great people and they taught me a lot because the best way to learn to play *son* was with Arsenio's group. . . . Imagine what an ear El Ciego Maravilloso had: his pianist at the time, Rey Coeña, was always trying to find time to push up his eyeglasses since they'd slide down all the time. Arsenio realized what was going on, and when the time came he'd tell him, "Push up your glasses." If that's not a sixth sense for time and rhythm, then I don't know what is. . . . Later, when I started with my own *charanga,* he'd come to see me from time to time and say, "Let me jump in a second," and he'd grab the bass and no one could get it away from him the rest of the night.

LPF: After you started your *charanga,* you invented *el nuevo tumbao de Pacheco.* How did that come about?

JP: The musical environment of the early 1960s was rather complicated here in New York, and it became very difficult for musicians and orchestras to survive. And since musicians stopped coming from Cuba, soon there was a shortage of instrument players, which affected the *charangas* quite a bit because the hardest thing of all was to find violinists who knew how to play in that special rhythm. Even so, the musicians who worked with me kept on earning good money because *charanga* bands were in vogue, and ours, which was one of the best, was always in demand. Nevertheless, just to be safe, I had a little group on the side that played in the style of la Sonora Matancera, Arsenio, and Chapotín, and in 1964 I joined on with this group full-time. That's when I started with that Cuban *tumbao,* but I added a *tres,* and instead of *timbales* I included a bongo drum, and that's the origin of *el nuevo tumbao de Pacheco,* which would later be known as *el tumbao* and later as *el tumbao añejo* [the old *tumbao*], because I've been working the same formula for thirty years. Ever since I learned my lesson from Cugat, I always say that when a formula works, why change it? And with that formula I've had the good fortune of recording many of the greats of Latin music: Daniel Santos, Julio González, Pete Conde Rodríguez, Héctor Casanova, and my divine goddess, Celia Cruz.

From *Charanga* to Salsa: Pacheco's Great Leap

The Pacheco sitting before me on this New York autumn afternoon in 1995 is a sixty-year-old-man with completely white hair and an arm that's recently been operated on. All the same, he never stops working on his projects and thinking about the future. Evidently his character has changed very little, which is to be expected since, as we know, if a formula works. . . . A cigar smoker, long-time driver of Mercedes Benzes, eternal band director, Johnny Pacheco has been the image of fidelity ever since he became a devotee of Cuban music. Since then he has been, without a doubt, one of its greatest practitioners, and not even during the golden age of boogaloo in the 1960s, nor during the recent fever of erotic salsa and Latin jazz, has he changed his style or his interests, which explains why even in his own country he's been called a Cuban on more than one occasion. But where Johnny Pacheco is concerned, the confusion is not the least bit offensive.

LPF: Let's go back to 1964: something very important is about to happen in the history of Latin music: the creation of Fania. How did this company come about?

JP: Since things were going well with the Alegre label, I decided to use the money from my records to become a partner in the business, and I started bringing people into the company. I signed Orlando Marín, Kako, and Eddie Palmieri. Everything was going great until Al Santiago and I had some differences regarding the royalty payments for the musicians and I decided to leave. Although I didn't have much money, I wanted to create a company that would respect artists' rights and pay them their fair share. So together with Jerry Massuci, who was my lawyer, I borrowed $2,500 to record an album by Pacheco y su Charanga titled *Cañonazo,* on which there was a Cuban number called "Fanía Funché," by Rolando Bolaños. And that's where the company name came from, because that word is catchy not only for Latinos but for Anglos as well, and we wanted to reach all markets. Then we started bringing in artists, and the first people who signed with Fania were Bobby Valentín, who was a trumpeter, and the Jewish fellow Larry Harlow—God only knows how he was able to play Cuban music on the piano. We also brought in Ismael Miranda and then Willie Colón and Héctor Lavoe, who at the time was known as Héctor Pérez. We were all young people with a desire to do big things, and I think we did them pretty well.

LPF: According to what I've been told, that was the "romantic" era of Fania.

JP: Well, just to give you an idea: we distributed the first records out of the trunk of my car, an old Mercedes that was about to fall apart. We kept at it like that for three years, and we shared the money that came in among all of us or we'd reinvest it in the company. We also kept signing artists who were fed up with their labels because my goal was to found a group that would respect the rights of musicians and make them feel like they were part of a family. And I think we achieved that in 1971, when we celebrated the first great performance of the Fania All Stars at the Cheetah Club. That's when I said to myself, "We've accomplished something." That performance was the basis for the movie *Nuestra cosa latina [Our Latin Thing],* and four albums were made from the concert, but most important of all, the music we were making started to take off. I recall that the recital was the idea of an American deejay known as Symphony Sid, and we had only two days to rehearse. The worst thing was that we didn't have any music, and Bobby Valentín and I had to lock ourselves in a hotel room for two days, right in front of the Cheetah, on 52d and 8th Avenue, to write the arrangements and even some songs, like the one that became famous, "Quítate tú, pa' ponerme yo," on which all the invited singers joined in. At the end, everything turned out all right because the room had a capacity for twelve hundred and we got four thousand in there. I remember the heat was unbearable.

LPF: As I understand, along with being the leader of the *charangas* of the 1960s, creating the *tumbao,* and founding Fania, you promoted the use of the word "salsa" for the music you were making here in New York.

JP: The word "salsa" came about when we started traveling in Europe with

Fania and I realized that, except in Spain, no one knew anything about Cuban music. After all, what we were doing was taking Cuban music and adding more progressive chords, emphasizing the rhythms, and highlighting certain aspects, but without changing its essence. And since the word "salsa"—just like the words *sabor* [flavor] or *azúcar* [sugar], for example— has always been associated with this music, it seemed logical to call it that. Likewise, since in Fania we had Dominicans, Puerto Ricans, Cubans, Anglos, Italians, and Jews, that is, a diverse group of condiments that would make a good sauce, this was another reason why the word "salsa" emerged as a label for what we were doing. It happened while we were searching for a name to designate all the music that in Europe is called "tropical". . . . But our intention was never to steal music from the Cubans by disguising it under another name, because I've always admitted that the roots are Cuban and I've learned everything from Cuba. And the best reward I've received from all this was that when I was in Havana with the Fania All Stars, a group of the greatest Cuban musicians told me they were grateful for our efforts because, thanks to us, Cuban music was being heard throughout the world.

LPF: Maestro, is there a certain rhythmic or melodic characteristic that identifies salsa?

JP: Just as I admit that the roots of salsa are Cuban, I should also confess that here in New York this music was enriched because there were people here from all over the place, and we brought our music with us and tried to put it in the same key. The influences are very diverse, and that's why there's diversity in the rhythm and melody. And that fusion could come about only in New York, which is a great melting pot. And since you look for musicians based on talent, not nationality, the confluence of different rhythms was inevitable. In the final analysis, I believe this is what distinguishes salsa: it's not a rhythm, or a melody, or even a style. Salsa was—and still is—a Caribbean musical movement.

LPF: And what's happening now with salsa?

JP: Different singers have emerged in the salsa sphere who, in my judgment, have nothing to do with true salsa. All the singers and all the arrangements are similar, and I can't even tell who's singing or which orchestra is playing. The most famous example is Marc Anthony, who in my opinion is nothing more than a balladeer using salsa out of necessity as a way to commercialize his stuff. But that's not going to last, and it won't maintain the tradition we established. Right now—without mentioning the old maestros and the

Cubans, who keep playing their music with an admirable fidelity—the only authentic young *salseros* I see are singers such as José Alberto "El Canario," Tito Nieves, and Gilberto Santa Rosa, who have the talent to do things with inspiration, because we all know that without inspiration, there's no *son.*

LPF: In your opinion, what's the reason for merengue's success throughout the world starting in the 1980s? How can you explain the worldwide success of Juan Luis Guerra?

JP: First of all, let me clarify that I hate merengue with a passion, but I'm also grateful to it because thanks to merengue, I came to New York when my father decided to seek his fortune here. . . . But to answer your question, I think the first reason for its success is that it's a tasty rhythm and is easy to dance to. And second—although I think this is the most important thing—its success is due to the humor in its lyrics, something that had been lost in Latin music. Merengue is from the street, it's got flavor and humor, and that's why it became successful when all that erotic salsa idiocy started, which is not salsa or anything else. And as far as Juan Luis is concerned, I think he's a true phenomenon, a musical genius, because he created something completely different. The first thing he did was to give merengue its needed tempo, and then he wrote some simply fabulous lyrics. That's how it all started.

LPF: As an artist, what dreams of yours have come true?

JP: My first great dream was to record with Celia Cruz someday. I first shared the stage with her at the Fania All Stars concert at Yankee Stadium in 1973, and later we got together and recorded several albums. The first one was called *Celia y Johnny,* and then came *Tremendo Caché, Unidos de nuevo,* and *Recordando el ayer.* I'm also thankful to God for having been born when I was, which allowed me to meet the best musicians that have ever lived in this part of the world. And I'm thankful to be working still at sixty years of age. I've worked with people like Celia and Tito Puente and almost all the great figures of salsa, and I've even played and recorded with some of the best jazz players and percussionists who've ever lived. Wouldn't you say that's a great privilege?

LPF: And as a musician who's participated in so many projects, who's played so many instruments, who's shared the stage with so many stars, what do you think your greatest virtue is?

JP: One of the things I'm thankful for in life is that I've been able to get along with everyone. And that gift helped me bring about Fania All Stars and so many other things. For example, I remember that in Puerto Rico we performed a tribute to Héctor Lavoe to raise money for the operations he needed, and I called the members of the Fania All Stars orchestra, including Celia Cruz and Rubén Blades, and everyone came. And I told them the expenses would be covered by the concert and the rest would go to Héctor. It was a great show, but the best thing was that when they left the hotel, the bill barely came to $300, because they all paid their own expenses. And we raised about $65,000. That was one of the most beautiful things I've done in my life, and I'm proud of it.

LPF: After such a long career, with so many successes, what do you have left to accomplish?

JP: I'd like to write a book, or several books, about different aspects of music, because I think I've got enough material to do so. And I'd like to dedicate more time to working with young people, because they shouldn't lose touch with their roots. A lot of them are playing Latin jazz nowadays, looking for new paths, but I insist on playing my music, because I know it's the music the dancers need, and that communication between musician and dancer cannot be lost. What's more, I refuse to let this music die.

New York, 1995

5

Juan Formell: It Ain't Easy, It Ain't Easy

I remember those ever more remote days of the early 1970s, when we refused to accept the news that The Beatles had broken up—it had to be
another joke; they'd get back together soon—and started listening to Elton
John; when we heard the first songs by Chicago, Creedence, and Blood,
Sweat and Tears; when the best parties in Havana had musical accompani-
ment provided by those semiclandestine groups that later vanished into thin
air, swallowed up by the cultural bureaucracy, groups with unforgettable
names such as Los Kent (idolized by the kids of El Vedado), Los Gnomos
(idolized by the kids of La Víbora), Los Signos, and Dimensión Vertical.

I recall those times and the infinite despair of my friends in Mantilla and
the adjacent barrios, unflappable dancehall dancers who insisted on putting
son steps to Creedence tunes. At a time when New York was giving birth to
"something different" that would later be baptized as "salsa," Cuban popular music—for the first time in nearly two centuries of tradition and just
a few years after the passing of Benny Moré, Arsenio Rodríguez, Cuni, and
Chapotín—had hit rock bottom and was pathetically waging a losing
battle (when not in outright retreat), with no hope in sight. Rock and roll,
which had become the vernacular of contemporary music, was overwhelming all comers—in spite of the more or less official restrictions, the more or
less drastic restrictions—and Cuban music was stagnating in a rhythmic and
melodic rhetoric dominated by those ephemeral "rhythms" whose names
this memory of mine can barely recollect: *el mozambique, el upa-upa, el pa-*

JUAN FORMELL

cá, el pilón, el cha-onda, el chiquichaca, and so many other melodic cadavers—none of them worth recalling, by the way.

But I also recall that when the desperation seemed greatest, we started to hear a name that was becoming more and more popular, a name that would soon be familiar to us all: Juan Formell, a young man born in Cayo Hueso in 1942, the same one who had revolutionized the Orquesta Revé in a matter of days and was now founding a new group called Los Van Van. With his new band, Formell was starting to make a name for himself at the local dances, and—without our realizing it yet—at the same time was starting to chart a new course for Cuban popular music.

Now, seemingly light years removed from the early 1970s, there's no doubt that those two names—Juan Formell and Los Van Van—constitute the most important, revolutionary, and sustained phenomenon of Cuban dance music of the last three decades, and this can't just be a matter of co-incidence. A boundless admirer of Benny Moré, Cuban from head to toe, a tireless and diligent soul, Juan Formell and his indisputable musical talent are directly responsible for an artistic phenomenon that Cubans have embraced with open arms for some time. The music of Los Van Van fills an important void in the history of contemporary Cuban dance music, and no Cuban nowadays can escape the refrains and cadences of their best numbers. From "Yuya Martínez" and "La compota de palo" to "La Titimanía" and "No es fácil," Formell has moved the feet of two generations of dancers, and, by all indications, he will continue to do so in the foreseeable future. Because unlike other orchestras that cling to one format and one melody, Los Van Van—while never losing its unique hallmark—is a group in constant evolution, thanks to the wide-open ear of its director and chief prophet, Juan Formell, who is always on the lookout for something new and something good.

Nevertheless, the importance of Formell's work also transcends music to delve into the realm of the literary. The lyrics of his *sones* and *guarachas,* inspired by the reality of Cuba and taking the form of catchy *montunos,* have gone about creating a unique chronicle of Cuban life. Beneath the apparent simplicity of many of his texts, disguised by the pleasant aura of a picaresque *costumbrismo,* Formell has managed to reflect a complex social circumstance to which, on more than one occasion, he has had to refer obliquely in order to tell truths that are well known but not admitted. Perhaps the most salient example of this is a *montuno* that proclaims *"Nadie quiere a nadie / se acabó el querer"* ["No one loves anyone / love is finished"], which caused the song to vanish from Cuban airwaves.

But Formell and Los Van Van have not only fomented their musical revolution in Cuba; recognized by *Newsweek* in 1992 as one of the five top salsa groups, thanks to their greatest-hits album *Songo,* and described by the *New York Times* as being on the top of the Latin music mountain, well known and danced to in Colombia, Venezuela, and Spain, whose songs are covered by all the salsa greats—including Rubén Blades himself—Los Van Van is also a definitive force in the history of Caribbean music and dance at our fin de siècle. How has this come about? Let's let Juan Formell explain.

From Cayo Hueso to Posterity: Confessions of a Van Van

JF: When I look back on my life, as you've asked me to do now, I realize that my destiny was to become a musician and nothing but a musician. . . . The truth is that I've been listening to music and watching it being made since birth, because my father was a copyist, arranger, pianist, and flutist, in sum, a man with a vast musical knowledge who also was the first person to try to dissuade me from becoming a musician. He was well aware of how musicians live here in Cuba because he had endured that hard life himself, so he encouraged me to become something else, a doctor perhaps. That's why I was never able to attend a conservatory or any music school, and I had to learn the guitar on my own, playing by ear: I was going to be a doctor no matter what. But the environment in which I was raised also had an influence on my real vocation. The 1940s and 1950s were a very important time in Cuban music, and I was born and raised in the Cayo Hueso barrio of Havana, which had been the home of many singers and composers and where there were hundreds of Victrolas constantly playing songs by Benny Moré, Pérez Prado, Arsenio, La Aragón, you know, the best of the best.

When I was in high school my old man finally realized there was no use fighting it: music was my true passion. And so he started teaching me some tricks of the trade, like copying music, arranging, and composing harmonies and instrumentations. That was my music school. I always remember that back then, when I already knew something about the guitar, what I most enjoyed playing was *filin,* songs by José Antonio Méndez, César Portillo, Marta Valdés, and all those people. And I also played a lot of rock and roll, Elvis Presley style, which I really liked. But at the same time, I liked to dance to Benny, Chapotín, Jorrín, and my tastes were formed by that mixture of styles—*filin,* rock, *son,* cha-cha-cha—which would later become my artistic interests and my style, the fruit of that tremendous concoction.

LPF: When and how did that vocation become a profession?

JF: My first job as a musician was playing bass in a septet with a bunch of my friends. We'd hit the different bars and spend the nights playing and passing the hat, and I think that experience helped me a great deal because the septet has its specific keys—a guitar, the *tres,* the bass, and the rhythm—and as the musicians say, you have to grab hold of anything you can. I spent about a year with that group, until November 1959, when I joined the band of the National Revolutionary Police and my professional career began. The band was my other school: there were people there like Generoso Jiménez, who did Benny's arrangements, a very capable musician who helped me a great deal. It also forced me to learn—very quickly—the band's format, which was quite demanding: its repertoire included everything from symphonic overtures to popular dance music. Later I had the opportunity to work with radio and TV orchestras that also accompanied cabaret shows, and in doing so I met a lot of people who taught me many things, such as Maestro Peruchín, Guillermo Rubalcava—Gonzalito's father—Somavilla, Adolfo Guzmán. . . .

Around 1965, after having played in cabarets for a long time and having composed some songs, I met Elena Burke and started doing some work that earned me more notoriety, including some arrangements for an album she recorded. But meanwhile I kept listening to a lot of Cuban music, and The Beatles as well, until I joined the Revé orchestra in 1967.

LPF: How important was your time in Elio Revé's orchestra?

JF: Just as things such as artistic vocation and destiny exist, so does chance, which changes everything. The truth is that I had never considered playing with Revé, but when I met him he asked me to join the orchestra, and soon things began to go so well and so badly that I managed to change the group's style and then was able to follow my own inspiration when I became in charge of not only the arrangements but also the musical direction of the group. The problem was that my head was full of music, new ideas, melodic solutions, and formats that clashed with some concepts of Cuban music at a time when it was becoming stagnant. And luckily, when I entered the orchestra, instead of adapting to what they were doing, I tried to adapt the orchestra to my ideas, and that's how I introduced a series of changes in

JUAN FORMELL

the typical *charanga* format, which opened the door to the road I'm still traveling.

LPF: So as you look back, would you say it was a conscious desire of yours to change the *charanga* format of people like Fajardo, of orchestras like Aragón's, to bring about a musical revolution?

JF: No, I think that everything was accidental, as I told you, because I joined a *charanga,* not an ensemble. The fact is that the big changes that have taken place in Cuban dance music have been the work of *charangas*—from *danzón* to cha-cha-cha—and *charangas* are very much a part of Cuban popular dance history. The *son* is a parallel tradition that culminates in the ensembles of Arsenio, Chapotín, and Roberto Faz, which have a different sound that, despite varying constantly, never alters the structure of the dance. So when I joined a *charanga* that wasn't very noteworthy at the time—in the 1960s, Aragón was the queen of the *charangas,* with Lay, Richard Egües, and all her musicians—and started introducing some changes in format and melody (including some rock), the orchestra began to sound different, which was exactly what I wanted. On more than one occasion, Jorrín and Lay complimented me for it; they said I had managed to create a *charanga* that, without abandoning its essence, didn't sound like Jorrín's or Aragón's, which were the two great models at the time. In the end, what happened was that, since I joined the band owing nothing to anyone, I had the freedom to do all the variations I wanted, and that's where the new sound came from; it was something different from the more rigid structure of the typical *charanga.*

LPF: So, then, why did you leave the orchestra?

JF: I didn't leave because of personal conflicts but rather artistic differences. I think it was all because Revé wasn't prepared for what I was proposing at the time, although in less than a year that practically unknown group started to become popular. But just when we were making that jump, things started to happen that I didn't like, and since I also was probably unprepared to handle that sudden popularity and wanted to conserve it at all costs, I got upset and I left. But a whole group of musicians left with me.

LPF: To form Los Van Van?

JF: Yes, to start a new group that we ended up calling Los Van Van. . . . But it wasn't easy to form that new orchestra. The violinists, pianist, and flutist all came with me from Revé's orchestra. We were all likeminded in what we wanted to do in music and we got along well, which is very important in a group like ours. And that's what's so difficult: we started to look for other musicians who shared our goals. The truth is we were lucky because we found a guy like Changuito, who for a long time has been considered one of the best drummers in this kind of music; we found a singer like Lele, who caused a great uproar with her style and was one of the people who helped give Los Van Van its initial style. So that's how we founded the group: looking for people here and there, always keeping in mind that we had to be very united, and so far we've managed to accomplish it, although it's cost me these gray hairs you see here. . . . And if there are some players who are no longer with us, it's because discipline is everything for our orchestra.

LPF: With Los Van Van you retained the *charanga* format, but with modifications. Why did you stick with a style that for many was definitely passé?

JF: Before I started playing with Revé, I had no plans to delve into the world of Cuban dance music, because, to tell the truth, at twenty years of age I was much more interested in jazz and rock than Cuban popular music. But the "accident" that got me hooked up with Revé, along with what I was able to accomplish there, seemed to win me over because I didn't even think of creating a different format for Los Van Van, although I was familiar with the *charanga*'s limitations. That's why we've been evolving throughout these twenty-five years. At the outset I introduced the bass and the electric guitar, which had never been a part of the *charanga,* and instead of the *timbal* I used a complete drum set, and later we enhanced things with synthesizers and trombones, which we introduced in 1982. In sum, I carried out a series of transformations that complemented the musical mélange we were creating: rock, Afrocuban music, beat. . . .

LPF: Was the addition of trombones to Los Van Van an influence of salsa?

JF: No. I didn't introduce trombones looking for a sound similar to salsa. The fact is that typical orchestras are weak in the midrange notes—one of the limitations I was talking about—while there are plenty of high notes and low notes. To fill that void, I bring in the trombone, using it in a different way than do the *salseros,* giving it a totally different sound. That's why the orchestra has such a unique sound, don't you think?

LPF: So the origin of your particular style lies in those transformations?

JF: Yes, I think so. And we now know that those changes have contributed to the evolution of the *charanga.* For example, the Original de Manzanillo is a product of that evolution, because Panchy Naranjo works out of that transformation, as do Ritmo Oriental and other orchestras. The evolution of Los Van Van has provided all of that.

LPF: Did you have a concrete plan or purpose when you founded Los Van Van and carried out those modifications?

JF: Look, I wanted people to dance, to dance to Cuban music, and that was my guiding purpose. But the melodies I liked had to be updated to satisfy the tastes of young people in an age when world music had been forever transformed by The Beatles. So Los Van Van is born as the more conscious result of a determination that, back when I was with Revé, was pure intuition. That's why the changes we make are premeditated, always trying to get people to dance, even at the worst moments of the crisis in dance music. And from the outset we had success. At the beginning of the 1970s people identified with us. They danced to Los Van Van, and they haven't stopped dancing yet for one simple reason: we're always evolving.

LPF: Nevertheless, people don't just dance; they also sing Los Van Van's lyrics. And more than singing them, they apply them to the events of everyday life. People say, "It ain't easy," just as your song says.

JF: That's right, because along with the changes in the music, I set out to leave behind a chronicle of my era, singing about what was happening in the country, using the ideas and attitudes of the people, saying what they say, talking like them . . . but always wanting them to dance. And it might seem like an obsession of mine, this dance thing, but they say that a Cuban will dance even to a tin can, which is true and false at the same time: the good dancer has a personality, a philosophy, and in the context of popular dance, he doesn't like to dance to just anything. That's why dance in Cuba lost its balance: as the national music industry was in a deep crisis, rock was showing its strength, and the people—the young people, who are the best audience, the audience that dances—started to prefer foreign music.

LPF: But it seems to me that music isn't fully to blame for this phenomenon. For example, [the Cuban novelist Alejo] Carpentier observed that in Havana at the beginning of the nineteenth century there were at least fifty dances every day, and by 1980 there weren't even five per week. What do you think about this?

JF: Of course, music wasn't the only thing responsible for all this. Actually, music was the victim, what with the indiscriminate closing of dancehalls and clubs, which provoked something much more serious: the loss of a series of uniquely Cuban traditions born from the confluence of people united around the country's music. And this is serious stuff, because when traditions are interrupted, they usually die. . . .

It's true that today a popular dance can become a real bad scene because people attend with a different mentality: there's more contained violence and fights break out; they throw beer at each other and shoot off fireworks, and that's no longer the spirit of popular dance where people used to go in search of diversion, friendship, and possibly love. But the solution created for this problem was the easiest one of all: to shut down the dancehalls. Because at a place like La Tropical, which has a capacity for five thousand, you might have an orchestra like Revé's or Adalberto's and eight thousand show up, which is fine; I wish that many people would go to all cultural events. But what happens is that they only let five thousand in and the others who are left outside have nothing to do and they get bored and start causing trouble, and everyone gets rowdy and fights break out, which is why they end up closing the places down. Just imagine, in the nineteenth century there were fifty dances per day—although many of them were private, of course—and now we're trying to put on just one.

But at the same time, a change in mentality is necessary. For example, how often do they tape a dance concert for TV? How often does the press report on our events and tell what really happened? Never, because there are a lot of prejudices. So all of this activity becomes marginalized, as if it weren't an important part of our culture, and in the end our initiative loses out to the argument that only "troublemakers" and "tough guys" go to these dances, when in reality in a country like ours the tough guys have no reason to dominate an atmosphere like that. We have to do away with those fears, and the solution cannot have anything to do with police repression, because when a fight breaks out at the place with the five thousand people I was telling you about, anyone at all can jump into the mix, no matter who they are. We have to think about all this in order to save dance, which is so important to a nationality like ours.

LPF: But there's some truth to the claim that a lot of orchestras incite violence with their songs and refrains. Does Los Van Van also foment this in some way?

JF: It's true that this happens, and the orchestras should take a good look at their repertoires, at what they're saying at the dances, and understand what the objectives of their music are. But I don't think it's fair to say that the lyrics of Los Van Van have incited violence in any way. We say the same words on stage as we do on the recordings, and I never add a chorus saying things like, "Let's kill each other," or "We've got to die," or anything like that. There are other groups that seek to connect with the crowd through violence, but we don't and we're not responsible for the violence that has already been generated.

JF: Changing topics a bit, tell me something about your creative process. Do you start with the lyrics or the music?

LPF: For me the most important thing is the story I'm going to tell. I can't do anything until I have the story, which I generally pick up by observing attitudes and the way people behave. I've never disconnected myself from the lives of my peers, not out of any sort of populism or a concerted effort, but simply because I enjoy being with my people, standing in line, listening to conversations. Food lines are great for this: you hear people talking about everything. . . . And Cubans have the virtue of often synthesizing a complex situation with one short phrase, which is often a sort of aphorism. For example, the saying "It ain't easy" in reference to their life situation. And starting with a phrase like that, I'll often construct a story. But after I have that story comes something that's very decisive for me: the chorus. I think the quality of the refrain is what decides the fate of a dance number. So, thinking about that story I'm going to tell, I search for a refrain that's going to get people dancing, that's really catchy. And just as vocation, destiny, and chance exist, there's a mysterious thing in life called inspiration, which comes to you one fine day, God only knows from where, and you start to write the number. But none of this is easy, and it never happens the same way twice, and life has taught me that when you try to fabricate a number without inspiration, that number goes nowhere.

Look, one example of inspiration was "La Titimanía." I already was familiar with the phrase, but one day I'm in my car and I see another driver, an older man, who pulls up next to a girl and opens his door to offer her a ride. And I say to myself, "This guy's got *titimanía*," and I started to sing the refrain right there, and I had almost finished writing the song in a matter of minutes. That's inspiration, no?

LPF: Nevertheless, sometimes I think that your lyrics—if we compare them, for example, to those of a Rubén Blades or a Juan Luis Guerra—are a bit on the simple side, less poetic, don't you think?

JF: Well, we first have to make a couple of distinctions based on the model you're proposing. Above all, I think that Rubén is a great lyricist, one of the best that Latin American dance music has ever had, and that's an advantage he's got in his favor. But you also must keep in mind that we reflect very different realities, and that's crucial. He's been immersed for a long time in the Latino community of the United States, with all their frustrations and nostalgias, the discrimination they suffer, and those are very rich and complex circumstances, very dramatic ones, in which the artist can easily find material to work with. On the other hand, our reality over here and the character of our problems are very different, and that's why I've opted for a humorous reflection of our conflicts and shortcomings, sometimes an ironic view of certain attitudes, sometimes a picaresque view, and that's why our styles are different. In any case, Rubén's strengths (and by the way, he's always been a great friend to us) are his own, just as Juan Luis's strengths are his, and my limitations are mine and no one else's, but don't ever confuse them with being facile.

LPF: In any case, I seem to detect a hint of *filin* in some of your music. Is that an influence from your childhood in the Cayo Hueso barrio, the birthplace of *filin?*

JF: Yes, I think *filin* left a mark on me, which was perhaps more evident in my early years, when I think my closeness to rock and jazz was also more evident. All those musical genres that play a part in the formation of an artist somehow revert in his work and rear their heads from time to time. But I think that *filin* not only left its mark on me, but in a certain way has also had something to do with recent salsa waves, from what was known as "erotic salsa" to the more bolero-like songs of Juan Luis Guerra himself, to offer perhaps the best example, because *filin,* as a movement, introduced a freedom of expression and interpretation that was a true revolution in Spanish-language romantic song.

LPF: Since we're talking about salsa: Were you one of those who recognized it as something original, or one of those who claimed it was Cuban music arranged in a different, more contemporary style?

JF: I've always said—and I'm sure of this—that salsa is born from the cultural necessities of a large Latino community that exists in the United States, now comprising several million people. So salsa is created in response to the need for a music in tune with that Latino community, and the result could in no way be an exclusively Cuban music, although from its outset it drew upon melodies very close to those of Cuban music of the 1950s—Celia Cruz and la Sonora Matancera, Arsenio Rodríguez. That's how salsa begins, but being created by musicians of Puerto Rican origin— along with Venezuelans, Dominicans, and Cubans—specific sounds and particular references begin to appear in the arrangements, in the way singers are used, in the trombones. This all culminates in a style initially composed of the contributions of that large Latino community in New York and throughout the United States. But I keep thinking that the foundation of all that is Cuban music, and it's not just my opinion; all the salsa greats also admit this. Oscar D'León himself, on one of his latest albums, performs a tribute to Benny Moré. And the most recent generation of *salseros* is working with music by Adalberto Álvarez and with my music, because they know that the principal base is here in Cuba. But salsa is a reality, a cultural reality, and a very significant one at that.

LPF: In some fashion, in recent years the process has become more complex, with the *salseros* now influencing the Cuban musicians. What do you owe to salsa, and what does it owe to you?

JF: Without a doubt we've evolved thanks to the *salseros*. I think that in the last five years the salsa ambit has influenced us greatly, and I think an excellent musician like Isaac Delgado is the result of this, with a melody that's very close to that imposed by salsa. I think that in my latest stage I've also been influenced a little by great songs by Willie Colón, Rubén Blades, and Papo Lucca that have intrigued me. For example, thanks to the *salseros,* I realized that my singers, throughout the 1970s, were not very inspiring and were weak in the *montuno,* and so we went out to find the right type of singers. In the same vein, I can honestly tell you that my trombones have nothing to do with salsa.

More recently, an element I've taken from them has to do with the recording criteria. We've got thousands of problems from a technical point of view: bad studios, deficient equipment, and so on. But in spite of that, we would mix the records with a very old criterion in which percussion stayed in the background. Listening to salsa, I realized that they use a very stable percussion—very close to that used in rock—and they keep it on almost the same plane as the vocals, which is very important for the dancers, most of all internationally, because they feel it much more strongly and can easily dance to it. We owe that change in strategy to salsa, and it's present on my latest recordings and has won me over because the band sounds fuller, more complete, so to speak.

But I think salsa owes more to my work than I owe to salsa, because when I started to work in dance music, what was to become salsa was just being born. And there's an anecdote that reflects this relationship very well: in 1974 we went to Panama to do a few performances, and the band was very well received. Then we met with a group of reporters and two of them approached us and said they liked how our orchestra sounded, but that our music wasn't salsa. Then I asked them what salsa was, and while they were explaining it to me, somebody brought out a record by Roberto Roena and the Apollo Sound as an example of salsa, and when I looked at it I discovered there were three of my songs on it, and when we heard them we realized the arrangement was almost identical. . . . At that time, more than twenty years ago, they were aware of what we were doing here in Cuba. I mean, they didn't just focus on the old repertoire of the 1950s, because Los Van Van was already a reality and Irakere was emerging at the time. In sum, the relationship was alive and well.

LPF: Collaborations between musicians are rather common in salsa. Why is that so rare in Cuba?

JF: I don't really know why here in Cuba the musicians and orchestras are so resistant to that type of collaborative work. A lot of people don't like it because they think that one figure can outshine another. What's true is that I support it, and my musicians have a great deal of freedom to record with whomever they please. I've tried to have Los Van Van record with other people—as I did with Gonzalito Rubalcava and Silvio Rodríguez—because that can do a lot for an album; it can help you make it a lot better. As you say, the *salseros* don't have this problem, and you'll often see, for example, a record by Celia Cruz with Tito Puente performing on it, and in the chorus you might even find Rubén Blades or another special guest, without that diminishing their work or causing people to step on each other's turf. Professional jealousy? Yes, maybe that's what's happening here in Cuba.

LPF: What, in your judgment, is the present state of affairs in Cuban music? What are its chances of success outside Cuba?

JF: Look, in the last three or four years we've been enjoying real good times. There was a time, between 1982 and 1985, when Los Van Van was practically an isolated case, but now there are several groups like Adalberto y su Son, Revé, la Original de Manzanillo, Dan Den, and NG la Banda, all of which are top quality. And if you look at the history of Cuban music, you'll see that even the best of times were like that: three or four good orchestras were the ones that set the tone, and a larger group followed that model. That's why I think we should take advantage of a moment like this to bring about the resurgence of popular dance.

But it so happens that Cuban music has the great disadvantage of a lack of adequate technology. For example, we recorded the compact disc *Songo—*

which was an anthology of our latest things—in England for Island Records, and it ended up selling very well in Japan. Later, by mid-1989, it achieved the impossible: it broke the Florida blockade by becoming the biggest-selling record in that state, which must represent a respectable number of sales, as well as providing clear evidence that in the United States there's a true fervor for Cuban music from Cuba. But the fact is that only in this way, by using state-of-the-art technology, can we compete with the *salseros* and the rockers. During all these years the records we've made here in Cuba have been lacking in technical elements that are fundamental nowadays. Our CD *Crónicas,* for example, was recorded on a twenty-four-track console, and three of the tracks were out of order; *Songo,* on the other hand, was made on a forty-eight, completely electronic. . . . And then you add the fact that in Cuba the mixing is done through the volume controls instead of the echo controls, which is a more advanced technology that gives you the highest fidelity. And after recording in those conditions you're more or less satisfied, and then it turns out that the disc cutter isn't very good and that the covers aren't made from very good cardboard, and the printing isn't very good, which ends up ruining the best design in the world. . . . The solution for a lot of people, therefore, has been to record outside of Cuba, typically in Mexican or Venezuelan studios.

Under these conditions it's very hard to succeed in any market, even in the domestic market, which has been in bad shape for quite a while as far as records are concerned. That's why I told you that it's not always the artists who are to blame; we've got to solve many nonmusical problems so that Cuban music, both on and off the island, can reach the level of competition and acceptance that its present-day quality and its hundred-year-old tradition deserve. We need to do this so we can keep singing and dancing. LPF: There's been a lot of talk about a blockade with regard to Cuban music, especially in terms of promotion, yet many musicians work within this situation or use it as a foundation. Do you think that by now you've been able to break that blockade and establish yourself in the international market? JF: Look, I don't think Cuban music has ever been blockaded. The ones who've been blockaded, for a long time and even today, are the Cuban musicians who live in Cuba, and that's why we haven't even come close to breaking into the big international record market. The problems with Cuban record production, which I was just mentioning, were always to blame for this, but even when we started to sign contracts with foreign companies like Island Records, which is a big multinational label, or with Fonomusic of

Spain, or Tophits of Venezuela, they ended up killing the record: either they don't promote it adequately or it doesn't reach the entire market, like any other salsa group from anywhere else does. That's the true blockade. Nevertheless, we're well known internationally, and for a lot of people we're one of the best salsa groups in the world, as an article in the *New York Times* recently stated. But this recognition has nothing to do with our place in the market, and the blockade continues.

LPF: In spite of this, in what countries are you having the most success right now?

JF: In lieu of a presence in the market by way of records, we've had to exploit our physical presence in determined places, and that's how we've gone about opening doors. This is what's happened, for example, in Spain, where we perform frequently and where we now have a loyal following. I'd say the same about Mexico, and certain strong Latino communities in Holland, Germany, Sweden, and Italy. But, in any case, our natural fan base is in the Caribbean: Venezuela, Colombia, the Dominican Republic, places we've not visited nearly as often but where I'm sure we're well known, because we get lots of airtime and sell records when they reach the market. Notwithstanding, what would be ideal for us would be to break into the New York market, which is very dynamic not only because of the number of people who listen to this type of music, but also because if you make it in New York, you get unparalleled recognition. But unfortunately, although many people in the United States are interested in our music, we've never even had the possibility of playing there because they've always denied our visa requests. I hope that someday things will change in this regard and that we'll finally be able to take our music there, because I know we'll be a great success. It ain't easy, *compay,* it ain't easy, but Los Van Van have what it takes.

Havana, Cuba, 1989 and 1992

6

Searching for Rubén Blades

Panama, November 29. The Panamanian singer and composer Rubén Blades was nominated as a presidential candidate by the Papa Egoro movement for the general election of May 8, 1994. The party's first national convention held its sessions with only two hundred delegates and did not provide access to the press.
—Notimex

This brief report, published in the Cuban daily *Granma*, was the penultimate piece of news I had heard about Rubén Blades. The last one, the real bombshell, the one I anxiously hoped would fill the headlines of many Latin American and European newspapers, never materialized. That last story, of course, turned out to be a "wasn't to be": Rubén Blades, the new president of Panama. But, regardless of what happened at the polls on May 8, 1994, that penultimate, definitive piece of news regarding the political and artistic career of the "Panamanian singer and composer" made me wonder when Rubén Blades started working toward that goal.

The summer of 1989 was particularly mild in Asturias. It even seemed like a real summer: no rain, no cold, no fog—although I remember responding with a resounding "no" when some friends invited me to take a dip at a beach on the Bay of Biscay. For a native of the Caribbean, the near-polar frigidity of that dark sea, in which the Asturians happily frolicked, could easily have provoked a case of pneumonia at the very least. I didn't want to take the chance of getting sick: at 9:00 that evening, as part of the program

RUBÉN BLADES

of the Second Noir Week of Murder Mysteries in Gijón—the reason I had come to Spain—Rubén Blades was going to play a concert, and there was no chance I was going to miss it. If my nonexistent finances had allowed me to do so, I would have willingly traveled to any point on the globe to enjoy a performance by "the most rational man in salsa." And now it just so happened that, while reading the program for the important meeting of mystery writers, I came across the following event, scheduled to close one of the evening sessions: "Concert by Rubén Blades and Son del Solar."

My excitement at the news of the concert I would attend was not, of course, the mere reaction of a music fan. For many years I had professed a true devotion to Rubén's music—the music that had allowed him to become the idol of millions of Latin Americans, the living hope of many Panamanians, and the artist who, through his enormously popular work, had managed to penetrate the souls and the harsh everyday reality of those millions of admirers who had transformed him into the most famous, the most listened-to, and the most promising singer in Our America.

And finally, at 9:25, the concert began with the sound of drums that seemed to be searching for the soul of America. Twelve hours later, with my tape recorder in hand, I would be the one to start searching for Rubén Blades.

This artist, the son of a Cuban woman who sang boleros and a Panamanian detective who played the bongos, born and raised in Panama, in the working-class barrio of San Felipe, came into the world as if predestined to wend his way to music and politics along the most unusual route imaginable. Perhaps this strange course was predetermined by his maternal grandmother, the Colombian Emma Bosques, a woman who had attended college, practiced yoga, and, according to her own grandson, "was wonderfully crazy: she practiced levitation and instilled in me the stupid notion that justice is important and we can all collaborate and be part of the solution," as she accompanied young Rubén to the premieres of American musical comedies. Or perhaps the person who led him to music was the colossal figure of Benny Moré, the singer most listened to in his home and the one who, when Rubén was barely ten years old, his parents took him to see during one of his tours through the isthmus. The truth is that music seemed very distant at the time, and it became even more distant years later when, after his first failure in the nascent New York salsa movement, Rubén Blades decided to return home to Panama to begin his law studies again. He had almost been defeated musically. Had he almost been defeated politically as well?

LPF: Rubén, between the day you went to see Benny Moré in the 1950s and your debut in salsa around 1970 with Pete Rodríguez, a lot of changes took place in Caribbean music. How did those changes affect your musical formation?

RB: Toward the end of the 1950s—and I think this happened all throughout the Caribbean—Cuban music was a powerful and attractive alternative in the face of the most popular music at the time, rock and roll, which had a great impact on the whole region. Cuban singers and orchestras managed to compete with the idols of rock and, at least in Panama, remained quite popular with the public through a strong presence on the radio and on records. I recall that when my father took me to see Benny Moré, he did so as if taking me to Mount Everest or the tallest building in the world, because Benny was untouchable. Nevertheless, starting in 1960, when the blockade against Cuba begins, a blockade that was very real and even included music, a void is created and several years pass without our really knowing what was happening musically on the island. Then something funny happens: Puerto Rico continues the Afro-Antillean musical tradition, and along with the more Puerto Rican genres like *bomba* and *plena,* it projects these rhythms throughout the entire Caribbean. And when my generation starts making music, in the 1960s, we're more influenced by the physical presence of the Puerto Rican bands that visit Panama and by their records than we are by the mere memory of a Cuban tradition that, without a doubt, has the same origins as that cultivated by the *boricuas. . . .* My musical formation begins in this framework: Puerto Rican music on the one hand, beat and rock on the other, and the Cuban tradition in my memory and on a few old records I always kept.

LPF: And later, what contacts did you maintain with Cuban music?

RB: Look, along with the problems of the blockade, you've got to consider the internal problems that Cuban music suffered. In the sixties, when certain composers started introducing jazz and rock forms into Cuban music, some people opposed this—there's always plenty of these types around. These were people who didn't understand this process as a logical form of enrichment, and they decried an unacceptable Yankee penetration in Cuba and other such things. I recall that in the seventies, when I started taking music seriously, I met Cuban groups in Panama that had no idea of what was happening musically in Puerto Rico, New York, or even Panama, and so they kept clinging to melodies that had long ago fallen out of international favor. But fortunately that situation has changed a great deal; the question has been restated, and as a result of that process we now see Cuban groups that are more competitive in musical terms, better informed of what's happening in Latin music. And, therefore, better singers and orchestras have emerged, along with more revolutionary musical agendas, such as those of Formell and Los Van Van, Adalberto Álvarez or Gonzalito Rubalcava, who plays very good jazz. And that's how my reencounter with Cuban music comes about, most of all starting when I record Formell's "Muévete."

LPF: Rubén, your road to success has been rather complicated, and you've been accused of many forms of treason. For example, some say the aesthetics of your music are more Brazilian than Hispanic, or that your lyrics border on political pamphlets. What do you make of such criticism?

RB: At this stage of the game, I'm very accustomed to living with criticism. In the salsa world of New York I had to work really hard to succeed with my style and my intentions as a composer. My songs were rejected a thousand times because they were too long and had too much to say and therefore weren't danceable, or they simply criticized me by saying they were "protest songs," and salsa wasn't for protesting. But the truth is that salsa, in its origins, was also that—a form of protest that was bitter and joyful at the same time. On the other hand, I believe that, yes, my project and that of the Brazilian musicians is essentially the same, not only in the lyrics but also in the way we conduct ourselves on stage, with the exception that in their case it's considered a virtue, isn't it? In my case, nevertheless, it has caused many people to think that I'm "aloof," and they say, "Look, he doesn't smile. He doesn't laugh much at all." And some critics always point out that I dress badly, but I think none of that has to do with the task at hand, with a love of music and a respect for the public. Just like Milton do Nascimento, Chico Buarque, or Caetano Veloso, I don't fit the model of the "soap opera" singer, the type of guy who worries more about his attire or his plastic surgery than his true task.

LPF: But although you've tried to be, let's say, "different," in the final analysis you ended up becoming a model.

RB: Look, this model thing is hilarious. I've gone to Panama, for example, and I've run into somebody, let's say a journalist, who hasn't seen me in four years, and in all that time I've recorded albums, made movies, won prizes, and worked on political programs for the country. And after I've done all this and after not having seen me in four years, the first thing the guy says to me is, "Wow, Rubén, you're going bald!" You know, they start off by throwing you a curve, they hit you over the head with something like that, and you just don't know where to start. So you say, "Yeah, that's the way it goes. What's a guy to do? I've tried everything, including spider pee, and nothing helps. The only thing that stops hair from falling is the floor. What do you want me to do? Comb it over and walk against the wind?" The truth is that in spite of doing this for so many years, I just don't fit into their image of the *salsero* or the *guarachero,* because the image I project is different. The same thing happened for a long time with my lyrics, which nobody liked because they didn't "sound like" salsa lyrics, and in the end the opposite occurred: my lyrics, for many people, became the only model for salsa, which is not correct either.

As I interview him, I try to come to grips with the fact that the man sitting in front of me is Rubén Blades. I'm watching him talk and say *"mano"* ["bro"] and *"fregao"* ["screwed-up"], I'm watching him gesture and laugh, and the night before I saw him perform. If I reach out I can touch him and verify that he's "real." And I still don't believe it. He's there, as relaxed and normal as a schoolteacher, anonymous and content, wearing a plaid short-sleeved shirt and very few pretensions, completely oblivious to my incredulity, which is exactly what any other Latin American would feel if he could speak, face to face, with the man who made him sing "Pedro Navaja," "Buscando guayabas," or "Tiburón."

But this sincere and affable man hides one of the most complex and vital personalities of the culture (and logically, the politics as well) of our continent. And he's well aware of this fact. He has known so ever since 1970, when he made his debut singing and composing for the album *From Panama to New York: Pete Rodríguez Presents Rubén Blades,* on which he included a number called "Juan González," an epic hymn to a guerrilla killed in combat, which caused the record to be banned in several Caribbean countries. Led by Rubén, politics had made its way into salsa, even though that young fair-haired man would have to accept an initial setback and return to Panama to become a lawyer, only to return to New York in 1974—thanks to the efforts of his friend Ricardo Ray, one of the founders of sixties boogaloo—to reenter the music world by filling a vacancy in the mailroom of the all-powerful Fania label: Rubén was in charge of sticking the stamps on the company's voluminous correspondence.

During those years, nevertheless, Rubén kept at his music and composed pieces that began to get him noticed, such as "Las esquinas del son," and especially "Cipriano Armenteros" (both recorded by Ismael Miranda), in which he tells the long, mythical tale of a Panamanian outlaw at the beginning of the nineteenth century. But his trumpet call would finally be sounded in 1977, when he was finally able to unleash his creativity by recording with Willie Colón the album *Metiendo mano,* which included numbers like "Pablo Pueblo" and "La maleta," and finally gave shape to what would soon be known as "conscious salsa."

"At one time," César Miguel Rondón has written, "when many salsa groups were reined in by the need to imitate the Cuban model of la Sonora Matancera, when New York salsa was starting to show signs of exhaustion, bogged down in a sterile and overly comfortable expression, the presence of 'Pablo Pueblo' was, more than a surprise, an authentic and consequential tour de force. This significant happening served as a reminder that salsa, in spite of the commercial boom, was popular music made to sing the circumstances of the barrio where it had been born, and that it simply had to continue doing so."[1]

LPF: Do you consider yourself a socially responsible person?

RB: I try to be, in all aspects of my life. And make no mistake: it's not easy.

LPF: In his book César Miguel Rondón writes, "In him"—in you, that is— "the themes that affected the daily life of an entire people were honed in upon with a very specific political position. Nothing was the product of chance or mere coincidence." How true is this?

RB: I spoke about that several times with him, and that's totally the case. And I told him I sing about what I see, what I feel, what I believe, and politics is seen, felt, and whether you like it or not, it affects all aspects of your life, and an artist should take the most responsible position possible toward it. And even more so if he's a Latin American artist.

LPF: How did you begin to think about participating directly in politics, as a politician, that is, rather than as an artist?

RB: That's the most complicated part of this story, you know? I'm going to

---

1. César Miguel Rondón, *El libro de la salsa* (Caracas: Editorial Arte, 1980), p. 313.

tell you how it all started. A journalist interviewed me once, and from the outset I could tell what he was up to because all of his questions were loaded. And so he asks me, "Are you a lawyer?" And I tell him that I am. "So what do you plan to do in the future?" And I tell him I plan to go back to Panama at some point and work there because I'm not going to spend my whole life making music and films outside my country. That's where everything started and that's where I want to end up, and I might even enter public life because if I don't, then why did I go to school and get my degrees? And then he says to me, "So, one of your plans is to run for president, right?" And I got so fed up with the guy that I told him, "Why not? Do I have some impediment that prevents me from running for president? I'm of legal age and I have my national I.D. card, which is required. Furthermore, in Panama right now you don't even have to be intelligent to aspire to the presidency. Or is being a musician a crime that disqualifies me?" And the next day the headlines read, "Rubén Blades Running for President of Panama," and of course, if a salsa musician says he's running for president of the country, well, everybody jumped all over that.

A lot of things have happened since then—including an invasion, the revelation of a connection between the government and drugs, and even the accusation by [President Manuel] Noriega that my family had ties to the CIA, which forced them to leave Panama—and now the idea of getting involved in politics in my country is a reality for me. But I've had to think hard and do a lot of work because I can't arrive and start a populist campaign by singing "Pedro Navaja" so people will sympathize with me and give me their votes. If I get into politics, I'll only do so with a coherent social program that will be useful for my country, so that people can find an answer to their eternal questions. But offering that proposal hasn't been easy in a country like Panama, and right now, in 1989, my political future is uncertain, although I no longer fear uncertainties. I always begin with uncertainty—the same thing happened in music, in film, in almost everything—but now I've decided to go ahead with politics.

LPF: Let's come back to the present and to music. In your case, would it be fair to say that there are no commercial conditions put on you when you go to record an album?

RB: Yes. My record label does not impose any criteria of that type. There's a mutual respect between us, and they know they can't make demands of me in that regard. Because where my work is concerned, I've always tried to remain independent, and that's given me the opportunity to write what I want without restraining myself or becoming a defender of a particular style, a specific idea. When I was with Fania, I had to put up with certain contractual imperatives, but that's over now. Musically, I'm free.

LPF: In that search for independence, you distanced yourself from Willie Colón. How do you two get along now after your artistic breakup?

RB: On personal terms, we still get along fine. We don't work together much, and perhaps that's for a practical reason: we're under contract to different record labels. But it's also because of a problem of style, because in order to work with Willie I'd have to keep repeating myself since the impact of the music we made together was so great. Otherwise, the separation had a very logical origin: he was fundamentally interested in music, and I was interested in other things besides music. I had the independence to say, for example, I'm going to get out of music for two years to write a novel, or six months to make a movie, or a year to get a master's degree in law at Harvard, as I did during the 1984–85 academic year. . . . But as I was telling you, although we see each other very little, we still have a relationship, even a working one, since I often do arrangements of old numbers for him. And I don't rule out the possibility of collaborating in the future, although I wouldn't want to rush through it, because we'd be working in a nostalgic, repetitive tone, looking back on a past that we both recall with great affection.

Twelve years after the fact, the separation of Rubén Blades and Willie Colón is to salsa what the breakup of The Beatles was to rock. And I'm not exaggerating as much as one might imagine. Works like *Metiendo mano, Siembra* (the biggest-selling salsa record in history and, in the words of a friend of mine, "the *Abbey Road* of the movement"), and *Canciones del solar de los aburridos* made this duo, for five years, the most effective, avant-garde, and imitated in all of Caribbean music, thanks to the fortunate encounter of these two leaders. Nevertheless, Rubén's ascendance as a solo artist could not be stopped. First came the creation, in 1980, of the impressive salsa opera *Maestra vida;* later, with his own band (los Seis del Solar, eventually enlarged to Son del Solar), came such definitive albums as *Buscando América, Doble filo, Nothing but the Truth, Antecedent* (a Grammy winner in 1989), or *Amor y control,* a record of astonishing maturity, full of political and humanistic content immersed in avant-garde melodic arrangements. A complete body of work to justify his title as "the most rational man in salsa" and his privileged position as one of the irreplaceable chroniclers of the Latin American spirit of our times. The long and winding road hasn't been easy: his music, a mixture of Caribbean rhythms, jazz, and rock, full of carioca inflections and *guaguancó* tempos, had to overcome the facile, catchy pitch of salsa that was often reclaimed from the old Cuban repertoire, and had to prove that music is a living organism and that salsa, within that vitality, was the expression of a circumstance in which, along with the fiesta, pain and uprootedness also reside.

LPF: But as you tried to make it on your own, they hurled all sorts of accusations at you. They say you're determined to make it in the United States, and that's why you make movies, music, and videos for that market. You know, they say you're a "crossover." What did it mean to you to work on the anti-apartheid video and album *Sun City*?

RB: I enjoy those accusations, because they have some truth to them: I think that *Sun City* made it possible for two cultural groups, which for some have little in common, to come into contact. I think it was important to insert into that project a Latin American point of view, which is increasingly strong in a U.S. society composed of millions of Latinos. In addition, it served to help me make good friendships and some plans for the future.

LPF: One manifestation of the future was the album *Nothing but the Truth*. What made you want to record an album exclusively in English?

RB: Look, that was a landmark album on many fronts. It was the first time, for example, that a salsa musician collaborated on a rock album. And collaborating, in this case, didn't mean I was invited to play just one instrument. This was something very different: I sat down to write the lyrics and music with Elvis Costello, Bob Dylan, Lou Reed, Sting, and a ton of people who generally don't make Latin music. That's how a truly close communication was produced between two forms of popular music—the most important in the present-day world—in a way that had never been attempted. On the other hand, the record responds to a need of mine to prove that people aren't prevented from doing something because of apparent cultural differences, that a soul doesn't need a visa, that when you sit down and write, you can communicate with another person even if you speak a different language and come from another culture because there's a point where you take each other's hand and travel together as individuals who inhabit the same world, where everything that happens affects us all—and there you have the themes for Nicaragua and El Salvador—in spite of the fact that we may have different points of view.

Of course, there were people who, upon listening to *Nothing but the Truth,* immediately assumed that the album represented a complete abandonment of music in Spanish for the chance of greater commercial success, and they even said, "This guy went too far. . . ." But that's nonsense; you can see that I haven't forgotten how to speak, write, or sing in Spanish, and the trail blazed by that record—that of true and necessary collaborations in this ever more homogeneous world—has been traveled again, successfully, by other Latino musicians who play salsa. But in the long run, it's been a very enriching experience for me personally, and I believe I'll continue to do this type of work in the future because I never finished my collaboration with Bob Dylan, for example, and the two of us are interested in doing something together.

LPF: Does all this mean that you're interested in some way in transcending the limits of so-called salsa music and are eager to try your luck at rock and jazz?

RB: A few years ago, when we were playing for the first time at the Playboy Jazz Festival, there were some purists in attendance asking what a salsa group was doing at a jazz festival. And I'll repeat now what I said then, which can apply to any festival where we might play in the future: It's a fact that, for us, jazz is an attitude, a proposal that takes freedom as its starting point, and as such, is a universal attitude—one that doesn't have to be from a particular place or from a particular culture in order to be considered legitimate. What's more, when we played at the Playboy Jazz Festival—which brings together the best people in jazz for two days—we felt that everybody was delighted with our performance, which was based on our traditional repertoire, so much so that we went back later and got the same positive reception. . . . Now, in spite of the distinct opinions everyone might hold, as musicians we always try to challenge the labels we're given, and we can show up at a concert and play rock, although that might feel like a bucket of cold water to those who can only conceive of us playing salsa. But we're not just jukeboxes that you can use to listen to what you want; we're not products, we're artists. Here, inside of me, there's a personality that's alive, that treats the public with respect. And our goal has always been to cross borders, in a way that no band from New York has ever imagined possible, and now a lot of people say we were right when they see it's possible to work in different places and on different stages. So, what do all those accusations matter?

LPF: In recent years you've been dividing your time between music and film. It's another border you're crossing. What brought you to film, and what intrigues you about it?

RB: Look, bro, the most important thing for me, right now, is to tell you this: The best definition of failure is not trying. Some might disagree and say that winning is everything and all else just talk. But not for me: you've gotta try. Ten years ago I didn't even think of making films. So why did I go into film? Well, that was another risk, another challenge, another possibility, not only in terms of working with people I'd seen on screen and had greatly admired, but also because it's a very different discipline from music, an artistic form upon which I as an actor have no control and in which I wanted to experiment. On the other hand, film came to be rewarding in terms of recognition, because people also saw my work on the screen. Furthermore, I'd always been indignant about the roles Latinos were given in American films. They were always the ones who were climbing up a tree to steal a TV from a second-story apartment, or the ones who were always on drugs or hanging around with prostitutes. And when I saw the chance to change that image a bit, I went into film big time.

LPF: And have you been satisfied with the roles you've been given so far?

RB: Although I've been involved in more than ten films, my best performance and my most well-known to date is *Crossover Dreams,* in which I play the role of a musician, although the problem was that many people thought it was my biography, that I was playing myself, and figured that's why I did such a good job. Then I had another interesting role for a cable network in a film called *Dead Man Out* with Danny Glover, who plays a psychiatrist who's attending to a death-row inmate—that's me, of course—and it was difficult for me, physically and intellectually, because the character is so complex. And other roles I've enjoyed have been the one I did for [Robert] Redford in *The Milagro Beanfield War* or in the comedy *The Lemon Sisters,* where I play Diane Keaton's boyfriend. This role, like that of the death-row inmate, was written for an Anglo actor, but I showed up, competed, and won. Just as I said at the beginning: You've gotta try.

Recently I had the great satisfaction of being offered a role by Jack Nicholson in a movie he was going to direct. This time, I wouldn't even play a Latino, but rather a Jewish lawyer from the thirties, which is why my hair's so short. What pleased me the most—how 'bout this?—was to discover that Nicholson's a fan of my music and that he's bought a lot of my records. That's pretty good, no?

LPF: How have you been able to combine your work in film and music?

RB: It's a difficult combination, bro. I'm intrigued by the possibility of working in live music, because it's one of the greatest satisfactions that life has given me. I was born dreaming about music and had to do many things before I finally got into it; I had to fight a lot, because when I started writing my lyrics, all the disco people in New York said I would never make it. But I insisted and people like Ismael Miranda and Ray Barreto recorded my songs, and then I had the good fortune to meet up with a band like Willie Colón's that really wanted to do some serious work, and that's where it all started. On the other hand, the bad thing about working in live music is the traveling. On many occasions I've had to perform one evening, catch a plane to the movie set the next day, and then return in the afternoon for another concert. Maybe I could postpone a few tours to concentrate on film, but music still means a lot to me.

LPF: So when all is said and done, will you be a musician or an actor?

RB: I'm an actor from time to time, if there's a role that interests me, and a full-time musician.

LPF: And a politician?

RB: That depends on the votes and not on my talent. But as I said before, bro: you gotta try.

Gijón, Spain, 1989 / Havana, Cuba, 1993

7

Cachao López: My Language Is a Double Bass

Life Is Full of Surprises . . .

And one of them was during a trip to Spain, where I had arrived as an invited writer to the Seventh Noir Week of Murder Mysteries in Gijón. I had just landed at Madrid's Barajas Airport. It was eight in the morning—two in the afternoon for my jet-lagged body—and my friend Paloma Saénz, after meeting me at the customs exit, invited me to have a much-needed cup of coffee. And as we drank and conversed she gave me the news: "Cachao's going to play at the Noir Week," she told me, and when I had not yet recovered from my surprise, she added: "I'll bet you're going to interview him, right?" "This time he's not getting away," I quickly replied.

Eight days later, at the Casa Pachín restaurant in Gijón, I was seated at Cachao López's table, sharing the exquisite *fabada asturiana* that they prepare there. I had a difficult dilemma before me: to eat *fabada* or talk with this transcendent musician whom I had fruitlessly pursued two years earlier from Miami to New York while he was somewhere between Puerto Rico and Los Angeles. Nevertheless, between *fabes,* chorizo, bacon, and potatoes—three plates worth, mercilessly scarfed down—I initiated a priceless dialogue with the mythical Israel López, Cachao.

CACHAO LÓPEZ

Myth and History

It so happens that Israel López, Cachao, is one of the living legends of the lengthy history of twentieth-century Cuban music. A witness of, and participant in, the transformation of *son,* somewhere in the 1920s; protagonist, together with his brother Orestes, of the renovation of *danzón* and the polemical germination of the mambo in the 1930s, with Arcaño y sus Maravillas; creator of some three thousand *danzones;* animator of the famous Havana dances of the 1940s; member, for more than three decades, of the Havana Philharmonic Orchestra; promoter of famous *descargas* in the 1950s that came close to fusing *son* and jazz, breaking the barriers for future fusion experiments; indispensable point of reference and leading figure within the salsa movement; indisputable master of the double bass and king of rhythm; and, most recently, protagonist of a documentary directed by Andy García in which justice is finally done to his story, Cachao is like a walking encyclopedia with too many pages devoted to the musical history of the Caribbean.

"The problem is not that I'm important," he refuted with his affable modesty, after taking a long swig of Coca-Cola. "It's just that I've been playing for sixty-eight years because I started very young, at the age of eight. I'm about to turn seventy-six, and I've had the good fortune of passing through all types of music in these years. In Cuba I did zarzuelas, operas, tangos with Libertad Lamarque, Hugo del Carril, and Alberto Castillo; I played mariachi music and almost all the Cuban rhythms: *son, danzón,* mambo, Cuban jazz, *guaguancó,* rumba, boleros. At one point, I decided to count the orchestras in which I had played, and I lost count at 248. . . . It's all been a blessing from God."

LPF: And what was the beginning of this whole story?

CL: Well, I think I was born to be a musician, like almost everyone in my family. My first memories are of my brother Orestes, who was six years older than I, playing with small groups in Havana, and in 1926 I joined a child sextet whose vocalist was Roberto Faz, the same one who later became the great *sonero,* the lead singer of the Casino Orchestra and leader of his own band in the 1950s and 1960s. At that time I was a bongo player.

LPF: But you changed to the double bass.

CL: I wanted to be a musician, and after playing the bongos I tried the trumpet, but that didn't last too long. We lived on Paula Street, in the same house where the apostle Martí[1] was born, before they turned it into a museum. With my borrowed trumpet I started imitating the bugle calls that they used to do in the police barracks that were near the house. I learned all the calls—reveille, midday, payday—and it was fun until the barracks sergeant grabbed me on the street and took away the trumpet. . . . Then I started to study double bass in 1927, and my first job was accompanying silent films at the Carral Theater, where Bola de Nieve also played. That lasted three years and was really a lot of fun. . . . Then things got serious, because in 1930 I joined the Havana Philharmonic.

LPF: How important an influence was your brother during your formative years?

CL: He was my idol, my inspiration. He's the reason I'm a musician, because I wanted to imitate him, I wanted to be like him. He showed me how to compose, how to study double bass, and he put the love of music and innovation in my blood. For example, he was one of the first to introduce the trumpet into *son,* with the Apollo Septet. To tell you the truth, I don't think there have been many brothers that have gotten along better than Orestes and I. That's why it was so sad for me to find out he had died three years ago. The worst thing was that they couldn't reach me from Havana, and I found out three months after the fact.

Danzón and Mambo: Fathers and Kings

Perhaps the most acute controversy in the history of Cuban music has as its protagonists none other than Cachao López and his brother Orestes. In the 1930s, when Cachao was a bassist and Orestes a cellist in the famous orchestra of Arcaño and y sus Maravillas—"A maestro on each instrument, and together a marvel" was their slogan—they introduced a *danzón* composed in 1935 and titled "Mambo," which has become the apple of musicological discord. While specialists such as Leonardo Acosta affirm that the seed of mambo (which would later make Dámaso Pérez Prado famous) was sown in those *danzones* by the López brothers, others, such as Odilio Urfé, claim that it was not until several years later, in 1949, with Cachao's danzón "Se va el matancero," that "the definitive consecration of the mambo rhythm

---

1. José Martí (1853–1895) was a poet and leader of the Cuban independence movement (translator's note).

ushered in the end of the danzones." Meanwhile, Radamés Giro affirms in a more recent text, "Orestes and Israel López, with Arcaño's *charanga,* made a *tumbao* that would come to be a characteristic rhythm of that orchestra and others of the same type, but it should not be identified with the mambo à la Pérez Prado." Finally, while Arcaño and Orestes López assured me that the mambo belonged to them, Dámaso Pérez Prado defended his paternity.

LPF: And what does Cachao think?

CL: Look, when I began to play in 1926, *danzón* was still a formal ballroom dance, very traditional, with very rigid steps, in spite of the fact that it had a final coda that allowed a more lively improvisation. But in 1937, when Arcaño y sus Maravillas was founded, we carried out a complete renovation of *danzón,* although without harming it: in reality what we did was modernize it, and in the process we started working with the mambo rhythm, which was the *tumbao* used to improvise in the final section and could last an indefinite amount of time as long as people were dancing. When the first "mambo" that sounded like *danzón* was created, what we did was to speed up the *danzón* rhythm, but without changing its structure because the dancers were not yet prepared for such a drastic change. Even that first "mambo" was too fast, and the following ones had to be slower, just like *danzón.* But by 1950, when Pérez Prado began working with the mambo, things had changed, and he was able to introduce the rhythm at its full speed. Besides, his goal from the beginning was to work with a more complicated, more active choreography. But the original mambo was our creation.

LPF: Nevertheless, Pérez Prado is always called the "King of Mambo" and is also credited as being its creator. Do you feel there's some injustice in that description?

CL: No, there's no injustice in calling him the "King of Mambo," because Pérez Prado was the one who universalized it and made it famous. That's the truth. He transformed the mambo from a ballroom dance into a true spectacle. Furthermore, I always got along very well with Pérez Prado. We were great friends and treated each other like brothers. We even worked together, as in 1962, when he came to Madrid and his bassist got sick. When he found out I was here, he came to ask me to do some shows with him. Then we did three programs together for Radio Madrid, along with other performances. But yes, there's a tendency among people to think that Dámaso and I were rivals, but that was not the case. On the contrary, I think we should be very grateful to Pérez Prado for what he did with the mambo: he universalized it. If it weren't for him, the mambo wouldn't have become known the world over.

LPF: How is it that a Cuban rhythm like the mambo achieved its greatest success in Mexico?

CL: I think it's because the Mexicans are very good musicians, and Pérez Prado was looking for musicians with good "lips," people who were able to reach the high notes that he demanded. When they performed live, Pérez Prado's main trumpeter would often move from first trumpet to fifth, because he could no longer handle it—he couldn't meet the demands of Prado's music. . . . And it's also because in Mexico, before the mambo craze, there already existed the tradition of dancing *danzones,* and the *danzón* is the natural father of the mambo.

LPF: And what relationship existed between *son* and the *danzón* that you two revitalized to the point of calling it a "new rhythm"?

CL: There wasn't much of a relationship, to tell you the truth. *Danzón,* as you know, has three very well-defined parts: the part for clarinet or flute, the part for violin, and the last part, which is for dancing more freely. That final part was what we worked on the most, making it more lively, introducing what's known as the *tumbao,* the *mambeo,* but without changing the structure of the rhythm too much, because *danzón* is already hard to dance in and of itself. *Son,* on the other hand, is freer, less schematic than *danzón,* and more open to any type of innovation.

LPF: You're said to be the creator of more than three thousand *danzones.* That must be a record, don't you think?

CL: In truth, it was my brother and I both, so you'll have to cut that figure in half: fifteen hundred for each, but that still might be a record. We were very young at the time and we had a lot of energy, a lot of things to say. And what's more, we had to work in order to eat, you know? I recall that at one point, between the two of us, we managed to write twenty-eight *danzones* in a week.

LPF: And where did you get the inspiration to write so much?

CL: That comes from anywhere: from a sound, an idea, a necessity. And we wrote so many *danzones* that one day something funny happened. I was at home listening to the radio, and they played a *danzón,* and I said to myself: "Boy, that sounds good. I wonder who wrote that." And at the end of the song the deejay said it was by Israel López, Cachao, and I didn't even remember writing it.

LPF: You were also a protagonist of the era of Los Tres Grandes [the Three Greats], in the 1940s: el Conjunto de Arsenio, Arcaño y sus Maravillas, and the Melodías del 40 Orchestra. What are your memories of that time?

CL: There was a tremendous ambience in Havana, and the different orchestras got along great. That was when Arcaño decided to form the musical alliance of Los Tres Grandes, and he called it that because it was the era of World War II: since there were three great political leaders at the time—Churchill, Roosevelt, and Stalin—there could also be three greats in music. And the impact it had was tremendous. I think we got the entire country of Cuba dancing.

LPF: What were the dances like at that time?

CL: They were fantastic, really hot, with big crowds, people sweating but everyone having a great time. For example, in the colored social clubs the dances couldn't end until four in the morning. God help you if you went home earlier. For whites it was different: they would dance until one or two in the morning, and they'd go home. But with the blacks . . . you were asking for trouble. Dancing is very important for blacks.

LPF: What was the relationship between the musicians and the dancers?

CL: Look, the dancers fed the musicians—and not only through their stomachs. The problem was that back then people knew how to dance, and the dancer would listen and if there was any sort of imbalance in the orchestra, he'd notice it. They had really good ears. There was always a tremendous silence at those dances, not like nowadays with everybody talking. You'd only hear the murmur of the feet because there were no microphones or any of that: the singer had only his lungs, and today if there's no microphone they can't sing.

LPF: What were the demands placed on musicians at the time?

CL: We were very fortunate that each orchestra had its own hallmark, its own style. For example, you'd be at home listening to the radio and they'd say, "That's so-and-so," or, "That's what's-his-name," and you could distinguish the style of each one. Not any more: they all play the same style, and if they're not singing, you can't tell who's who, you know? In addition, everything in my case was more complicated, because when the Orquesta Radiofónica de Arcaño was founded, with fourteen musicians, I had to write for each one of them. You have to write *danzón;* it's not like *descarga,* in which each player takes off from the same beat and does his own thing. In sum, you really had to work quite a bit. Perhaps that's why in 1949 I left Radiofónica and went to play in the fifty-member orchestra of the Blanquita Theater, a Radio City–type orchestra, accompanying Broadway-style musical revues. . . . With them I was just another musician, without so many responsibilities.

Like His Rhythm, There's No Other

And I was a witness to that. The night Cachao played in Gijón, he did so as a special guest of the Spanish tour of the Orquesta de la Luz, the most famous Japanese salsa band. When the Asians started playing, in all truth, those who hadn't heard them before were in for a pleasant surprise: they knew how to play salsa. But when Israel López was announced and the maestro joined the group, his double bass at the ready, a true miracle occurred. Suddenly a light went on for the Orchestra of Light, because their rhythm changed—becoming intense, earthy, definitively Caribbean, thanks solely to the rhythmic riffs that the seventy-six-year-old maestro unleashed from his double bass.

LPF: Cachao, it's well known that good dancers dance to the bass, and you're considered the most important bassist in Cuban music. What does it take to be a good bassist in Cuban music?
CL: Since the bass is the instrument that sets the rhythm, a good bassist has to know how to dance. The thing is, there are two ways of dancing: one is dancing to the backbeat and the other is dancing in time. . . . In Santa Clara the people would dance to the backbeat, and in Havana they'd dance in time, and an argument broke out as to who danced best, but all of them danced to the bass. That's why the bassist must have a great sense of rhythm and a lot of imagination, because it's a coarse instrument, a rough one, and if you don't play it well, it sounds like an elephant throwing stones. It's hard to be a good bassist.
LPF: Do you think that to understand the rhythm of the Caribbean you have to have been born there?
CL: In part, yes, you have to be born in the Caribbean, because it's a matter of blood. In Cuba everyone knows how to dance *danzón,* but in the United States, for example, only the Jews, who have an incredible sense of rhythm, know how to dance it. You see a Jew dancing and you think he's a Cuban, but if you look closely you realize he's studied it and he does a good job, but he lacks the final cadence of the rhythm.
LPF: Maestro, how did your connection with jazz come about?

CL: In reality, when we wrote those *descargas,* starting in 1957, we weren't paying too much attention to jazz, but rather to Cuban music itself, to *son.* That was a reunion of well-trained musicians who had the desire to do some new things in music through inspiration and improvisation. The first *descarga* we did was at 4:00 A.M., at the Panart studios, and we did it at that hour because everyone worked at night in orchestras or at nightclubs. But no one paid any attention to that *descarga,* and the record just hung around and nothing came of it, just as happened to Jorrín with "La Engañadora," which was under wraps for two years, without the cha-cha-cha ever becoming known.

LPF: What were those nights like in Havana?

CL: There was a lot of happiness, a lot of movement, a lot of nightclubs like El Gato Tuerto, La Gruta—small places that would be packed, often until dawn.

LPF: And have you made any more *descargas?*

CL: Yes, of course. I love to do *descargas,* to improvise freely over a theme. I recall that at one point we had a quartet in which Miguelito Valdés sang and Tito Puente played the *timbal,* Charlie Palmieri the piano, and I the bass, but unfortunately we never recorded that music. If memory serves me, it was very good.

LPF: Lately you've gotten a lot of recognition, thanks in part to the documentary directed by Andy García titled *Cachao, como su ritmo no hay dos [Cachao, Like His Rhythm There's No Other].* How did your encounter with Andy and the idea for the film come about?

CL: Well, you know, Andy left Cuba at the age of five and was raised in Miami. But he always maintained his connection to Cuban music, and I even think he's more of a musician than an actor. So one day, when he was filming *Godfather III,* he had a one-week break that coincided with a concert I was playing in San Francisco with Carlos Santana. He came to see me and proposed the project to me right there. When we started talking, it turned out that for more than fifty-five years I had been a good friend of his father's—René García—who, by the way, died shortly after the movie was filmed, and I had the privilege of taking my orchestra to the church to play his funeral mass. Then Andy paid for a concert that would form the basis of the documentary, and from the beginning it was done with cultural goals in mind, planning for it to be shown mainly at universities. But then things got more complicated: it turned out really well and was shown all over the world. It was a great success. But the truth is that the whole thing was filmed in two weeks, without a script or anything because I'm not an actor, and Andy realized we should work in the most natural way possible.

LPF: And what do you think about him?

CL: He's a very noble kid, very decent and humble, and his fame hasn't gone to his head. And now, well, I'm sort of like the father he lost.

LPF: Another of the great figures of Cuban music in the United States was Mario Bauzá, who died recently. What can you tell me about him?

CL: That Mario Bauzá is the father of Afrocuban music. I met Mario in 1930, when he was leaving Cuba because he wanted to play jazz and do other things, to have more musical freedom. At that time he played the clarinet with the Havana Symphony, and in the United States he started playing the trumpet with Chick Webb and Cab Calloway, and later he created Afrocuban jazz with Machito and had a lot of influence over the creators of bebop, such as Dizzy Gillespie, who considered him his musical godfather. Mario's career is, therefore, one of the most important in Cuban music in the United States.

LPF: What has African music contributed to Caribbean rhythms?

CL: The richness of African music has been decisive in this entire process. Although it's often an intuitive music, played by nonprofessionals and often for religious purposes, its variety of rhythms and its strength have been fundamental in the music that's been made in America. That's why its influence is not new, but rather can be found at the very origins of all Latin American music in which there's a black root.

LPF: And do you feel any longing to return to Cuba?

CL: I have those longings just like any Cuban, although I don't plan to return for now, and if I did so it wouldn't be to stay. I've gotten used to living in the United States and it would be very difficult to go back knowing that all my friends are dead, my brother Orestes, old Arcaño. I think that after thirty years I'd no longer know anyone. But yes, I'd like to return because it's my country.

Pour Some Salsa on It . . .

When Cachao left Cuba in 1962 to try his luck with his music in the United States, he was already one of the most famous instrumentalists in the entire universe of Cuban music. From the *danzón* to the *descarga*, his fame had grown along with his prestige. That's why during the 1960s he was recruited by several orchestras—among them the famous Tito Rodríguez band—at the same time that his work as an arranger and composer was making its mark on the origins of what would later be known as salsa music. This fact is acknowledged by the renowned scholar César Miguel Rondón, who even affirms that the percussion sections of salsa bands "owe a great deal to the first steps taken by Cachao in the 1950s in Cuba: a fundamental trio of *tumbadora, timbal,* and bongo, along with the occasional use of maracas, guiro, and claves." Nevertheless, his picture does not appear on the most important album covers of the period until 1976, when the Puerto Rican musicologist and producer René López forms a large band that, under the Cuban's direction, records two groundbreaking albums of the era: *Cachao Uno* and *Cachao Dos,* two significant salsa works that enjoyed only modest commercial success. So it seemed that Cachao's best days had passed while at the same time salsa was coming into its own. But a lot of salsa has passed under the bridge, and Cachao is still there.

LPF: What do you think about salsa? Does salsa exist?

CL: Salsa, as Tito Puente has rightly observed, is the tomato sauce that's used for cooking. . . . What happened with that other "salsa" is that it was used to commercialize Cuban music in the United States. But as a musical genre, salsa doesn't exist. Look, if you hear a *guaguancó* with a bit of an arrangement, they tell you it's salsa, and the same thing happens with rumba or bolero or whatever. But the truth is that in 1926, Ignacio Piñeiro was already singing *"Échale salsita"* ["Pour some salsa on it"], and Yeyo, the famous bongo player, later shouted *"Más salsa que pescao"* ["More salsa than fish"]. The fact is that when you say a certain music has *salsa,* it's like saying it has flavor, or that it has swing, or like saying it has salt, as they say in Spain. But to go from there to saying that salsa music exists is quite a leap.

LPF: So what do you think about the *salseros,* the salsa musicians?

CL: Right now there are a lot of very good orchestras that play "salsa" in Puerto Rico and Colombia, which are the two countries where it's most often played. I'm always impressed by the quality of the group Niche and by Guayacán. But there are other very good groups such as Oscar D'León's or even Tito Puente's, and it would be very hard for me to say which is the best.

LPF: Let's agree that salsa doesn't exist. Nevertheless, when talking about the essence of salsa people often mention you and Arsenio Rodríguez. What's the relevance of Arsenio in the music made nowadays?

CL: He's a very important figure because he was a great creator, the founder of a style that many people of today have copied. But there's a huge difference. Arsenio had an incredible clarity, an original flavor, and salsa can't reach that. Nevertheless, although they've recorded a lot of his music and some people have rendered him tributes, he never got much recognition in the United States, nor did he enjoy the success there that he did in Cuba. Because for a musician to distinguish himself in New York at that time, he really had to polish his image and have someone backing him. And Arsenio's image just didn't sell: he was like a museum piece, and it was more profitable to take advantage of him than to promote him, that's the truth.

LPF: What relationship do you have nowadays with the Cuban music that's made in Cuba?

CL: I really have very little information, but I know they're doing good things because Cuban musicians are excellent. Every time I hear something by them I think they're great. Just recently I heard something by NG, and I think they're really good, as is Irakere, although now there's more influence from U.S. jazz, unlike before.

LPF: And if the Cubans are good, why didn't you mention them when we were talking about salsa?

CL: Because of what I told you at the beginning: Cuban music is Cuban music, and not salsa. That's why I think it's a mistake for some Cubans to consider themselves *salseros,* even though that might help them commercially.

LPF: We've talked about several Cuban musicians, and yet we haven't mentioned the two greatest voices of the island: Celia Cruz and Benny Moré.

CL: The incredible thing about Celia is that she began her career singing tangos in a contest, and that's how she became well known. Then Rogelio Martínez takes her to work with la Sonora Matancera and introduces her to the popular rhythms, which is when her career takes off, and she's remained in that vein even to this day. And I don't think there's anyone else who has the voice that she has: a voice of clarity, force, and permanence.

Benny was my friend, and we loved each other a great deal, but I couldn't work with him because his *compadre*[2] was the bassist for the band. He was a genius: he didn't know how to read or write music and he had to verbally explain to the arranger what he was thinking, but eventually he achieved what he wanted. And add to that his sense of rhythm. And his voice. Having worked with all the great singers of Cuba, I can tell you that no one has

---

2. *El compadrazgo* is a special relationship in Hispanic countries between a father and the godfather of his child, who become *compadres* after the baptism (translator's note).

or will ever come close to him: Fernando Collazo, Abelardo Barroso, Panchito Risset, Alberto Aroche, Paulina Álvarez, Barbarito Diez. All of them were good, but none was like Benny.

LPF: And why did you leave Cuba?

CL: For artistic reasons, fundamentally. I wanted to work in another environment, to try other rhythms. Besides, I had no interest in politics; it's never interested me. When you're really into music, the only thing you want to do from morning till night is to make music, and the only thing that's ever interested me in life is exactly that: making music. That's why I never talk about politics, nor do I enjoy being interviewed. I prefer to talk with the strings, because my language is a double bass.

Gijón, Spain, 1994

8

Wilfrido Vargas: I Am Merengue

The King of Merengue climbs onto the stage. He runs across it, and, with his back to the crowd, he raises his shiny trumpet, demanding silence. Finally, he lowers his arms and the madness begins: *"¿Qué hiciste, abusadora, qué hiciste?"* The deafening merengue rhythms enter through your ears and leave through your feet, and you've got no choice but to dance.

For many people he's the true King of Merengue, and his name is Wilfrido Vargas. He plays the trumpet, composes songs, sings, dances, has been leading his band of Beduinos [Bedouins] for the last twenty years, and he proudly affirms that merengue is the strongest Caribbean rhythm of the last decade.

The King of Merengue is a forty-year-old mulatto who tends to suffer from insomnia and who, in order not to reveal his identity, answers the phone with the name Tony when staying at hotels. He likes to smoke but hates cigarettes because they're bad for him, and he practices his anti-tobacco proselytizing at every opportunity. He speaks in long pauses, which are foreign to merengue, as if thinking twice about everything he's about to say. But above all, this man, who has triumphed on all the stages where he's performed, who has revolutionized his country's national rhythm to the point of "Wilfridizing" it, displays the sincerity of all great artists. This explains why when his brother Juan, manager of the group, told him a Cuban journalist wanted to interview him, his answer was straightforward and la-

WILFRIDO VARGAS

conic: "What time tomorrow do wanna take care of that crap?" he asked, and we agreed to meet at his hotel for breakfast.

Before our encounter in the beautiful Mexican city of Guanajuato—which we would repeat later in the capital, during the intermission of a successful performance—I knew of Wilfrido only by ear: I had heard some of his most famous works (such as "El Barbarazo," the long ballads "Enrique Blanco" and "Desiderio Arias," "El Africano," "Abusadora," and the double entendre "El Cucu"), but I did know that this young musician had been perhaps the person most responsible for what was happening with merengue since the end of the 1970s: first, its musical conquest of the entire Caribbean, later, of New York, and finally, Europe.

Starting with Wilfrido Vargas, the history of merengue had begun to change forever, its face completely open to the world. This Caribbean rhythm, which had long resounded on the beaches of the Dominican Republic, had truly become an international phenomenon, bursting on the scene through the breaches in quality left by a salsa music that was becoming repetitive and worn-out.

And now, hearing him speak, I understand why Wilfrido Vargas was able to don his crown fifteen years ago and is still wearing it today: this man respects his music as one respects the sacred. And he knows that each day, each concert, is a challenge he must meet—and he always plays to win.

Merengue and Life

LPF: Wilfrido Vargas is synonymous with merengue. What should we talk about first—it or you?

WV: About merengue, because it's the star. . . . Look, merengue has had a long and difficult evolution, but a very interesting one because somehow that national dance reflects the history of my country during the last hundred and some years. They say that in the nineteenth century merengue arrived in Santo Domingo from Haiti, although it wasn't very popular there. It was a rhythm of the country folk, rather humble in origins, that was played with the Spanish guitar, just like Cuban *son.* But soon it started bringing together more instruments for a very simple reason: more volume was needed to play at parties, and so they started incorporating the accordion, the *guiro,* and especially the *tambora* to create what was called the *perico-ripiao.* That's the era of pieces like "Jovinita," "A la gallera," or "Arroyito cristalino," when merengue is still a rural music, although starting to gain in popularity.

So then, when the United States invades Santo Domingo in 1916, merengue suffers along with the entire nation, and that strong country music with a syncopation already marked by the *tambora* is forced to become a pleasing rhythm because, as the story goes (and it must be true), the Yankees couldn't dance merengue (and they still can't), and so merengue had to be played in a way that was danceable for them. That's why its evolution didn't stop but took a rather circuitous detour, through a half-hidden route, which is the same one it follows when Trujillo takes office and becomes the "benefactor" of a certain type of merengue, a rather inoffensive and significantly transformed variety. That's the beginning of the big band era in Santo Domingo, and these groups were sponsored by the dictator who, like all good dictators, had a paternalistic attitude toward his nation, his "plantation." While taking away some things from the people, he gives them back some less dangerous ones, like music, even though that music was no longer quintessentially Dominican. And the truth is that during the dictatorship, subsidies for municipal bands were never lacking, nor were impeccable military uniforms with kepis, which was what gave some pizzazz to the parades on national and personal holidays.

Later, with the fall of Trujillo, many social and political values fall along with him, as well as, of course, cultural values that responded more to his caprices and personal tastes than to the expression of a nationality. And the subsidies for municipal bands also dry up, which is logical given the lack of food, electricity, and water in the country. Meanwhile, for a people who had never renounced their true music, another door is opened for merengue, the national dance that had first been transformed by the Yankees and later by the dictator and the bourgeoisie, who disguised it in order to take it into the ballrooms, where it was considered inferior to the waltz, the *contradanza,* and the *danzón* of the big orchestras. After all, to even talk about playing a *perico-ripiao* at the quinceañera[1] of a high society girl was a bit out of bounds, no?

LPF: So authentic merengue doesn't reappear until the 1960s?

WV: It happens almost the same day Trujillo dies, when it becomes impossible to maintain a thirty-piece band. With the disappearance of the big or-

---

1. The *quinceañera* is the traditional coming-of-age party given to Hispanic girls on their fifteenth birthday (translator's note).

WILFRIDO VARGAS

chestra, which he encouraged as a way to disguise the accordion and the *tambora,* everything becomes smaller, everything needs to be reconsidered, and a type of group emerges that is barely larger than a *sonora*—the combo. *Sonoras* typically have two trumpets as their melodic voices, along with two saxes—one alto and one tenor. But given the economic conditions of the time, even that reduced format was difficult to sustain, and what becomes more common is what was called the *ven-tú* ["come on, you"], because I'd say to you, "Hey, what are you up to? What do you play?" And you'd say, for example, "The trumpet," and I'd tell you right there, "Okay, come on, because I need a trumpet for a *picoteao*"—which is how parties are referred to down there—and that's how we started out: *ven, tú* and *ven, tú,* until we got a short-lived group together with no preparation and no fixed format. That's how the *ven-tú* format was born, the defining characteristic of Dominican popular music of the 1960s.

But if one of those *ven-tú* had a little luck and played quality music, it generally underwent a transformation: the musicians stopped being chosen at random and started to become more or less permanent members. This is what happened with groups such as el Negrito Trucman's, maestro Johnny Ventura's, Rafael Solano y sus Amigos, and Félix del Rosario y sus Magos del Ritmo. Frank Cruz is no longer a singer who goes wherever he's called, but instead plays only with Félix del Rosario. The orchestras start wearing suits again, and Johnny Ventura, a few years later, gives merengue a stage show by creating choreography for his numbers. He becomes the biggest star of that era in which a national space is reclaimed for merengue and, without people realizing it, an international boom is about to occur.

LPF: While all this was going on, where was Wilfrido Vargas?

WV: I was in front of a TV in Altamira, my hometown, watching everything that was happening with music and life . . . and dreaming. But still a long way from merengue.

LPF: And who was that Wilfrido who had yet to turn twenty and didn't play merengue?

WV: Wilfrido Radamés Vargas Martínez was born in Altamira in 1949, the son of Bienvenida Martínez and Ramón Emilio Vargas. My father was the typical village bohemian, a guitarist who liked to drink and who fell in love one day with a girl who ran a small store to get by and sold oranges, cabbages, and the like. That girl, Bienvenida, also sang and played the guitar. Can you imagine what the relationship was like between those two people, in which the suitor tries to win his girl over with the guitar and his sweetheart responds with a guitar of her own? She also played a little flute, and he a little accordion. So, they get married and the first thing to come of that union—in addition to music—is yours truly. My first breath, the first oxygen I breathed, was infused with what was going on in that home: the meals, the sorrows, the joys, and even the tears were all melodic in my house. When I got a little older and started to feel an attraction to music, my father taught me the notes used to compose a typical song from a harmonic point of view. The style of playing he taught me ranged from Los Panchos to Benny Moré—most of all El Benny, who was our daily bread, our touchstone. It's only later that I start listening to different types of music and I discover Los Tres Ases and the Los Reyes trio. I also start listening to Brazilian music, and I discover the creations of a man named Miguelito Méndez, who creates harmonies from a more complex and richer point of view, and that really impressed me.

LPF: When did you become a musician? And when did you start making your living from music?

WV: In 1966, during the first administration of President Balaguer, I wasn't a political activist, but I was a member of the losing political party, which meant that I also lost my job as the lead trumpet of the municipal band and postman of Altamira, a job that was more coveted than I could have ever imagined. Then I had to emigrate to the capital, where I started working with the *ven-tú* bands, and in one of them I met a young man named Chely Jiménez who had a rock group, and since he liked how I played the trumpet, he told me about a restaurant that needed several musicians. But the place served Arab food and had Arab decorations, so the group had to play Arab music and dress like Arabs, like Bedouins! So off I went, and you can just imagine that my trumpet playing Arab music, along with a little obligatory merengue, sounded a bit strange in such a small group.

The interesting thing is that my style of playing started to intrigue the other musicians because my phrasing didn't seem typical of Altamira, and people noticed it right away. That group, which was called Ali Baba and His 40 Thieves—what an imagination, no?—soon became, by order of the restaurant manager, Wilfrido Vargas and His Bedouins, and we even recorded a little number titled "Samba alegre," on which I revealed my potential as a trumpeter who could play fast notes. This was in 1972, and, as you can see, I still hadn't really started playing merengue yet.

LPF: So how does your marriage to merengue finally come about?

WV: My formation, as you can see, is a bit removed from merengue per se:

there's Cuban music, boleros, jazz, and even Arab music, but very little merengue, although I'd grown up hearing it every day, because in Santo Domingo merengue's in the air and people live their lives to the rhythm of merengue: the mailman walks along to a merengue beat; on the bus or in taxis you hear merengue all the time; in the cantinas and clubs, as you have a drink of rum, merengue's always present. . . . That's my environmental education, but not my musical education. So, when I finally throw myself into merengue, there's no rhythmic idea, no inspirational element from my background, that has anything to do with those of a Johnny Ventura or a Cuco Valoy and the other orthodox *merengueros,* because that's not who I am: I'm not classical, I'm not typical. Therefore, since I have a different type of formation, a different way of thinking, when I start playing merengue it sounds different—newer, they say, with a special accent, perhaps more universal. But strangely, instead of being rejected because of this novelty, we were immediately admired.

I think it was an advantage for me to reach merengue by a road other than merengue itself. This Dominican rhythm always had one of the limitations of a folkloric genre, which is the fact that it doesn't transcend the spirit of that folklore. In its harmony and melody, merengue was only trying to inspire dance, and its lyrics, always relegated to a second level, barely reflected the daily chronicle of the people—something that did in fact happen back during the years of the War for Independence, and with one or two isolated musicians. So then we searched for a melodic scheme based more on the conga, and I gave free rein to Luis Mondesí, our conga player, to invent anything he wanted. In addition, the rhythm of the *tambora* starts to speed up, the trumpets are relentless, and to top it all off, the singer we chose was a falsetto who sang like a girl, who had nothing in common with the power of El Negrito Trucman, Johnny Ventura, or Frank Cruz. And that little group of "Bedouins" started to attract fans as well as detractors, of course, because some people accused us of being something akin to the antichrist, anarchists who were going to do away with tradition. But I held my ground and I was real stubborn—a rabid defender of what I was doing. And today I can state, with all the strength of arrogance, that my determination was what gave rise to a radical change, so much so that to learn to play merengue today, you've got to go through us—whether you're Juan Luis Guerra himself or Las Chicas del Can.

LPF: That's what was called the "wilfridization" of merengue, right?

WV: That's how the "wilfridization" began, along with the supremacy of Los

Beduinos, a group that adopted particular ways of playing that have continued to evolve, because we're no longer the same as we were fifteen years ago. Starting in 1975, when we recorded *Así, así,* every year we've done an LP and every year they've been different.

The most important thing, in my judgment, is that the national rhythm, which was decidedly local, became an export that, during the height of the salsa boom, first took off in the Caribbean, and then Latin America and New York, before finally arriving in Europe. That's why we've been able to do openings for festivals like the one in Rome, where people such as Paul Simon and Miriam Makeba were playing. We were also the group most hounded by the Parisian press while we were still under contract only as a fill-in band. We were the top attraction at the Rotterdam carnival, and at the Zurich carnival we even got the Swiss people dancing, and they had no idea that something called merengue even existed. We've been the top-selling merengue group in the United States ever since we entered the market because people know we always give them top quality. And during our first tour in Mexico we were the best thing going at the Cervantes Festival in Guanajuato, an event at which music has never been the main attraction.

And I want you to write this down: merengue had never enjoyed the level of acceptance that it's had during recent years, when its power transformed it into the revelation of the 1980s, the most influential genre in all of Caribbean music and the most celebrated export from Santo Domingo.

LPF: So, you haven't been considered the antichrist of merengue for quite some time.

WV: Look, Fafá Taveras, the Dominican labor leader, has said that merengue is the only movement that unequivocally unites the most diverse sentiments of Dominican-ness, that merengue is the cultural product that gives us the most worldwide notoriety and is the element of national identity that flourishes with the most pride in the country. And he, like many intellectuals and journalists, has recognized that we've been the ones most responsible for this process of universalizing merengue.

Furthermore, I think that what's really important in all this is the dignity we've bestowed upon the rhythm. A while back, the person who played the *tambora,* that instrument made of wood and goatskin tied together with rope, represented the lowest step on the social ladder within a genre that was already marginalized to begin with. He was the lowest of the low, and today the *tambora* and the *guiro* have been transformed into national symbols for Dominican youth, and that's due to a musical movement that be-

WILFRIDO VARGAS

gins with us and takes merengue to the young people and makes them feel Dominican when they sing and dance it.

LPF: I believe there are two important elements in your conception of merengue: on one hand, aspects of the polyrhythm of jazz, and on the other, rhythms and melodies of Cuban music. How did Cuban musicians influence you?

WV: I think Cuba was the best melting pot in which the rhythms brought from Africa by the slaves were mixed with and adapted to Spanish music. So, Cuban music—in genres like *danzón, son,* and mambo—is the model of the Caribbean, and that's why all Cuban music reigned supreme, as a musical dynasty, over all the nations of the region. Let's say, for example, that in a sweet, subtle way Benny Moré was the musical dictator over all of us insofar as rhythm is concerned. Today it's even more evident, because the tendencies in lyrics, musical information, tonal inflections, and harmony are highly influenced by artists such as Silvio Rodríguez and Pablo Milanés. Even today, very few people understand the importance of Cuba thanks to the recovery of Cuban rhythms by what is known as *la nueva trova,* the country's new generation of musicians, who did great things in the musical and poetic planes once they overcame a rather propagandistic period. And even though this might seem a bit demagogic to a lot of people, my harmonic code is much more in tune with that of Chucho Valdés, the director of Irakere, than it is with that of U.S. jazz musicians. I must be the type who's more inclined to follow in the footsteps of Chucho Valdés, Paquito D'Rivera, Arturo Sandoval, Pablo, and Silvio, and I sincerely think that Cuba exerts a stronger influence today than it did thirty years ago, during El Benny's heyday, because they're creating the freshest music in the entire Caribbean.

LPF: Wilfrido, what are you like offstage?

WV: Can't you see that I drink coffee like everyone else? . . . Look, the autographs, the applause, the kisses from the girls, are all a drug that has a direct influence on the conscience. I think artists have emotional problems and generally turn to the trappings of fashion—which can range from a blonde girl with a great big ass to a fancy car, or eccentric clothes and an earring—to get noticed. But the musician uses his art to do and say things, to be useful, and I think I'm in that group.

LPF: And how does one fight against vanity?

WV: By just doing the math: the results of that vanity are always negative. And that's the idea I've instilled in my group, where each individual is selected from a musical point of view, of course, but also for his moral character. You've got to be a good person and have self-discipline, and you've always got to put your work first, because it's everything.

LPF: Now that you're famous and make good money with your music, and are recognized at home and abroad, how grateful are you to your parents for bringing you to music?

WV: I almost never look back. But my relationship with my parents is removed from all financial calculations, and I've never thought about how those little tones they taught me turned into X number of dollars. They're still my parents, and I thank them for giving me a peaceful childhood. I'm still the oldest son, the first fruit of the love between the bohemian Ramón Emilio and the store clerk Bienvenida, who met one day in Altamira and sang together such a beautiful love song that made it possible for me to sing many other songs. Life's as simple as that.

Guanajuato, Mexico, 1989

9

Papo Lucca: From Ponce to Heaven (without a Doubt)

The Winner: Papo Lucca . . .

Those of us who had the privilege of being present at the Plaza de la Reforma on the opening night of the Fourth Festival of Caribbean Culture in Cancún left with the impression of having attended a rare and brilliant musical combat in which there were—this one time—winners and losers. Although no one had presented it as a *mano a mano,* the festival stage served as a veritable ring in which blows were exchanged between two of the greatest figures of Latin American popular music of our time. In one corner, Tito Puente with his group, having arrived in Cancún with the glory of his 102 albums, the fame he had earned by recording the soundtrack for *The Mambo Kings,* and his landmark career as an exceptional *timbalero,* a career full of memorable collaborations with other musical greats. In the opposite corner, Papo Lucca, the diminutive forty-seven-year-old pianist who has led la Sonora Ponceña for more than twenty years, one of the most sought-after salsa arrangers, and, for many, the most accomplished and dynamic pianist of the entire contemporary Caribbean musical movement.

Rather than go into the details, I'll merely comment on the results: while Tito Puente was making delicate golden jewels on the *timbal,* he was badly accompanied by an indecisive orchestra that wavered between jazz and salsa in spite of the quality of its performers. For his part, Papo Lucca, leading a band in full command of its talents, clearly showed—with his piano fugues

PAPO LUCCA

ignoring musical borders as they ran the gamut from the exquisite phrasing of jazz to the impetuous attack of a *son montuno,* with keyboard wizardry reminiscent of Chopin—why he was the leading pianist of the Fania All Stars for more than a decade, and why he's one of the most brilliant practitioners of salsa. His victory, on points, was the victory of a strong, well-armed music in which Papo Lucca moves about like a man possessed between the outermost limits of salsa, stealing sonorities from *son, bomba,* bossa nova, and jazz in order to make—to create—a Caribbean flavor that took the crowd to the verge of frenzy.

On personal terms, I was thankful for the fight and left the arena content with Papo Lucca's victory, because I believe that, starting in 1972, the year in which this native son of Puerto Rico recorded for the Fania label his LP *Desde Puerto Rico a Nueva York,* contemporary Caribbean music received one of its most solid and creative figures, as he would prove in his future recordings, great hits by his group la Sonora Ponceña that Papo Lucca never abandoned: *La conquista musical, El gigante del sur, Explorando, La orquesta de mi tierra. . . .*

Enrique Arsenio Lucca Jr., "Papo," in the Puerto Rican tradition of renaming the firstborn son when he carries the father's name, agreed to meet me two days later at the pool of his Cancún hotel, friendly and unconcerned about time, to talk about music and his Cuban friends, his frustration at not having played more baseball because of his piano studies, and his hopes that his son Papo Lucca II might realize his father's athletic dreams and become a figure like Roberto Clemente, Pachín Cepeda, Cheo Cruz, or Roberto Alomar, "that boy from Ponce who did so much to help the Toronto Blue Jays win the World Series this year." This is the Papo Lucca with whom I spoke, and I learned more about why he had emerged victorious the night before.

The Explanation of a Winner

LPF: How important was it for you to have been born in the midst of an orchestra that's about to celebrate its fortieth anniversary?

PL: The day after I was born there was a rehearsal at my house, and when I turned seven I attended the inauguration of la Sonora Ponceña as a special guest, because my father was the director of the group. I recall that back then the group didn't play original music, but instead did remakes of songs from albums he would get from abroad—especially Cuban ones—and I participated in this process, playing the bongo and the *tumbadoras*. And when my father saw the interest I had, he sent me off to study music.

That's when I learned to listen to the music that came from Cuba: Benny Moré, Arsenio, Chapotín, el Conjunto Casino, Rumbavana, those groups that were the great influence on all of us who are now in this type of music and that marked me, at least, forever. So it was a great blessing to have been born into a family of musicians who educated me with their tastes, which soon became mine.

LPF: But in some way the elder Enrique Lucca continues to be your musical guide, because he still accompanies you to all your performances.

PL: My father is always there at my side, and I hope he will be for a long time to come—for a lot of reasons. He's the founder and director of the orchestra, and he's the one who more or less steers the ship. He's the one who imposes respect, because the guys and I were practically raised together, and at times I don't have the strength, or the desire, to say how things should be, to impose discipline, and I prefer that he continue doing it so I can avoid other problems. Besides, that way I can concentrate more fully on the musical issues.

LPF: La Sonora Ponceña was your first school, so to speak. But how did you become a musician?

PL: I began to study at the age of six with a musician from Ponce, Señor Julio Alvarado, a very dear and respected man, who was the director of the Banda Municipal de los Bomberos [The Firefighters' Municipal Band] and taught voice at the Escuela Libre de Música [Free School of Music]. One day my father took me to see him and said, "Look, this boy plays the conga and the bongos and has good rhythm. I think you can do something with him." Then Julio gave me a newspaper and saw that I could read well, so they agreed that the following week I would start to study music. I did two years of voice, as was the practice back then, and at the age of eight I started with instruments. And since things were going well, my father hired my own private piano teacher, with whom I studied about six hours a day. I recall that my first piano lessons were in classical music, and only later did I begin to copy from albums by Cortijo y su Combo, solos by Rafael Ithier, Noro Morales, Peruchín, and numbers by Lili Martínez, although I never had the sheet music. But I think that helped me a lot later on, as an arranger, and it gave me an idea of the freedom with which the popular musician should work.

LPF: Papo, it seems to me that there are three distinct stages in your career:

first, before joining Fania; later, when you sign with the company and play with the All Star Orchestra; and finally, the stage you're in now. What happened with your music in each of those three stages?

PL: I think there's one more stage, which now looks almost prehistoric but was very important for me and la Sonora Ponceña. I'm referring to those beginnings in which we directly copied from the records that came from Cuba and the United States. We'd take any number we liked and that more or less corresponded to the same style and ended up making it our own. This happened more or less from 1960 to 1968, before we were asked to do our first audition for Jerry Massuci, the director of Fania—an audition, by the way, that never took place. It was then that a Cuban meat-market owner from Miami, Pedro Páez, who had gotten into the record business and had recorded the Tommy Olivencia Orchestra from Puerto Rico, decided to record us, along with Eligio Peña and Willie Rosario y su Orquesta. A label was created with these four groups, and we recorded our first album, *Hachero compadre,* which is now out of print. Then we made *Fuego en el 23,* almost at the same time when Fania became interested in the groups that were recording for Pedro Páez and bought the label. From then on we had to start working with greater professionalism, and since the budget allowed it, we added a fourth trumpet to the group. And instead of one or two singers we started to use four, and the group began to become popular outside of Puerto Rico. That's our second stage. Then I joined the Fania All Stars, which was very beneficial because at each performance I did with the band, I also got work for my group. And starting in the 1980s, la Sonora begins to make a name for itself, and that's the beginning of the period we're in now, when we can perform in Europe, the United States, and South America, and our records are distributed everywhere.

LPF: You're known as one of the most accomplished salsa pianists, as a man who literally attacks the piano in a unique style. Who have been your models as far at this instrument is concerned?

PL: I've always studied Cuban pianists a lot. People like Lili Martínez, Peruchín, Emiliano Salvador, and Chucho Valdés have had a great influence on my formation, as have musicians like Eddie and Charlie Palmieri. A special case is that of Jorge Dalton, a Puerto Rican pianist you don't hear much about, but who was one of my greatest teachers. I had to substitute for him several times in his orchestra, or I'd accompany him at his performances and was forced to adopt his style. And, of course, I've learned a lot from jazz pianists like Oscar Peterson, Scott Tainer, Bob Powell, and Peter Nero. In other words, I've taken something from everyone who's offered me something interesting. As far as attacking the piano, I should remind you that for me the piano is a percussion instrument—it's the link between percussion and melody—and my attack, my style of key striking, perhaps has something to do with the fact that I was a bongo and conga player before I became a pianist, and something must have stayed with me from the way I struck the drumheads.

LPF: During your years with Fania, you were known not only as a piano virtuoso but also as one of the most important salsa arrangers. Have you abandoned that work?

PL: At the beginning I did a lot of arranging because I was just starting out as a musician, and I had a desire to make a name for myself and take every job I was offered. I recall that often at dances or recitals, while the people were resting during the intermissions, I'd remain seated at the piano with a notepad, making arrangements for musicians in Puerto Rico and New York. But that was a big sacrifice. There came a time when la Sonora started to get a lot of work, and I needed more time to attend to the business, promote the group, and work with the musicians. For five years I was in a virtual whirlwind, which was truly exhausting. Then I decided to do less arranging, but the requests kept pouring in, however—from Celia Cruz, Johnny Pacheco, Cheo Feliciano—until I decided to stop doing that work because it was so draining. It was very hard to travel, rehearse, direct a group that was becoming more popular all the time, prepare recordings, and on top of it all, arrange for several different people. You just can't give your all to everything.

LPF: What influences do you recognize in your music?

PL: Not only for me, but also for everyone who plays this music, the Cuban orchestras of the 1950s were a more than obligatory point of reference. There was Arsenio Rodríguez, Chapotín, Benny Moré, La Aragón, la Casino . . . whose music even people starting out today have to use as a point of departure, because if you don't start from there, I don't think you've had a complete education. It's the same today: you've got to study the work of Adalberto, Los Van Van, Irakere, Revé, and Emiliano Salvador, the first pianist of this era that I listened to and whose death I greatly regret, because in addition to the admiration I have for him as a musician we were united by a good friendship. I recall that the first time I went to Cuba, he was one of the people who came looking for me. We talked for a long time, and that's how our great friendship and mutual respect were born.

LPF: What most interests you in Cuban music today?

PL: What interests me most is Adalberto Álvarez's orchestra, first because they have a format similar to mine, with four brass instruments, a piano, a bass, and percussion; and second, because they know how to do things very well. They execute a more modern *son,* closer to salsa than any other Cuban orchestra. But I listen to them all: la Original de Manzanillo, Irakere, Los Van Van, Revé. . . .

LPF: And have you recorded Adalberto a lot?

PL: At least one number on each record, because he's the best, just as I said. I've recorded somewhere around fourteen or fifteen songs by Adalberto, and they've all been hits for la Ponceña. What I do with his numbers is change the arrangements, the melody, and I work the choruses in a different way, although I insist that Adalberto has the best understanding of the salsa sound of all Cuban musicians. On personal terms, Adalberto's like a brother to me, and we're united by a great friendship, in spite of the fact that we've seen each other very few times. What we do is send each other messages and records with mutual friends whenever possible. If you can, say hi for me and tell him I send a hug to him and his daughters, who are virtually my nieces.

LPF: In addition to Adalberto, you've done a lot with Pablo Milanés. What attracts you to his songs?

PL: One of the ways we've attempted to avoid the somewhat artificial themes of erotic salsa has been to use the solid lyrics created by people like Pablo Milanés, who's an incredible poet in the music of this century, in our language. That's a good enough reason, don't you think?

LPF: I see in your music an eternal struggle between tradition and experimentation. How would you define this confrontation?

PL: Look, if tradition becomes a model, I think you're going down a dead-end road. That's why, without losing tradition, you always have to keep searching. So, without disrespecting Caribbean music, we're always proposing innovative variations, incorporating elements of other musical traditions, from the United States, Brazil, or from anything that's artistically related to our ideas, because if you draw from only one source, you can get stuck on that dead end.

LPF: What is salsa? Is it the old Cuban music with contemporary arrangements?

PL: Although there are different versions, I think the real people responsible for the acceptance of this term are Jerry Massuci and Johnny Pacheco, when they founded Fania and began to cultivate and promote all the rhythms of the Caribbean under one umbrella. So they grouped them under one label, in one style, which was called salsa. But behind all that, more than anything else, it's a more contemporary treatment of the Caribbean music that originated in Cuba. When the Cubans became a bit marginalized during this evolution, however, I think it was the Puerto Ricans—those living on the island as well as those in New York, like Willie Colón or Héctor Lavoe—who did the most for this movement's success. Nevertheless, salsa has been influenced by every possible genre, and that's why it has elements of jazz and pop, of *bomba* and *plena,* of merengue, and even of Brazilian music. In fact, Frankie Ruiz's first hit, the number that made him, is "La Rueda," a Mexican song. So, salsa has been enriched with elements from everywhere, not only from Cuba, and at this stage of the game it's not fair to say that it's simply old Cuban music with contemporary arrangements. Because even if you can't speak of salsa as a genre per se, it's obviously a movement that has transcended all national affiliations to become a musical phenomenon of the entire Caribbean.

LPF: Clearly you consider yourself a *salsero.* What do you owe to salsa?

PL: A lot. For example, the fact that I was chosen to be part of the Fania All Stars gave me tremendous exposure I would never have achieved otherwise—exposure that, I think, has had a lot to do with the success that la Sonora Ponceña began to enjoy. Furthermore, salsa has had the virtue of giving our music the recognition it deserved. In the case of Puerto Rico, until a few years ago, all you heard about were people like Daniel Santos, while excellent groups like Orquesta Mercado could never get off the island. Not any more; now we're heard throughout all of Latin America, in many parts of Europe, and a few days ago we even got an offer to do some performances in India, a country I would have never thought would be interested in our music.

LPF: What's happening with popular music in Puerto Rico? Is there room for experimentation and variety, or do the commercial models dominate?

PL: It's true that commercial music always has greater exposure, and one example is erotic salsa itself. But in the case of those of us who make more traditional salsa, this has turned out to be an impetus for us to recreate ourselves and to set out in search of new things—to make our musical work more interesting, for example. La Sonora, to give you an idea, has just recorded a Latin jazz album on which we experiment a great deal with our musical potential, while at the same time trying not to do away with vocals so much, because our style depends a lot on the lyrics. And although this record is a commercially risky venture, I believe it's worthwhile to dive headfirst into unknown waters.

LPF: In your judgment, who are the most important *salseros* in Puerto Rico right now?

PL: El Gran Combo, which is the best known worldwide; Luis Enrique, who, although he's not Puerto Rican, lives there with his group; and orchestras like Willie Rosario's and Bobby Valentín's. But there are a lot of other groups that don't enjoy the international success we've enjoyed but that, in my judgment, are first-rate.

LPF: What do you think of so-called erotic salsa? Do you think that in some way it detracted from the hard, streetwise character of 1970s salsa?

PL: Look, I think it's salsa, to the extent that the music is salsa, because as a movement salsa is capable of encompassing everything, and the lyrics can just as easily be romantic as they can be humorous or social. And although it's definitely not my thing, I have to recognize that it's had a lot to do with the revitalization of salsa on a worldwide scale because international record labels have become interested in these new talents and they've launched them very astutely, which has helped to avoid, perhaps, a true crisis in salsa. Remember that in the 1980s, with the merengue boom, there was a notable decline in the acceptance of salsa by the public. Then, whether it was due to the wide exposure or the quality of the musicians—after all, you've got to recognize the work by many talented arrangers for the stars of this genre—it's undeniable that erotic salsa has been responsible for opening doors in faraway places like Europe, which today is an important market for our music. That's why I think the new talents in salsa, such as Johnny Rivera, Frankie Ruiz, and Luis Enrique, have helped to save the movement. Of course, the image they've created for the contemporary *salsero* is very different: ours is still a very macho image, while they've proposed something akin to a unisex model, as much in the attire as in the very concept of the music, a distinct image that the labels have insisted upon highlighting. In the end, it's just a passing fancy. In the meantime, I'll stick to my own thing.

LPF: It's clear that salsa is beginning to conquer Europe and other places that until recently were completely devoid of Caribbean music. How was this conquest carried out?

PL: I believe the origins of this acceptance in Europe date back to 1976, when Jerry Massuci, the director of Fania, called together the Fania All Stars and proposed that we do a European tour. I recall him telling us that it was a promotional tour and, as such, there wouldn't be much money involved but it could be decisive for our future: it was a long-term investment. So we traveled through European cities for about two months, performing, selling records, making commercial contacts. During this tour, for example, we played for the first time at the Cannes Film Festival, a venue that no Latino orchestra had ever before played, but a meeting place for the most important music moguls and record producers in the world. And what happened there was wonderful, most of all because we didn't expect it: we were received with a tremendous ovation by a crowd that danced as if they'd been waiting just for us. And the reason I remember everything so clearly is because when I saw that we'd won over the crowd, I couldn't control myself and started crying in the dressing room.

Without a doubt, that was the beginning of the frenzy that exists today in salsa music outside America and of the penetration of those markets, where we even have distributors now. That's why I insist that if there's anyone to thank for this boom, it's Jerry Massuci and the Fania label, who organized those first tours in 1976 and 1978.

LPF: Did the collapse of the Cuban record market some thirty years ago diminish the competition?

PL: Look, if Cuba had been open to the music market, I definitely believe there would not have emerged many of the groups that exist today in salsa. But at the same time, I believe the relationship with Cuba would have been more direct and the influence greater, if that's possible. The other side of the coin is that the collapse of that market also affected Cuban music, and although they still do a good job, there were times when what was being made in Cuba wasn't top quality.

LPF: Recently Tito Puente claimed that if it weren't for him and other Puerto Rican and Cuban musicians in New York, Cuban music would have completely fallen out of favor with the public. What do you think of this?

PL: You've got to look at that from two perspectives: music and business. In the international market, it's true that people like Tito, Celia Cruz, Johnny Pacheco, and others always kept the faith in Cuban music. Musically it's a different story because the reality is that a space always opens up and the good stuff always ends up coming to light, which is what's happening now with the music made in Cuba, which has once again become an obligatory reference point for all of us. In any case, Tito's opinion is his own and mine is mine, and I think that by now you've realized that I'm an admirer of contemporary Cuban music, because I know it well. But even in the most difficult times, when the records stopped coming from Cuba, the blockade was relative because we could still tune in the radio.

LPF: What music do you like to listen to?

PL: I listen to the music that's being made in Cuba right now, just as I enjoy listening to the old records of the Cuban orchestras, because it's material you should review constantly in order to avoid bad habits and because every time you hear it you find something new, small details that make all the difference, and you start to discover its richness even more. But outside of that I barely listen to the radio, whether I'm in New York or Puerto Rico, and that's how I avoid contaminating myself. I recall that a few years ago, during a time when we couldn't get any records from Cuba, I used to listen to Radio Rebelde a lot in order to tape Cuban music.

LPF: Do you think this is a good time for Caribbean music? Are we in a period of recovery?

PL: Yes, definitely. This is a complex process in which anything can contribute to the greater diffusion of our music. A perfect example is what was achieved by the movie *The Mambo Kings,* which, while being a bad movie—according to what I've been told, because I didn't dare see it—has excellent music. And in addition to earning a lot of money for those who recorded the soundtrack, especially Tito Puente, this movie helped open up markets that are beneficial to all of us. One of those markets is film itself: recently I've seen several pictures in which salsa music is prominent, old music from Fania during the 1970s, and there's one that has a scene in a Miami barrio in which they're playing my music on the radio. This also helps take our music to places we've never been before.

LPF: Speaking of places . . . if there's one important place in your life, it's this town called Ponce, in Puerto Rico. What does that little town mean to you?

PL: Well, I was born in Ponce, I live there, and I'm going to die there, which is enough for one life, don't you think? It's a town I owe a lot to, as do the many other salsa mainstays who are *ponceños,* such as Cheo Feliciano, Ismael Quintana, Héctor Lavoe, and Pete "El Conde" Rodríguez. In other words, Ponce is a land of musicians. But all of them had to leave Ponce for San Juan, and San Juan for New York, to get exposure and achieve success. And yet I myself never had to leave the town because I had the good fortune of making my career there: you had to go there to find me. It goes without saying that living in Ponce had its inconveniences because it's not the capital of the country, and that was a limitation for some people. I imagine the same thing must happen between Santiago and Havana, or between Maracaibo and Caracas, no? In Ponce, for example, we had to play for less money, and you had to work harder if you wanted to make it, although in the end you could reach the same level as others. And that's what I did: I rooted myself in Ponce and I said, "From here to heaven." And he who has strong wings makes it to heaven, that's for sure. There's no doubt about that, don't you think?

Cancún, Mexico, 1992

10

Adalberto Álvarez: Sonero in a Car

It seems that Adalberto Álvarez is capable of making a *son* from anything at all—daybreak, María, a *sonero*. I'd like him to dedicate his next *son* to the telephone because, thanks to that sometimes marvelous invention, this interview almost never took place. But after fifteen days of persistence, a timid ring—which to me sounded more like wind chimes—announced that I would finally be able to question this artist, who is writing a fundamental chapter in the history of contemporary popular music in Cuba and who has worked the miracle of making Cubans from Santiago, Camagüey, and Havana agree, not on questions of baseball, of course, but on questions of dance, because Adalberto Álvarez, like no one else on the island, sings to the feet of Cubans.

The founder of two essential orchestras in Cuba's recent musical history (Son 14, in 1978, and Adalberto y su Son, beginning in 1984); the author of numbers that drape themselves in the delicate clothing of unforgettableness; a revolutionary of contemporary *son* and a writer in great demand by the leading figures of salsa—from his friend Papo Lucca, Oscar D'León, Andy Montañez, Roberto Roena, and Ismael Quintana to the less orthodox figures of contemporary salsa, such as Willie Chirino and Juan Luis Guerra—Adalberto Álvarez is also one of the classic names in salsa throughout the entire Caribbean because he achieved—along with Juan Formell, although by a parallel path—an important and seemingly impos-

ADALBERTO ÁLVAREZ

sible feat: to make Cuban music, specifically *son,* an obligatory reference for salsa once again, as was once the case with the melodies produced by the great Cuban maestros of the genre.

The miracle of the recuperation achieved by Adalberto Álvarez has only one origin: his overwhelming talent, of which we've been well aware ever since those remote days of the 1970s when he wrote his first numbers and arrangements for the Rumbavana orchestra, pieces in which we discovered something that would become patently clear upon his debut with Son 14 and a permanent reality with Alberto y su Son: the music of this creator, in the purest tradition of Cuban *son,* had what it took to reinsert itself, from Cuba, into the salsa universe that for the last twenty years has dominated the entire Caribbean and New York. And this revival of *son,* undertaken from its native land, just might be a breath of fresh air for salsa, and its cultivators know so.

In 1992 Adalberto Álvarez reached the height of his success in Cuba and in a good number of places where his music has been played: an LP titled *¿Qué tú quieres que te den? [What Do You Want Them to Give You?],* with its title track dedicated to the wise and practical everyday philosophy of Afrocuban religion, which managed to remain at the top of the charts for more than a year and became a virtual hymn of the harsh Cuban realities of today, as its chorus insists: *"Yo voy a pedir pa' ti, lo mismo que tú pa' mí"* ["I'm going to ask the same for you as you ask for me"]. In reality, more than a catchy *montuno,* the phrase repeated by his admirers disguises the dimensions of a true artistic project that, through dance music, expresses the human concerns of this musician: those of a contemporary Cuban who, while not renouncing fun, reflects—happily, but profoundly—upon the particular moment fate has chosen for him to inhabit this earth.

Nevertheless, the fundamental expression of his program is not in the lyrics, but rather in the very concept of music that guides his work: the recuperation and modernization of the venerable Cuban *son* tradition, often forgotten on the island and frequently slighted beyond its borders. In all truth, it is thanks to this project that Adalberto Álvarez travels by car, no longer toward Bayamo, but toward that evasive altar upon which Cuban music has placed names such as Benny Moré, Arsenio Rodríguez, Mario Bauzá, and Félix Chapotín: the altar of the greats. In the meantime, I'll just ask that this be the case, and I hope Adalberto also asks for good things for me.

Questions for a *Sonero*

LPF: When you hear people talk about Adalberto Álvarez, they always say *"el sonero."* How did your fondness for *son* come about? How did it first manifest itself?

AA: My fondness for *son* is something genetic, it's in my blood. I was born by accident in Havana because my mother happened to be here then, but in reality I'm from Camagüey. There my father had, and still has, a *son* ensemble, and I always recall my mother singing *trova* songs. That's how I grew up, in the social gatherings at my home and the dances where my father performed, always in contact with lots of musicians who were friends of the family, some of whom were important *son* figures at the time: Miguelito Cuní, Félix Chapotín, la Orquesta Casino. . . . My father's group, which was called Avance Juvenil, was for a time the best *son* ensemble in the province, and some of its members went on to play in very important orchestras, such as la Sonora Matancera. Also, being a headline ensemble, Avance Juvenil was always one of the bands—along with Benny's band, Riverside, and Chapotín's group—that traveled from Havana to play at town festivals. At the age of eight or nine I was already playing the guiro at those dances, and that's how I started to imbibe the ambience of *son:* an image, a togetherness, a necessity that my current work is merely the result of, because *son,* more than a danceable musical genre, is a way of looking at music and understanding it.

LPF: When and how did you become a professional?

AA: After graduating from art school, I went back to Camagüey to do my social service teaching musical literature at the Provincial School, and that's when my father told me to take over the musical direction of Avance Juvenil. Together with a few friends of mine who had graduated with me, I changed some things within the orchestra, and we quickly started to make a name for ourselves. As we carved out our niche, I believe we began to surpass what the provinces could provide in terms of exposure. Our numbers started taking off, and many musicians in the capital, as was the case with Rumbavana—for which I had written two or three pieces, such as "Con un besito mi amor"—came to get things from our repertoire. This is a curious phenomenon because it occurred during a time when Rumbavana was enjoying a lot of success, and suddenly almost everything they played was my music. It no longer made sense for us to be a practically clandestine band in the provinces, not recording and with no access to television, while our

ADALBERTO ÁLVAREZ

music was having so much success here in Havana, where it was being played on the radio and TV. But that's when a friend from Santiago, the composer Rudolfo Vaillán, made us an offer to form a group in Santiago. And from that point, I started to think very seriously about how to make this a reality: what the group would look like, how it would work, and what format it would have. I even started to compose some songs, until the name Son 14 occurred to me, although I still didn't have a group. In the meantime, the rivers of Cuban bureaucratic hell kept flowing smoothly until the Artists' Guild of Santiago de Cuba, thanks to the help of Antonio Orúe and the insistence of Vaillán, found a way for seven musicians from Santiago and Havana to get together and finally form Son 14. And on November 11, 1978, we made our debut.

LPF: Were you out to revolutionize something with Son 14?

AA: The first thing I tried to do was to make sure my style was different from Rumbavana's, with whom I had identified at one point and had molded some of my songs in their image. That's why I introduced the trombone, and why when I went to record I invited Pancho Amat, with the *tres,* always searching for a different sound. Although I wasn't exactly sure where I was going with all that, the truth is that I was trying to find a personality, to achieve a hallmark that would set me apart.

LPF: What information did you have about salsa back then? What did you think of this musical phenomenon?

AA: Look, I think that even back then I was one of the most well-informed people about salsa. From my time in Camagüey, when there was not yet much mention of salsa here in Cuba, I had a real old radio which got good reception of several stations in Venezuela and Colombia, like Radio Rumbas from Caracas, and which kept me informed of what was happening in the salsa world when the boom started throughout the entire Caribbean. Trying to tune in stations that played salsa became a sort of hobby or obsession, but the important thing was that I kept myself informed. It's nice to remember those times, when I wasn't even thinking yet of having my own orchestra, nor did I even dream that one day I'd have the opportunity to share the stage and be friends with many of the people who were my idols at the time. I recall that the first experience I had in this regard was when Dimensión Latina came to Cuba and brought along Andy Montañez as a singer and performed with Son 14 in Santiago. At one point Andy came up to sing with us, and when he finished he said something very nice, which in a certain way helped reverse our fortune: he said it was a pity that a true

Cuban orchestra like Son 14 couldn't go to Venezuela or Puerto Rico, to the places where our music was played and danced to.

LPF: Did Andy Montañez's wish come true?

AA: Yes, our first trip to Venezuela was the result of the great time we had performing together at Guillermo Moncada Stadium. One of the people in attendance was Orlando Montiel, an important record mogul who, together with Ali Kó (who at the time was Oscar D'León's manager and today is my manager), had the foresight to take Son 14 to Venezuela, when Venezuela was the center of Caribbean salsa. And this country would become our greatest venue in the history of the orchestra. We even played at the Caracas Poliedro, and when Oscar D'León was selling 110,000 albums, we managed to sell 70,000 or 80,000 with less promotion and less tradition. We were the only Cuban orchestra to achieve that.

LPF: This information about salsa, does it have to do with your group incorporating a melodic style that wasn't common in Cuban music?

AA: At that time I was attempting to create an atmosphere with a connection to original salsa, to the atmosphere of the 1970s, when 90 percent of salsa was composed of Cuban music, whereas now it's closer to 70 percent, because people no longer draw so much on the old repertoire. The arrangements have changed a great deal, and there's a greater influence of jazz phrasing on the piano, as well as other elements that distance salsa a bit from the way Cuban music was traditionally made. Nevertheless, at that time people like the Palmieri brothers or Tito Puente had something in the cadence, in the construction, that was a bit different from what was done in the 1950s. So I started to identify myself with some of their pieces, songs of Puerto Rican or Venezuelan origin, and I decided to put a similar stamp on what I was composing, attempting in some way to do to their music what they were doing to ours. That's why Son 14 sometimes seemed to be a Latin American group—that is, a Cuban group able to please the tastes of any Latin American country—because we were closer to the general style of dance music that was being made in Latin America. But after listening to Son 14 recordings again after many years, I was finally able to discover one defect that we had: our music was a lot faster than that of the other *salseros,* which is to say, geared more toward the tastes of Cuban dancers. And I think that if I had it to do all over again, I would have made Son 14 more settled for the dancer, closer to this cadence I use now with Adalberto y su Son.

LPF: As a movement, what's the legacy of salsa?

AA: I think salsa has had highs and lows. I have great respect for the first generation, which made interesting contributions. I'm talking about Rubén Blades and Willie Colón and their record *Siembra*, which is one of the masterpieces of the movement, as well as Cheo Feliciano, Eddie Palmieri, Papo Lucca with la Sonora Ponceña, and Oscar D'León. I think that was a respectable body of work, where music was always the protagonist of important social and cultural events. Later, because of commercial pressures, there was a tendency in erotic salsa where you couldn't tell who was arranging or who was singing, and at least to me it all seemed the same. The music stagnated in the models of a particular style and a lot was lost: the *timbal* and piano solos disappeared, along with the strength of the rhythm, because everything was reduced to one little mechanism designed to make songs in only one style and at the service of one figure alone. Fortunately, however, I think now we're getting back to the bold music that is true salsa. The public is clamoring for a salsa with vitality, with guts, and the experience I've had in recent years, even in Europe, is that people want bold salsa, to see the singer truly giving his all, to hear a good solo, to hear lyrics that talk about life, in sum, everything salsa had at the beginning. And proof that this is happening is that many people who made their fortune from erotic salsa have disappeared, while an excellent singer like Gilberto Santa Rosa—whom I admire a great deal—is writing romantic lyrics but with aggressive music, with strong arrangements, with lively melodies that stimulate the listener and the dancer. Other musicians, such as Luis Enrique, are creating very well arranged music from the point of view of tone color. But people still prefer how El Gran Combo plays, how Willie Rosario's orchestra plays; they like to see a *timbal* solo by Tito Puente, a piano solo by Eddie Palmieri, with the musician giving his all and making the most of his talents.

LPF: What role can Cuban orchestras play in this recovery?

AA: Cuban orchestras have had an important role in this avant-garde in spite of the fact that we're blockaded in the promotion and distribution of our records. But I think that those of us who've managed to break through the blockade and penetrate that world, as is the case with Los Van Van or ourselves, have been influential in that recovery. This became clear to us when we performed at the World Expo in Seville, where there were a lot of groups from Puerto Rico and other countries, and the people agreed that we had something different—perhaps more explosiveness, less rigidity, or that we made fewer concessions to commercial pressures. Our case has been a fortunate paradox: we need to penetrate that market, but we don't live off it, and that gives us greater creative freedom. If we manage to penetrate that market in a big way, something very interesting might happen, because salsa is enjoying a great moment and I think there are a lot of young people out there with the desire to do big things, and you've got to exploit that situation by making strong music, like the old school that packed the Garden or Yankee Stadium and is still able to do because they're going to make real music.

LPF: Adalberto, much has been written about the crisis in Cuban popular music after 1959. People talk about a period of decay in the 1960s, and another in the 1970s, when only Formell and Los Van Van stood out. What provoked this crisis? What effect did it have on the domestic and international diffusion of Cuban popular music?

AA: The crises were real, and no one can deny that, and I'll tell you that the first mistake was made by Cuban musicians themselves. I think the level of quality dropped, and there you have the origin of many problems, regardless of other phenomena such as the lack of promotion, which brought about a true invasion by rather mediocre Spanish groups that we endured for several years during the 1970s. Nevertheless, there was a great lethargy on the part of composers and musicians at a time when it was still possible to make good recordings, before the technical problems began at the studios, and when it was still possible to get things on the radio. But the musicians got comfortable and worked with worn-out models that, even while satisfying a certain sector of the public, were artistically condemned to death. And as the lyrics were becoming encased in repetitive, facile refrains, the music was increasingly less elaborate and less ambitious. The musicians were the only ones to blame for that phenomenon, and that's why the international diffusion was practically nil at a time when salsa was at the height of its boom and when many Latino musicians were working at it very seriously.

But there's another important element: at that time, around 1970, when I was still in school, I recall there were also a lot of places to dance in Havana, and although we were apparently in the midst of an internal music crisis (and in the midst of a belated invasion by The Beatles and other rock groups that were finally beginning to be heard because it was impossible to "hide" them), the truth is that, at the same time, Cuban music was being danced to all throughout the island. These paradoxes make me think that the crisis was also due to the radio. This favorable situation for dance continued until 1978 or 1979, when we first came to Havana with Son 14.

LPF: Nevertheless, in the 1980s the situation changes. While many dance-halls are being closed, the orchestras begin to improve, which is a contra-diction. Do you think this improvement is due to the acceptance and dif-fusion of salsa in Cuba starting at that time, after the anti-salsa offensive that was carried out during those years, which denied its existence and ig-nored it in terms of promotion?

AA: Yes, for a long time we denied the importance of salsa, but I've always said that when you analyze the phenomenon, you have to start with the fol-lowing calculation: the majority of the *salseros* who became famous in the 1970s openly admitted that a good chunk of their repertoire was Cuban music and that Cuban music had determined their style of composing and even their stage presence. And it wasn't coincidental that they recognized the influence of Benny, Arsenio, Celia Cruz, and Chapotín. They did so with a respect that deserved a better understanding on the part of Cuban musicians and scholars, who, on the contrary, became entrenched and felt offended and robbed of their tradition, when in cultural and artistic reality salsa was providing a continued vitality for Cuban music understood as part of the cultural makeup of the Caribbean. But that artificial and chauvinis-tic negation of something so important in the field of Caribbean popular culture couldn't last forever: after all, salsa was a reality and was becoming stronger all the time. Then it so happened that Dimensión Latina came to Cuba, followed by Oscar D'León in 1983, and I believe Oscar's perform-ance triggered an explosion: first because he was accepted by the public in a way that no Cuban orchestra could achieve at the time, and later because he gave back to us, from his perspective, many elements of the Cuban music of old. But the important thing was the recognition created for this music, which for the first time was played on radio and TV on a massive scale. It was then that we tried to recover elements that we had abandoned and that nevertheless still worked, such as the sense of showmanship, the singers dancing on stage to choreographed moves, something which salsa always had, in addition to purely rhythmic and harmonic recoveries.

LPF: In Cuba you're known as the first musician to approach the melodic realm of salsa, its tempo, and to play music in a style that's typically salsa-ish. How did this come about?

AA: Look, although I kept myself well informed about what Latin Ameri-can *salseros* were doing, my models were the originals: Arsenio, Benny, and Chapotín, my lifelong idols. It was only much later that I learned to ap-preciate the modern salsa musicians, most of all because I realized that the salsa avant-garde was looking for essential elements in the old maestros, things that went beyond lyrics or melody: Papo Lucca imitated Lili Martínez on the piano; Oscar owed much of his strength to what he learned from Benny; Arsenio was an obligatory conceptual reference for the first *salseros*. So there you have the true source, and as I started listening to the *salseros*, I began incorporating elements, perhaps intuitively, that had to do with what I was looking for. In other words, there was an artistic communication at work. But there's something that finally consolidated this approach, which is when I began to hear my numbers played and arranged by the *salseros*. They were arrangements done from their perspective and with the tastes of their dancers in mind, and that's when I began to understand many things, like what I was telling you about the tempo at which we play. Then came the more conscious process of analyzing the phenomenon, because the knowledge that more than twenty of my numbers were in their repertoires and that I was being played on lots of radio stations meant that I was doing something right. I think the first reason for the acceptance of my work had to do with the fact that I always tried to avoid localism; I tried to make the most universal songs possible, songs that would appeal to diverse groups of people. In addition, I began to work my songs from a perspective closer to the versions that the *salseros* had done of my music: that's the key to why my sound has managed to identify itself with salsa and has approached that melodic atmosphere more closely.

LPF: Tell me a little more about your influences. In what way did Benny Moré, Félix Chapotín, and Arsenio Rodríguez influence you?

AA: The influence of Arsenio and Chapotín is a decisive element in my work—from my time with Son 14 to the present with Adalberto y su Son—because my fondness for the music played by these people was complicated by the oblivion to which they had been relegated here in Cuba. The most evident manifestation of this affinity is the fact that on all my records I've included numbers by Arsenio, from the era of Chapotín, as a sort of tribute to these greats of Cuban music. It's also true, however, that these pieces didn't always work well at the dances and that my popularity suffered among the youngest dancers, who started to consider us a traditional *son* ensemble, and that's why I decided to undertake a true offensive with *¿Qué tú quieres que te den?* in order to prove that this wasn't the case, that I could be at the forefront doing innovative and fresh things as well as those tributes I enjoy so much. Furthermore, if I've had to resort to these maestros so often it's because in terms of rhythm, flavor, and the secrets of the *son* *montuno,* everything is in Benny, Arsenio, and Chapotín, and whoever wants to make this kind of music has to drink from those fountains.

LPF: And in that respect the *salseros* beat us to the punch.

AA: Yes, they've had two moments of brilliance, and one of them was precisely when they discovered the goldmine lying there, just waiting for those who wished to exploit it. And the other was thanks to a terrible error that we Cubans committed: while having people here like Pablo Milanés, Amaury Pérez, and Silvio Rodríguez, excellent lyricists, we insisted on singing about banalities and weren't capable of creating things like those by el Gran Combo with Pablo's numbers or Ismael Miranda with those of Silvio. Then our reaction, in both instances, was to raise the banner of chauvinism and criticize the *salseros* for another purported looting, when in reality what they did was to appropriate a cultural treasure that we, its most direct inheritors, were spurning. The *salseros* proved that this music could be played, and now one of the hits on my latest record is precisely my version of a number by Amaury Pérez, made in my style, in my way.

LPF: Music and dance. You make music for dancers, thinking about them, about earning their approval. How have you been affected by the reduction in the number of dances in Cuba?

AA: Just imagine, dances are the barometer of the popular music orchestras, and right now, if you're lucky, you can play two or three dances per month, tops. So, how can the dancers check out what you're doing? How can you tell if your music really gets people moving? But add to that the problems that exist with the recording studios, which make it difficult for many orchestras to get their numbers on the radio, which is another important means of reaching the public. I think there's a serious problem in this respect, because even though we're in a good creative period, the communication with the public is at perhaps its worst level ever, and you can't always blame the notorious objective problems, which aren't always the same but always take the heat. That's why I think we have to find solutions to this problem, for the dancers as well as for the musicians. One solution might be to create places like the so-called *salsotecas* that exist in other countries, have a capacity for three or four hundred dancers, and can be established with a minimum of expenditures. The most important thing is that the musical quality exists to achieve this.

LPF: What do you consider your most accomplished records?

AA: Two albums, most of all. The first one I made with Son 14, *A Bayamo en coche [To Bayamo by Car]*, on which I did things like "El son de la madrugada" ["The Daybreak *Son*"]. I've got another number that I'm very fond of, which is "Son para un sonero" ["*Son* for a *Sonero*"], which, incredibly, was rejected at a Guzmán contest but has nevertheless become sort of an anthem for this new music and has earned a spot in people's hearts and is played a lot in Colombia, Venezuela, and Mexico. And the other is our latest record, *¿Qué tú quieres que te den?*, which, as you know, has been very successful and is making it hard for me come up with my next record because I raised the bar so high, and I don't want to disappoint the public.

LPF: What do you plan to call your next album?

AA: *Dale como e'.* I'm already working on it; I plan to record it in Caracas at the TH studios, and it'll come out on the PM Records label, like the last one. And I've got a lot of faith in it so far.

LPF: And what success have you had in the United States and in Europe?

AA: In the United States my work has a level of acceptance that sometimes surprises me, and right now we've managed to sell more than four thousand copies of *¿Qué tú quieres que te den?* in Miami alone. What's happening, in my judgment, is that since the majority of the *salseros* who've recorded my music live in the United States, they themselves have gone about opening doors for us, first for Son 14 and now for Adalberto y su Son. And I think that's going to be our most important market.

LPF: And do you think this acceptance transcends the borders of the Latino community?

AA: Yes, I believe we've also been able to cross that boundary. And in the case of Europe, Spain in particular, what happened at the concerts we played in Seville and other cities has been very encouraging, so much so that we're thinking of doing a follow-up, because that's another very important market.

LPF: Adalberto, the treatment of religious themes was almost a constant in Cuban popular music. But later, for almost thirty years, this mainstay disappeared (from music and from every other public manifestation of culture). Do you think the return of those themes is merely due to a political crossroads or to a cultural necessity that has finally been accepted?

AA: Look, that music has even had its classics, like "Que viva Changó" ["Long Live Changó[1]"] by Celina, a piece that everyone identified with her and that she and I recorded again on an album we made with Frank Fer-

---

1. Changó is an important deity in Santería, a religion that combines West African Yoruba beliefs with elements of Roman Catholicism (translator's note).

nández. Síntesis also made some attempts, but more with folkloric music than with pop. But it's not until ¿*Qué quieres tú que te den?* that the return is consolidated with such an impressive level of acceptance. And I'll tell you something: I didn't write that number because I'm religious, but simply because I thought it was cute and that it didn't pressure anyone to believe or to stop doing so, and because it had an informative way of explaining some things about religious syncretism, without proselytizing. And the fact is that the song worked so well that it stayed at the top of the charts for a year. But I'll tell you something else: the song predates the new treatment of religion that's been adopted as an official policy in our country. What happened with the song, its success, opened the door a bit to a lot of people and now everyone sings to the saints, and I think they're starting to bore people now, because in addition, many songs are badly done—they're aggressive and disrespectful at times. And on the other hand is the need to take advantage of the opportunity that the political view of religion has changed in Cuba. . . . But I assure you: if the saints exist, they must have thrown a fit with some of the songs you hear being played nowadays.

But I have a clear conscience: no one can accuse me of political opportunism or of proselytizing. I only wrote a *son,* a good *son,* I believe, that could have just as easily been inspired by daybreak or by a *sonero.* In any case, don't worry: I'm going to ask for you the same as you'll ask for me— health and good luck.

Havana, Cuba, 1992

11

Juan Luis Guerra: With and without Hat

Havana, April 13, 1994
Señor Juan Luis Guerra
Santo Domingo

Sr. Juan Luis Guerra:

On May 28, 1993, by way of my friend the poet Alex Fleites, I delivered to you in Santo Domingo a letter and questionnaire for a possible interview. I am now sending these to you once again with the hope that, perhaps having a bit more time, you will agree to an interview.

Thus began, four years and two months ago, the pursuit that would eventually lead me to interview Juan Luis Guerra with the purpose of including him in this book. Of course, the letters accompanied by questionnaires that I sent him every six months, more or less, produced no response, and my hopes were only revived when my first trip to Santo Domingo became a reality. Even so, I knew that Juan Luis, absent from the stage and even from the recording studio for almost two years, was now much less accessible to the journalists who, even when he was doing nothing, always wanted to interview him. But I had a true ace up my sleeve: my host in Santo Domingo would be the ineffable and infallible Freddy Ginebra, director of the prestigious Casa de Teatro, a man capable of opening

JUAN LUIS GUERRA

every door in the country, including the front door of Juan Luis Guerra's house.

And six days after arriving in Santo Domingo, I finally achieved the impossible: after a systematic pursuit throughout the entire city, under the direction of Freddy and the no less insistent Thimo Pimentel—with several fruitless stops at Mango, his radio and TV station, at the court where he likes to play basketball in the afternoons, and even at his home in Arroyo Hondo—I arrived with Freddy at Juan Luis's house and we were told he was there. And that was when the best side of Freddy's personality came to light: "Well, then tell him to cut the crap, get over here, and sit down, because Leonardo Padura has come all the way from Cuba to do the best interview anyone's ever done of him in his whole life."

And Juan Luis came down, hugged Freddy and greeted me, vanquished by the inevitable: The king of the *bachata,* the most universal of all Dominicans, the most timid man who's ever gone on stage to sing and dance merengue, the musician who made the entire world ask the heavens to let it rain coffee, agreed to tell me his story and his dreams, in a long conversation during which he would repeatedly put on and remove his hat, all the while never ceasing to be Juan Luis Guerra.

Juan Luis, with Hat

LPF: Juan Luis, I've heard it said that when you were a kid there was a guitar in your house that was destined for your two older brothers, who were supposed to be the musicians in the family.

JLG: Yes, the guitar was there, but my brothers were deaf, completely tone deaf. As we say here, they ran on diesel, because they had a hard time getting started, and I was the one who was crazy about that guitar. The guitar belonged to my brothers until one day when they were trying to play a Beatles song but couldn't hit a note, and I told them I didn't know why they were having such a hard time since it was really easy. And I got them so upset that one of them gave me the guitar, and they watched me hit the melody right away. From that day on, the guitar was mine. Today, one of my brothers is a surgeon and the other is an economist, to the good fortune of music.

LPF: What do you owe to The Beatles?

JLG: A lot—both to The Beatles and to George Martin, who was their arranger and who's almost never given the credit he's due. Since that first song I played on the guitar was one of theirs, I think that marked me forever. Later, I continued playing almost all their songs, and I learned George Martin's arrangements very well. On "Ojalá que llueva café," for example, there's a tribute to the cornets on "Penny Lane" and to the violin arrangements on "Eleanor Rigby." And if you look at the way I arrange the voices on any of my *bachatas,* you'll also see the influence of The Beatles.

LPF: And how does the influence of merengue enter into that predominately pop universe?

JLG: If you're Dominican, and a musician to boot, the influence of merengue is something that touches you without your realizing it, because our musical roots are very solid. If you put a *tambora* and a guiro to a rock or jazz tune, what comes out is merengue with rock or jazz influences, but it's still merengue because it has a very strong sound. An example is our merengue "Tú," which starts out like a rock song, with rock harmonies, but is still merengue. And this is true in spite of the fact that merengue was very poor until the arrival of Johnny Ventura and Wilfrido Vargas, who opened up its structure and bequeathed to the musicians of my generation a much richer and more diverse brand of merengue.

LPF: Is there a moment you can point to as the beginning of your career as a musician?

JLG: Yes, and a place as well: it was at the Casa de Teatro in 1976. I think that for more than twenty years everyone who's had something to do with music has gone through that institution. Freddy Ginebra is an exceptional man who, all by himself, created a house for those of us who were starting out and had nowhere to go, those who wanted to accomplish something and didn't know where to start. That's where I gave my first performance as a singer-songwriter, with my guitar, when the Casa de Teatro project was just getting underway. But I should also tell you that it was my only solo concert, because I was so embarrassed. And Freddy Ginebra was also the first person to get me on TV. This is why I have a bond of unconditional gratitude to that institution and to the man who founded it, has sustained it, and has transformed it into something so important to contemporary Dominican art—my great friend Freddy Ginebra.

LPF: Even though you've probably told it a thousand times, I'd like to have your personal testimony: Tell me how the idea for your group 4:40 came about.

JLG: The formation of the group was a process more than a conscious effort. It so happened that while I was studying in Boston, I'd come back to Santo

Domingo regularly to make TV commercials, which is how I paid for my studies at the Berkeley School of Music. And in doing those commercials I got together with Roger Zayas, Maridalia Hernández, and Mariela Mercado, and when I finished at the academy, in 1983, I decided to do some arrangements using what I'd learned there about the transmission of vocal quartets. At that time I was very taken with the style of Manhattan Transfer, and so I made four montages in their style in order to sing them with these friends of mine. And I think that was the first step of 4:40: getting together to do those songs. That's when we started to realize we had vocal potential and that we could really accomplish something, and the idea emerged of forming a more stable group. The following year, in 1984, we recorded our first album, *Soplando,* and if you hear it you'll realize we owe a great deal to the harmony of North American vocal quartets like Manhattan Transfer or Pathfinder, as well as to the influences of big bands such as Count Basie's, with four trombones, four trumpets, and five saxophones. But we were trying to do the record in a merengue fashion, and the closest thing to our style at that time is the modality known as *el palmbiche,* which is a slower type of merengue, perhaps more commercialized. That was the genesis of 4:40, which didn't cause much of a stir because we didn't have a lot of success or become very popular. After all, we didn't even manage to get a single record label interested in us. But finally we decided, based on the advice of a record seller, to make a faster merengue, a bit more orthodox, and that's when I wrote "Si tú te vas," which was 4:40's first real merengue, and which is on the second record, *Mudanza y acarreo,* from 1985.

LPF: And before that time, would you say that you already had a particular fondness for merengue, that you were interested in doing it?

JLG: No, not at all. Before that time, I wasn't a *merenguero* and I had no interest in becoming one. I was a rocker, and I liked all the rock groups, although I always listened to a lot of merengue. In my childhood and adolescence I heard a lot of merengue; I grew up listening to musicians such as Johnny Ventura, Félix del Rosario, and Joseíto Mateo before the rock influence arrived. Since merengue was in my cultural formation, I was able to sing solos by artists like Félix del Rosario, but I would never have considered doing so professionally. Later, when I decided to play merengue, it was as if something deep inside of me was emerging, something I'd ingested long ago. Just as in any other Dominican home, at my house you heard a lot of Caribbean music by people like Joseíto Mateo or Benny Moré, whom my father loved. Since my father was a basketball player, he would visit a lot of other countries, and he always brought back music—from Mexico, Panama, Cuba—and that allowed me to grow up in that musical atmosphere.

LPF: In that first stage of 4:40, you developed a style called *el guaberry*. What was *el guaberry*?

JLG: Well, *el guaberry* is a little seed used by the people of San Pedro de Marcorís to make a liquor. At that time we were making our third record, *Mientras más lo pienso . . . tú*, and I tried to create a type of merengue based on aspects of the folklore of San Pedro and the culture of its people, combining it a bit with the *gulolla* tradition, which is that of the immigrants from the Tórtola Islands. And so I made a version of merengue using two *gulolla* instruments, the triangle and the snare drum, and the rest was just letting my inventiveness and imagination run wild.

LPF: In some way, did you start to revolutionize merengue at that point?

JLG: Yes, because the *gulollas* speak English, and that's why there are moments when we sing lyrics in English, and there you have that mixture, which is perhaps one of the best mishmashes of all my merengues. And I accomplished that with *el guaberry*, in which I started using the saxophone again.

LPF: The saxophone is not a typical instrument in the original merengue, right?

JLG: Well, the saxophone has been in merengue from the era of the *pericoripiao*, in which the harmony comes from the sax. But the original merengue had the guitar as the harmonic instrument, until it was replaced by the accordion and the sax. There are many versions and theories regarding the origins of merengue, and one that I learned in Santiago de los Caballeros is that the format of saxophone, accordion, *tambora*, and guiro was the format of a group that played at a place in Santiago called Perico Ripiao. Now, whether that theory is true or false, I can't say. What I am sure of, however, is that we reclaimed the saxophone for merengue starting with our first record, when we invited the great saxophonist Tavito Vázquez to play with us.

LPF: Where would you place yourself in the renovation of merengue with regard to figures like Johnny Ventura or Wilfrido Vargas? Are you someone who continues the tradition or breaks it?

JLG: It's difficult to compare oneself to these musicians who've been so important for merengue, because Johnny is virtually the symbol of merengue, he's the sine qua non. I wouldn't even be able to say what's more important in him, his music or his style of dance and scenic presentation, because he consummated what had been accomplished by all the great *merengueros* who preceded him, like Joseíto Mateo himself. But he's the one who definitively modernized it. And then Wilfrido came along, who was also a great innovator, and he enriched merengue and exploited its full potential and started to make it competitive outside the country. But each did at his moment what his moment allowed and demanded: Johnny and Wilfrido enriched merengue in their own way, as I did later in mine, and that's why I consider myself a continuer, more than someone who tries to break with tradition. But, without a doubt, there's an evolution in the merengue we make because we contribute a lot of new things. And I'm sure that whoever comes along next, if he has talent and drive, will also do his own thing.

LPF: Juan Luis, how do you explain that such a congested and even repetitive rhythm as merengue has enjoyed a true international boom starting in the 1980s and that, thanks to 4:40, it has become popular all over the world?

JLG: The first thing we did was to make a conscious decision to be open with merengue. We began with those jazz influences of the big bands and the vocal ensembles that I mentioned, but we also opened ourselves further and brought in elements of rock and pop, and even elements of gospel choirs and of bebop, and that's how we greatly enriched the harmony and the arrangements of merengue and managed to give it another amplitude, more potential, so it was no longer so monotonous. And I think that stirred up the entire sound of merengue. But in addition you have the lyrics and the melody, both of which we decided to take a bit farther. In the lyrics, for example, we incorporated the teachings of people like Silvio Rodríguez, Pablo Milanés, and Rubén Blades. All those factors have caused a larger public to embrace merengue, and, at the same time, have allowed merengue to evolve and become more competitive and diverse.

LPF: One of your innovations is to incorporate music from the English-speaking countries of the Caribbean as well as from Brazil and to mix them in with that distinct merengue you've created. Has this been a conscious effort?

JLG: Yes, it has been completely conscious, and it has also been the result of a musical ambience. There are even influences of African and Haitian music in my work. But I think the essence of everything, perhaps the most important element, is returning the guitar to merengue, because once it stopped being played, it never again became a harmonic or even a melodic instrument in merengue. But since I'm a guitarist, I started using it, and that provided one of the most important changes to merengue that I made, because those who preceded me, like Johnny and Wilfrido, used the piano. And then I come in with the guitar twang on pieces like "Si tú te vas" or "Reina mía," and I change the sound that was in the air quite a bit.

LPF: But where your intentions are most evident is in the lyrical innovations you make to merengue.

JLG: My goal was to make music for the feet and for the head, hoping that merengue would have this duality. When I started to work I already had the model and example of Rubén Blades, who had written those beautiful chronicles he brought to salsa, and I decided to do something similar with my songs and merengues. I wanted to give them a communicative significance, to be able to sing about any circumstance at all—from love to hate to social themes or whatever, all through merengue—and I think I've proven that you can.

LPF: An example of that possibility is a number like "Ojalá que llueva café" ["Let it Rain Coffee"], which is a hymn to poverty and happiness that was played the world over. What does a piece like that mean to you?

JLG: Well, I think that "Ojalá que llueva café" was something akin to a hymn. You know, I heard that metaphor in Santiago de los Caballeros in a folk poem that talked about the need for it to rain chocolate, and it struck me as so beautiful that I decided to develop that same poetic idea. And so I started to work on that number, and when it was finished I put it on my fourth LP, which was the one that really put us on the map on a worldwide scale.

LPF: Have you ever considered transferring your talents as a lyricist to poetry and publishing your verses?

JLG: Well, maybe someday I'll give it a try, but I haven't decided to do so yet. I've got a lot of papers with verses, but they're always written as a function of melody and harmony because what I know how to do is to write songs. What I try to do is to get as close to poetry as possible, by playing with metaphors, with images, and if someone considers it poetry, that makes me even happier.

LPF: What about the recovery of what in Cuba was known as the *bolero-son* and in the Dominican Republic as *la bachata?* Is that also a conscious effort?

JLG: I think there's an influence there from the Dominican *bachateros,* who have cultivated that musical form for many years. But when we took up that genre, we were also accepting melodies from Cuban *son* and Mexican *ranchera* which the *bachateros* had already processed. And that type of pre-formed music is what I take on and try to recreate—with more elaborate lyrics, of course—and that's how 4:40's *bachata* comes about. But to be honest, I should say that we *son*-ify it even more than the Cubans, who make it more similar to bolero than to *son.*

LPF: What's your relationship to Cuban music been?

JLG: Well, as a Caribbean I have an inescapable relationship with, and influences from, Cuban music because it's too important to ignore. I also know it very well because I grew up listening to it. I already told you my father had records by Benny Moré and other Cubans from the 1950s, and later, when I went off to study jazz at Berkeley, I discovered Machito and Chano Pozo and their collaborations with Dizzy Gillespie and Charlie Parker. And then, without a doubt, I was influenced by the figures of *la nueva trova,* like Silvio Rodríguez and Pablo Milanés, most of all in the lyrics, through those beautiful metaphors of theirs, which have made their mark on the lyrics of almost all of us. But in this regard I'm also very indebted to Rubén Blades, although in his case it's via salsa, because his narrative and his musical chronicle are a true model of what could and can be done with popular music.

LPF: And what type of a working relationship did you have with Gonzalito Rubalcava?

JLG: I had an excellent relationship with Gonzalito, most of all when I tried to do something closer to salsa and Cuban music. It was an interesting experience because he has a great command of tempo in the salsa genre, and at one point, when we were recording "Ojalá que llueva café," he completely overshot the rhythm, and that was the quality of his that I liked the most. Since he was a percussionist and had an impeccable command of Cuban rhythms, he could violate the tempo at his whim, and that's had a big influence on me as far as the closest music to salsa that I've made, because what I play has never been true salsa.

LPF: So then, what relationship do you see between your music and salsa? Are you sure that what you do doesn't fit within the salsa movement?

JLG: In reality, I don't consider myself a *salsero,* but rather a *merenguero,* although this is a bit complicated because it's not easy to define the limits between these genres or styles. I play salsa without being a true *salsero,* and the *salseros* play merengue, often times very well, although we both transform those rhythms according to our idiosyncrasies.

LPF: But beyond specific genres—a *guaracha* or a *merengue* or a *plena*—it's said that salsa is the popular dance music of the Caribbean today. If we use that definition, would you be a *salsero?*

JLG: Look, I admire the good salsa musicians a great deal, especially the Puerto Rican–Nuyoricans and the Cubans, although in their case the definition is also more complicated. I already spoke of my esteem for people such as Rubén Blades, or supersingers such as Ismael Rivera, Bobby Cruz, Oscar D'León, or the late Héctor Lavoe. But my music is different from theirs because of its principal base, which is merengue. That's why when I recorded certain things close to salsa, I decided to use Seis del Solar, which was Rubén's group. In the recordings I respected a great deal what they were doing, and I would barely indicate the tempo to them because they have a much stronger command of the meter and key of salsa music. There were moments when they would argue about whether they were crossed up or ahead of time, or whatever, and I just let them be, because that's their territory. And the same thing happens with merengue, because if you're not a *merenguero,* you'll never know which way is up. That's why I never considered myself a *salsero,* although I gave it a shot.

In any case, I do share other concerns with these Caribbean musicians, and if what they tell me is true, that the Cubans now consider themselves more as *salseros* than *soneros,* well then I could also be a *salsero.* But I'm not too sure about that.

LPF: And what do you think about the Cuban musicians of today?

JLG: Well, they're masters. Formell and Adalberto are two big-league musicians. I also like NG la Banda, which has some impressive arrangements. I recorded Adalberto's "Bayamo en coche," which is a beautiful number. But I think the best band in Cuba is Formell's: that's as good as it gets.

LPF: You've said that your first loyal fans were the Dominicans in New York. What was it like to perform for them?

JLG: I think it was all as simple as them seeing in me a singer-songwriter who spoke to their circumstances, their story, and they identified with what I was singing because it was also their cultural and social experience. For example, "Visa para un sueño" ["Visa for a Dream"] is nothing more than a portrait of the life of Dominicans that applies to both those living here as well as those living in New York. It's the same thing with "Elena." I think that the identification of experiences was the first step, and from there sprang the support they gave us and the popularity we reached with them and through them. But all of this is my opinion, what I think happened, and it may have been something else, no? But it's true that they were my first loyal followers.

LPF: How did you go about creating the stage show for 4:40?

JLG: There were two important moments from a stylistic and scenic point of view. In our first era, when Maridalia was with us, we shared the different vocal parts but she did the majority of the solos. But when she left I took on the role of the soloist because somebody had to fill that vocal function. The choreography and stage show were also a process in which we were looking for a different style of making merengue, more in tune with what we were attempting to do with the lyrics and the music.

LPF: And how did the hat come about?

JLG: Out of necessity, I guess. I think hats and caps look good on me, and since my hair was starting to betray me. . . . One day my manager saw me with my hat on and he suggested I sing with it, and that was it. I think I'm going to continue using it because it's part of my stage personality: now if you put a hat on stage all by itself, the people know I'll be coming right out.

Juan Luis, sans Sombrero

Perhaps the most interesting thing about Juan Luis is not his (frustrated) basketball player's height, nor his sense of artistic and civil responsibility, or even his exceptional talent as a musician, but rather the contrast that exists between the man who goes on stage to sing *bachatas* and merengues and the same Juan Luis far from the limelight. It's almost impossible to believe he's the same person, because the Juan Luis Guerra who's talking with me now, even from the height of his fame and prestige, is a reserved and timid man who's still amazed at how far he's come, all by his own effort.

Juan Luis has a sad face, even while smiling, and he talks about his successes with a serene modesty. He tries to live like a normal person and, without a doubt, what he most enjoys is being at home with his wife and son, shooting baskets with his old friends, and, if his fans let him, riding around Santo Domingo on his bike. Composing songs, alone in his studio, is another of his satisfactions, although it's not always completely enjoyable.

At forty years of age, Juan Luis is a mature and accomplished artist, yet still unsatisfied. He's waged a terrible war not to stop being the person he is: fame, money, and showbiz could have changed him, but he resisted all the temptations, conserving the shyness of the boy who sang alone with his guitar and who now insists he's finally found the most essential peace and tranquility: that which comes from the divine.

LPF: How do you write your music? I have the impression that the creative process makes you suffer. Do you write and rewrite?

JLG: To me it's difficult and tedious because I'm very insistent, and I don't recommend that anyone come near me when I'm in the midst of the creative process because I can be insufferable. I recall a number of ours called "La Gallera" that we mixed more than fifteen times, which is a real torture for any sound engineer. And that was only one song on the album, so that gives you an idea of what I'm like. But the results proved I was right, because "La Gallera" was at the top of the charts for a long time. I must be a bit of a compulsive perfectionist. That's why I tend to take so long between records, because I don't have goals of time or quantity, but only of quality. The song "Como abeja al panal" took an entire year of work. The same with "Bachata rosa," and it took me almost three years to finish the album *Ojalá que llueva café*. I'm definitely not one of those musicians whose goal is to make a record each year in order to always be on top. I never know when my next record is going to be ready, and my label knows this is the only way I can work, and they've accepted it because the important thing is the final product.

LPF: And by the time you put out *Mientras más lo pienso . . . tú*, 4:40 had a lot of new members. How were you affected by the departure of your friends and the arrival of new members?

JLG: The departure that affected me the most was when Maridalia Hernández left, which happened before we recorded that album, after she won a soloist award at the Viña del Mar festival in Chile. And that was really hard, because she was not only one of the founders of the group but also the lead soloist, and so I had to reformulate the entire style of 4:40. That's when I took on the role of lead vocalist. And then came the departure of Mariela Mercado, around 1989. But the rest of the group encouraged me to keep going, and we had the good fortune of having people like Marcos Hernández and Adalgisa Pantaleón join the group, and we've stuck with that new format all these years.

LPF: You've had an antagonistic relationship with fame. How did you accept it at first, and how do you accept it now that you're quite removed from the stage?

JLG: It's difficult, very difficult, to assimilate everything that goes along with fame. I was a person who rode around Santo Domingo on my bike, and suddenly the explosion happened and I found myself immersed in a terrible machine. And so I tried to adapt the best I could, although at times, unfortunately, things got out of hand and I had to go with the flow and play the game, because if you don't, you simply disappear. You have to throw yourself into that tremendous competition that is the record world. You've got to put on the show, promote your record, smile when you've got to smile, because if you're out there, you've got to be on top, you've got to give it your all; if not, you better get out. And that causes you to live in a constant state of anxiety. . . . That was really rough on me, because my personality has nothing to do with that struggle for popularity and money. What I tried to do was to keep being myself, the person I've always been—somewhat distant, rather aloof—and I think that made things worse: the more aloof I became, and the more I tried to hide, the more they sought me out. You have no idea what that was like: I felt so overwhelmed, so hounded, that everything was getting out of control. I had to change things if I wanted to keep being myself and if I wanted to keep my life from becoming a living hell. That's what fame can do to you. Powerful stuff, no? Just imagine, they started talking about me as "the Dominican par excellence," crazy stuff like that. . . . What I do know is that while I was inside that system, I did what I had to do as best I could, I gave it my all, and I represented my country very well. To use a baseball metaphor, every time they threw me a decent pitch, I'd hit it out, and when I get back to work, I'd like to hit it out again, but in artistic terms, or course, not in terms of the typical showbiz hype.

LPF: You've been silent since your album *Fogaraté* came out in 1995. What's 4:40 doing these days?

JLG: Well, right now we're basically on a sabbatical that's lasted more than a year. One of the problems when we decided to stop was with the orchestra that accompanied us. Since we don't have an established group, a lot of the people who collaborate with us for a time eventually leave in search of other jobs and join other groups, as did our last percussionist, Chichi Peralta, who has made an excellent record with Son Familia. . . . But when we come back, I hope to have a good group together because right now I'm preparing a record with a recompilation of *bachatas*—it doesn't have a name yet, but it has four new songs—and after that I'll start recording more frequently. But I needed to take this break, to think things over, to get centered and recover that intimacy I had lost.

LPF: And in all those decisions that are so important for an artist whose livelihood comes from performing, how have your cohorts from 4:40 helped you?

JLG: They've always been very steady, and very good friends. For example, Roger Zayas, who's always been my closest friend in the group, was a great help when Mariela left 4:40, because I was determined to dissolve the group. But he encouraged me to continue, to look for new people, to keep my spirits up. Furthermore, he's always been the hardest working and the most organized of us all, and I've learned a lot from him. And I also owe a lot to Maridalia and Mariela. Later, when Adalgisa joined the group, I felt I'd met a great friend, someone who was capable of doing great work and who offered me her sincere affection. And another important thing has been their ability to relate to me, because I'm not an easy guy to get along with. But they accepted that I was the brains, the one who did the arrangements, who handed out the parts, and that was clear, so from the beginning everything worked great.

LPF: Recently you've become more religious. What are you looking for in religion, and have you found it?

JLG: No, I haven't become more religious: I've gotten closer to Jesus. I don't think religion is good for anything if you don't get closer to Christ, which is what I'm trying to do. I understood that I was very far from the Lord, and I was living in a perpetual state of anxiety, in a tremendous state of worry. I'd always been a believer, but very much in my own way. I was like everyone else: a big believer when I got on a plane, but after we landed okay, I went back to my own thing. But due to my work, the success I had, I was very overwhelmed, with no peace or tranquility, although I had all the other things that many people desire—fame, money, popularity—but I was lacking what I needed the most. And I looked for peace in him, the true peace, because the peace of this world is based on circumstances: it implies that your business is going well, that your family is okay, but the Lord's peace transcends all those contingencies. If you're at peace with him, you're truly at peace. That's how I began to understand the Lord's peace, wisdom, and goodness, and I accepted him as my guide and savior, and he gave me what neither money nor fame could. And now I feel good, thanks to him.

LPF: And is that newfound peace reflected somehow in your music?

JLG: Of course it's reflected, but my music hasn't changed. The Lord wants me to keep being a musician, and that's part of my path to God because he doesn't ask you to stop being yourself. In addition, my music fulfills a social function that I believe is necessary. Pieces like "Visa para un sueño" and

"Ojalá que llueva café" were true blessings, because they're the songs that people identified with because they were truly necessary.

LPF: Do you consider yourself a socially committed musician in some way?

JLG: Of course I do. From the moment you sing a protest song, you're giving some people happiness, but you're saying the things you think should be said. I've always said that's an attribute and an advantage that we musicians have over politicians, because they don't sing. Can you imagine a speech in merengue? We make denouncements, sometimes very strong ones, at other times more sublimated ones, but the people hum them, they repeat them, they learn them by heart, and in this way, rather sweetly, they reach their consciousness. And many times we take advantage of irony, double entendres, and metaphors in order to say things.

LPF: What's your view of Dominican culture and society right now?

JLG: Right now they're creating a Ministry of Culture here in my country, and it's the first time I've seen a government with a desire to work for the culture. There are even musicians living abroad who are coming back to work here, to create philharmonic orchestras and other such things. Now what's indisputable is that we need to work a lot harder and invest more in all sectors of the culture. We've got to create a cultural system, and I think it's good news that a man as sensitive as Víctor Víctor is working for the Ministry of Culture. We'll see if he's going to get the support and the resources he needs to do his job.

LPF: The Dominican Republic is a country of tremendous social contrasts. What's your view on this very contradictory reality?

JLG: I'm a product of those contradictions and those circumstances, and everything I do comes out of that, you know? There's a merengue of mine that analyzes this problem very well, which is "Me enamoro de ella" ["I'm Falling in Love with Her"], and it's very autobiographical. In it I talk about my girlfriend at the time, who's now my wife, and I tell how we lived in different worlds: she studied at the rich people's university, and I was at the one for people with no money. She drove a Mercedes and I rode the bus or my bike. And all those contrasts, perhaps, spark the imagination and creativity as well, and that's something one should take advantage of as much as possible because if you're even a bit realistic, you understand that society today is so full of contrasts that it's not going to change. But I say that in the midst all this hardship, you can be optimistic and see the good things that our misfortunes offer us. For example, the lights go out a lot here, and no society in which the lights never go out knows the feeling of happiness when the lights come back on: it's amazing to hear the shouts of joy an- nouncing that the lights are back on. . . . But what we can't forget is that, individually, we can each help in something, and I'm always ready to pro- vide that help. What I say is that if you're looking for me, I'll show up ready to work—and you've seen this is the case, right? Just recently they called me to rearrange the national anthem, and I'm happy to do so because I want my hymn to sound good, no? I'm very sensitive to those types of things, be- cause I feel the pride and the responsibility of being an artist and being a Dominican.

Santo Domingo, Dominican Republic, 1997

12

Nelson Rodríguez: With Salsa until 2000

He's just thirty-three years old, and he has tremendous power. He's driven and never satisfied, always demanding more from himself and his work. Nevertheless, the image projected by Nelson Rodríguez, the young Puerto Rican who for the last year has been at the helm of Ralph Mercado Management—the emperors of New York salsa today—is not that of the ruthless yuppie of *The Bonfire of the Vanities,* but rather that of an enthusiastic man who has dedicated his intelligence to a project he believes in with the fanaticism of the chosen few: that of helping salsa triumph in the Big Apple, which is the same as saying in the entire world.

From his office in Suite 806 at 568 Broadway, Nelson Rodríguez moves the visible and invisible strings of the world's greatest salsa emporium, helping to create images, figures, styles, and tendencies—dictating, in sum, the commercial directions of salsa music and casting the tentacles of the genre toward the furthest corners of the globe. Because, from Tito Puente and Celia Cruz to today's newcomers, almost all the figures of the movement have abandoned their fate to the company led by this young Puerto Rican man.

Musically educated in the tastes of his Puerto Rican parents (diehard fans of Daniel Santos and Benny Moré), the definitive formation of Nelson Rodríguez occurred when he made his debut—at the tender age of fourteen—as a disk jockey in the Latin clubs of New York. There he learned to mix records older than himself, combining them with pop and rock to satisfy diverse tastes. But most of all, he learned how to take advantage of the

NELSON RODRÍGUEZ

pauses between songs to invite into the booth veterans like the venerated Machito (Frank Grillo) and his compatriot Tito Rodríguez, who made him hear the old Caribbean rhythms in a different way and revealed to him important and forgotten names, surrendering to him, day by day (or more accurately, night by night), the secrets of this long musical history. Later, for nearly ten years, Nelson was head of promotions for the TH company, until Ralph Mercado managed to steal him away to the headquarters of RMM. His years with TH, however, were decisive ones, because in addition to handling promotions, he had the enviable opportunity to accompany the orchestras of Oscar D'León and Andy Montañez on their European tours, working as a translator. The time he spent with these two stars allowed him not only to learn about the inner workings of the business, but also to familiarize himself with the intimate ambience of salsa and to forge a close friendship with these two musicians who now trust in Nelson—as do so many others—as the Greeks did in the Oracle at Delphi.

This is why today, in addition to being an excellent promoter and sales agent, Nelson Rodríguez is considered one of the most knowledgeable figures on the past, present, and even the future of salsa, and why his articles frequently appear in the specialized magazines of the genre. And in New York today, they say that his word is law. And from his words during a two-hour interview, I obtained this revealing salsa exposé that uncovers the most inaccessible back streets and alleyways of this cultural project which, at the same time, cannot forget that it's also a commercial enterprise. The cards are on the table.

The Game Begins

LPF: Nelson, people talk about a deep crisis in salsa during the 1980s, after the commercial boom of the 1970s. Beyond the obvious, how did this crisis manifest itself? Has salsa completely emerged from it?

NR: There was a crisis, and it was terrible. It started right around 1980, when Fania's longtime empire started to crumble, more or less. That's when Sergio Bofill, Adriano García, and Roberto Torres got into the music business to form the SAR company, which was exclusively dedicated to working on old Cuban songs, with the only modification being that they updated the arrangements and extended the length of the numbers to satisfy the dancers. The period of crisis that broke out at that time had to do with people no longer attending salsa dances, both here in New York as well as in Puerto Rico, Miami, and the rest of the United States, because what was happening in New York was reflected in the other areas. The response by the promoters, however, was more commercial than musical in nature, and they contented themselves with bringing to market a very elemental salsa, meant to please the dancers, with very little musical sophistication or lyrical depth, but that at the time turned out to be effective for the typical dancehall crowd, those who, after the commercial demise of Fania, had nowhere to go. There were also a few *charanguitas* at the time that cultivated the old Cuban songs and very little else. This is the general state of affairs from 1980 to 1983 or 1984: with the exception of SAR, no other company was doing much of anything. There were, of course, companies such as TH, which had good music but were not promoting their artists because many of them had reached an age that was considered a bit advanced in commercial terms. I'm talking about people like Willie Rosario, Andy Montañez, Oscar D'León, and Ralphy Levi, who weren't arousing much interest because people were looking for something new, something different from what was imposed by the Fania empire. I recall that at La Décima, where I was working as a deejay in 1983, the TH people came looking for me and they hired me as a promoter, in spite of the fact that many people were saying that during that period of crisis it didn't make much sense to hire a promoter. The majority of professionals in radio, showbiz, and distribution were very skeptical and thought that Latin music would eventually end up being swallowed by some monopoly. They expected a CBS or some other megafirm to buy up all the small labels, and they expected that the salsa market would be centralized in the hands of people outside the movement. My opinion at the time—and a lot of people now recognize that I was right—was that we had hit rock bottom, as low as we could go, and things just couldn't get any worse. The only thing we could do was to get back in the saddle, and in that spirit I joined TH.

LPF: Do you think this fall was only due to the excessive commercialization that occurred toward the end of the 1970s, when experimentation and innovation were abandoned?

NR: I think so, without a doubt. In order to make more money, certain commercial criteria were established, many figures were invented, and each singer in Fania was given his own orchestra. A time came when that repetitive sound saturated the market because it became a formula that only imitated itself, and the people weren't interested in a music that offered nothing new. In addition, in the 1980s the merengue invasion takes place, which had a devastating impact with people such as Wilfrido Vargas, Johnny Ventura, who was really played a lot here, los Hijos del Rey, and young people who were making really good merengue. Furthermore, salsa was having internal problems, such as the *salseros* not taking care of their image: they no longer dressed like before, and had lost the pizzazz that characterized the music of the 1940s and 1950s, when Machito, Tito Rodríguez, and such people performed in tuxedos. That look was abandoned, and the reasoning was that it wasn't fair that in order to attend a dance you had to dress to the nines and pay $80 for a round of drinks and a $30 cover to watch an orchestra play in T-shirts and tennis shoes because the musicians had come straight from work. In any case, the quality of the music suffered, the charm of the show was lost, promotion evaporated, and finally, merengue came on the scene with a livelier rhythm and with a sense of choreography, having their people dance on stage, something that had been lost in salsa—with the exception, perhaps, of the Puerto Rican orchestras like El Gran Combo, which always danced.

People also complained about the banalization of the lyrics. The conscious salsa of the 1970s, with Rubén and Willie at the forefront, proved that you could say very important things, and suddenly all people were talking about was *"un rico guaguancó"* ["a smooth *guaguancó*"], and saying *"yo tengo azúcar"* ["I've got sugar"] or *"vamos a guarachar y a rumbear"* ["let's dance the *guaracha* and the rumba"] at a time when a new generation was entering the picture. It also coincided with the fall of disco, which had affected us so profoundly in the 1970s. I was a witness, as a deejay, to the fact that what the young people wanted to dance to was disco, not Latin music, and the lack of new models for these new dancers completely distanced them from Latin music, as became evident around 1982 or 1983, when we hit rock bottom.

LPF: And by that time, were the most important figures of the 1970s—Rubén Blades himself and Willie Colón—no longer popular? And what about the old masters, such as Tito Puente and Celia Cruz, for example?

NR: As the saying goes, when it rains it pours: Tito and Celia didn't sell during the entire decade of the 1980s, and at one point Tito even decided not to record any more salsa, opting to devote himself entirely to Latin jazz until Ralphy Mercado suggested he record his hundredth LP as a tribute to salsa with the label's best singers. Celia, for her part, had the loyal following of a large sector of the Cuban community, but that was about it. Meanwhile, people like Rubén and Willie still enjoyed a certain amount of popularity thanks to the quality of their music and lyrics, but things weren't going well even for them.

The situation became even worse when a new generation of musicians came on the scene and dealt the salsa veterans the most serious blow of all. The arrival of talents like Frankie Ruiz, Eddie Santiago, and Luis Enrique began to change the panorama of Latin music with what has come to be known as erotic salsa, which for many was a betrayal of the very character of salsa, a macho, streetwise, strong music. The curious thing, however, was that this erotic or sensual salsa had the virtue of regaining the attention that had been lost, and it helped improve the situation. But even so, a war still broke out because there existed an old school of *salseros* who refused to accept the sensual stuff, most of all because they said it was a facile music, with no melodic elaboration or challenges for the singer.

LPF: So why, then, did this new tendency work? In the long run, was it an important tendency in salsa?

NR: Look, this is a complicated issue because there was a lot of truth in the accusations made by the veterans. The fact is that several of these erotic salsa singers stayed within a very comfortable range, and the reason they were able to continue working was that they were performing a music that wasn't very demanding. If you analyze the style of many of these young people who were fresh from Puerto Rico, you realize that they sang trombone music, which was sensual and lethargic, but without trumpets, and the reason they couldn't use them was because the powerful sound of the trumpet would drown out what little voice they had. They simply couldn't sing over the trumpets. Nevertheless, in the midst of that desolation, the public enthusiastically welcomed this new wave, first of all because they were pretty boys who were heavily promoted, and second, because they had something new, which was a lot easier to dance to than the previous music or merengue. Many people from the *charanga* period discovered that this music was almost the same style—soft, slow, perfect for not breaking a sweat—and you could be very sensual while dancing it. All these factors influenced the success of erotic salsa, but I think they were also decisive in the commercial strategy of TH to make idols out of these boys: you saw their faces everywhere, we promoted their records, and they became very successful. In short, we just kept at it.

What happened five years later—around 1988—was that we realized this sound was saturating the market, because all the labels were recording this kind of music and even the veterans had to sell out to this tendency.

Oscar D'León went to Puerto Rico to record sensual salsa, Andy Montañez recorded similar things, and we at TH started to become alarmed by the saturation phenomenon, which got so extreme that you couldn't even distinguish between one singer and another because everyone was doing the same thing. In the meantime, the only ones who stayed their course were the *merengueros,* who were becoming more popular all the time, so much so that if you went to Puerto Rico, the music you heard the most was merengue, and you'd find discos that would be packed every day with people dancing to merengue, and if you went to a disco with good salsa bands, there'd be four souls in the audience. To top it all off, the cover charge for a salsa show went down to $7, and now you've got to pay at least $50 to get into a show with three bands. But the result of all this has been that today, for every twenty orchestras in Puerto Rico, nineteen are merengue bands—and a lot of them don't play a particularly good brand of merengue.

Another of the problems created by erotic salsa, I believe, with its lack of complex musical compositions, was the flight of many musicians to jazz. There were orchestras like Luis Enrique's that had excellent players, but when they saw that they weren't being used or appreciated for their true worth, they went over to jazz in search of the freedom and creative potential that jazz provides. I think some of the figures of sensual salsa caused a lot of harm to the music, because when it came time for the *descarga,* they, as the band leaders, were the ones who went and played the piano and the conga, and the image that stuck with the crowd, of course, was that they were tremendous musicians because they could play all those instruments, and that therefore they should do the solos. And any self-respecting instrumentalist surely won't stand for this, and a lot of people didn't. . . . So, considering all the pros and the cons, sensual salsa has to be given the credit for bringing the spotlight back onto Latin music.

LPF: You were saying that around 1988 there was a saturation of sensual salsa. What happened then?

NR: Another change. What started happening around 1988 was principally due to the efforts of Ralphy Mercado's RMM company, which was founded that year. He began to sign kids like Tito Nieves, Tony Vega, and José Alberto, who all had their respective orchestras, and he transformed them into soloists. José Alberto had already been a soloist, but he hadn't had the success he's enjoyed here because previously he'd mostly made records mixing merengue and salsa, a mixture that didn't work because it was obvious you had to stick with one genre or the other. When Ralphy signed him, he asked him to play only salsa, and that's what they recorded, and the result was the gold records this kid has earned since he made that decision.

That was the beginning of a return to salsa that we were waiting for and in some way preparing for. Then we went to look for the old sound, the old arrangements, that were really catchy with the dancers, but we wrote new lyrics for them that said more than "Let's go do the rumba and the *guaracha*." What most interested us was the musical concept of the old masters. The success of this change can be seen through a negative example, such as that of Oscar D'León. TH asked Oscar to keep recording sensual salsa, even as his sales were declining with each album, at the same time that I was recommending he drop that style and go back to his own thing, "macho" *son*. The terrible part was that the companies accepted these downfalls as something inevitable in the case of a veteran singer, because their interest was mainly in the young kids, the only ones that they thought could sell 100,000 copies, while these people from the 1970s had become catalog standbys who barely sold 20,000 or 25,000. That's when the exodus from TH of people like Oscar himself, Andy Montañez, and Tony Olivencia began, in spite of the fact that they hadn't enjoyed the success of before. A case in point is that of Willie Rosario, who kept putting out very good records and barely sold 20,000 copies owing to a lack of promotion on one hand and to commercial demands on the other, demands that come from radio program directors and the discotheques, which require an artist work in a particular genre. The beginning of the change introduced by RMM had a lot to do with that, because we didn't accept such interference. I think it's the public that should decide if a product is good or not, and other people have no right to manipulate the public's taste and the artists' work.

So, what Ralphy's company did, after working with those young people, was to begin recovering the veterans, and now we have Cheo Feliciano, Oscar D'León, Celia Cruz, Tito Puente, and Eddie Palmieri on our roster. And combined with the company's newer talents, they've managed to reach the young people. Because—and here's another important detail—in reality, until very recently, all the Latin music companies, including this one, had forgotten about the young people, and the young people preferred to listen to American rock and rap rather than Latin music.

In our company we started to make the change with the work we did with a very young singer, La India, and her husband, who's a world-famous deejay, Leduc Louis Vega, a man who's very well connected in the American music business, where currently, for example, he's in charge of mixing the greatest-hits album that Michael Jackson is recording. Being interested in Latin music, Vega came to see us since he was thinking about making a record with certain fragments of works by people like Tito Puente and Eddie Palmieri. But we proposed an idea to him that immediately won him over: instead of fragments of songs, he could use the artists themselves, and the result was several records of American music with Latin musicians giving a special flavor to the tunes, which at times are rock versions of old numbers of theirs.

That was when the idea came about for India to do a record of American music with two or three salsa numbers. They hired Eddie, and when Eddie heard her, the idea changed completely and they decided to make a pure salsa record titled *Llegó la India, via Eddie Palmieri [India Has Arrived, via Eddie Palmieri]*, on which a veteran of Latin music shares the stage with a young girl who has the virtue of bringing with her the young fans who heard her in the American atmosphere and who, in this way, can get to know our music. And this is very important in attracting that audience because no one can deny the fact that those young people can no longer look at Celia Cruz or Oscar D'León as idols, because for them, they're simply too old; but it's different with young singers such as India, Rey Sepúlveda, and Tito Nieves, who are almost their same age.

LPF: So, have you proposed a strategy for capturing that "other" audience?

NR: Look, the only Latin music that had great success among the young people here in New York was the boogaloo rhythm led by Pete Rodríguez in the 1960s, because the people who played it back then were young kids of seventeen singing in English to kids their own age and talking about things on the street, their daily life, and mixing elements of *son* with pop. Nevertheless, the producers of Latin music weren't capable of viewing boogaloo as a means of penetration, and instead viewed it as an enemy and began doing everything in their power to take it off the market. The example of how boogaloo was handled is very relevant for us: if you want to attract young people, you need singers who are young themselves and speak the same language as their audience. We already have three kids who are doing that, and we take them out to the streets, the plazas, the beaches: they are Marc Anthony, a Puerto Rican who has a great talent for salsa but who comes from an American musical background, where he sang with Leduc Louis Vega's group and reached the top of the *Billboard* charts, selling 200,000 copies (which is very little for an American company, and that's why they let him go without renewing his contract); India, who was part of the chorus of that same group; and the third is another girl with a similar background, Crezy, who we just made a record that was produced by maestro Luis Perico Ortiz. In any case, the good thing about these musicians is that they already had success in another musical ambit, but they have excellent traits for salsa, and whoever listens to them now has no idea they're singing salsa for the first time. This is the company's new marketing strategy, which has been imitated by other production outfits, like TH itself, which is managed now by Oscar George, or Tony Moreno's Musical Productions.

LPF: Obviously, along with a musical change, there's been a change in mentality among the promoters. Are we witnessing a generational change in the marketing of salsa?

NR: Without a doubt, there's new blood in all the Latin music companies, and a generational change also provoked a change in mentality. I think that the new generation of promoters has emerged from those of us who worked for several years for TH. That's where I came from, as well as people like Sammy Vargas, who's the head of the Sony's Latin branch; Frank Torres, who was TH's magician in Puerto Rico, the one who made the company's hits there and who's now founded his own house and is with VMG, a subsidiary of RCA. César Delgado, who was a sound engineer on a lot of the important salsa records, is the head of EMI Capitol in Puerto Rico. And all of us came from the same TH school during the 1980s, when TH dominated salsa.

LPF: And do you feel personally satisfied with what you've achieved so far?

NR: I think I'm the ambitious type, the type who's never satisfied. I'm always aspiring to achieve something more. . . . I never feel, even with the things I've achieved, that I've made it. And the day I feel I have, the best thing for me to do will be to retire and lie down on a beach somewhere and get a nice tan. The good thing about life is that one can do something new each day, and thanks to God, I'm in a position in which every week my job requires me to invent new things, because here, whoever stops doing so is finished.

LPF: So do you think that with promoters like you and Ralph Mercado, there will once again be a climate favorable to salsa?

NR: I believe so, and for several reasons, although our responsibility isn't that great: it's mostly in the hands of the musicians. Erotic salsa, which was saturating the market, has started to subside, and the producers are allowing people like Tony Olivencia, Willie Rosario, and Oscar D'León to record their own thing, which is strong salsa. If you listen to the latest record by José Alberto, "El Canario," you'll see that along with sensual numbers there are also streetwise songs, with a lot of swing, masculine music. The most recent albums by Tito Puente, including his hundredth, also go back to the strong stuff, to *salsa brava,* so to speak. The same goes with what we've got planned for the upcoming months: the new records by Celia Cruz, Tito Nieves, Tony Ortiz, and Antonio Cartagena—a new talent from Peru who, in my judgment, is very promising and whose style is reminiscent of Adalberto Álvarez. In addition, the philosophy of salsa has changed, and this can be seen in the results: if before it was a virtue to be a streetwise musician, today it's important to be an accomplished artist, and many of the new talents are exactly that, having studied music at prestigious schools, as in the case of Juan Luis Guerra. Another element of the change is the strong influence of Latin jazz, which we're also recording and producing, because we'd have to be very stupid not to record what's played at the concerts we organize, even more so knowing that this music has a large market the world over.

LPF: So salsa's definitely not going to die?

NR: Salsa's not going to die. The only thing you can expect in this music are changes, a lot of changes. I think that in the future you're going to see a lot of collaborations between artists because, for many of them, to record a record all by themselves, as famous as they might be, won't produce the sales they want. But if you put Eddie Palmieri together with Ismael Quintana, they'll sell because Ismael is fresh now, doing new things. A good singer who sold twenty years ago will sell today if he's got good music. We're going to work with those combinations a lot. We've already got plans for new concerts in which we're going to hook up Celia Cruz with Oscar D'León; Oscar's orchestra with José Alberto; Cheo Feliciano with Antonio Cartagena from Peru; Marc Anthony with India; Van Lester—whom many people compare to Héctor Lavoe—with Ismael Miranda, in a tribute to Lavoe we're going to do. We're starting to discover that salsa today is going in that direction and Musical Productions is also.

But the key to success for this project is the ability find new things, new music, although you're also trying to recover the tradition, as we did with Tito Puente's recording at Village Gate, a place where an album hadn't been recorded in twenty years. And you've got to keep looking for young kids, not to invent them but to promote them, that is, people with real potential for success because of their voice and their artistic sense. When I started out with TH, they used to say you had to record a singer because he was the only thing we had, and today that's not the case. There are a lot of musicians with good voices, who've studied music, such as Eddy Ruiz, for example, a Cuban who was living in Puerto Rico and who's coming here shortly to do his first dance performances, and who's got an excellent voice.

LPF: In addition to joint efforts, what other elements are helping to revitalize salsa?

NR: There's a little bit of everything, like in the Lord's vineyard. It just so happens, for example, that all the Latin music companies are putting out their old records on CD, which is prolonging their commercial life. They have technology now that improves the sound, which is a good thing, because a lot of those records were an embarrassment, like those by la Gema, and now they can clean them up and they sound a lot better. Fania, West Side, and SAR are living off those archives right now. So, whoever has a catalog of five thousand records will be around for the next five years.

Another important wave that's helped to revitalize this music is salsa from Colombia, which deserves a lot of credit, because they were one of the few who in 1988, when only sensual salsa was being recorded, kept playing their own thing, old salsa with its rough edges. And the people who liked that music danced Colombian salsa because it was the only kind that sounded different, the only kind that spiced things up a bit, and today a lot of good tunes are still coming out of Colombia. The reason, in my judgment, is the immense popularity that salsa enjoys there: in Cali alone there are around two hundred salsa groups, and although not all of them record, somehow they manage to get by. And in Barranquilla there are another fifty-five groups, and in Medellín about thirty. . . . In any case, they have more groups than the United States and Puerto Rico combined.

LPF: And what about Cuba? Doesn't it enter into the equation?

NR: The case of Cuba is the most contradictory of all: it's always been on the margins of salsa, at least commercially, but it's always set the musical standards. And now there's a new school in Cuba, which is no surprise to those of us who know music, but which is a revelation to those who hear these things for the first time and then say, "Those people are up to something down there." What do you mean, *up to something?* Can't you hear them? Those people are on the cutting edge. And it's not just one orchestra: it's Adalberto y su Son, NG la Banda, Den Den. We've recorded a lot of things from Cuba here, such as "Te regalaré" by NG, which Johnny Rivera recorded to great success, and "Tú me quemas," by Pablo Milanés, which was one of the hits on Tony Vega's first album. Rey Sepúlveda just recorded two numbers by Isaac Delgado, who used to be a singer with NG la

Banda. Cuba was always a veritable music school, and it still is, and we're all very interested in what's happening down there. In the meantime, my dream is that some day music will speak its own language again, and that we'll be able to freely record musicians from here alongside Cuban ones, and when that happens, salsa is going to take an important step. That might be the key to salsa's future. Just be patient and you'll see.

LPF: Nelson, would you be so bold as to offer a definition of salsa?

NR: Although I'm Puerto Rican, I admit the truth, and every time people talk about salsa as something new, I ask them, "What side of the bed did you get up on today?" And although there's always a debate about this topic, I don't think it's worthwhile to discuss it. I remember that when I was little, in Puerto Rico you'd hear *bombas* and *plenas*, music by trios and quartets, but the music that was later called salsa—or that gave birth to true salsa, to be fair—was made here in New York, by people like Machito and the two Titos, Rodríguez and Puente, but even more so, it was made in Cuba, by Arsenio, Arcaño y sus Maravillas, and Benny Moré. I think, in truth, that the music is still the same in its morphological structure, although certain things in the lyrics have changed along with some aspects of the rhythm, as well as the brass section. . . . But the origin of all that is in Cuba. In any case, I think that even when you reduce all of that to a name, salsa has been a very important movement in terms of exposure, because at least it made our music known in many parts of the world. And nowadays no one can deny that, along with *son,* rhythms like merengue, *bomba, plena, cumbia,* and several others have had a remarkable impact on the formation of salsa, which is a hybrid.

LPF: Earlier you mentioned the search for a market within the United States. What about Europe? Does it make sense to talk about a salsa conquest of the Old World?

NR: Right now we're determined to enter the European market. It's true that in Europe there have always been salsa tours, sometimes with big crowds, because they like our rhythm and have a good understanding of music. But Europe was never considered an important market for record sales, and for the first time we're working on it cautiously but with great interest. Right now RMM has made some distribution deals in France, and we signed a contract with a German company, Belafon, that represents us in thirty-eight countries where salsa has never been introduced, and that's how we're going about entering Finland, Switzerland, Italy, Germany, and Australia. We've even received distribution proposals from Russia, and we have companies in Japan, Mexico, and Central and South America. Something that's helpful in this sense is that the interest in cultivating salsa has spread through many of those countries, and the work of Orquesta de la Luz has been important in this regard, because they've proven that not only Latinos can make this music. And now groups are appearing in Europe and are creating an atmosphere conducive to the cultivation and consumption of salsa. In Spain there are around ten or twelve salsa orchestras, and there are groups in other parts of Europe. And in 1992 the first salsa festival was held in Japan. It's clear that more markets are opening up all the time, but you've got to work them intelligently and gradually to avoid another saturation phenomenon and the artificial creation of orchestras and figures. In the short term, this means we'll be doing lots of tours in these parts of the world, because if the records sell they'll want to see the orchestras. I think that with such a favorable climate, with those new markets, with the Cuban music that's being made now, with what's coming out of Colombia, the music from Santo Domingo, which is still really strong, and with the collaborations here, salsa has a long life to look forward to. I think this favorable history is covered until at least the year 2000.

New York, 1992

13

Radamés Giro: The Tangents of Salsa

adamés Giro has a *sonero*'s past: in his native Santiago de Cuba, where
he was raised in a family of musicians, Radamés learned the secrets
of *son* perhaps before those of the alphabet. This explains why, long before
becoming a musicologist, he was a traveling musician in his city, and with
his guitar on his back, he drifted through different ensembles, trios, and orchestras in search of his daily bread. Radamés the musician, however, had
a serious problem: his hands, which were too small, made it impossible for
him to exploit the richness of his chosen instrument, and so he abandoned
music as a profession and instead devoted himself to its study.

But that *sonero*'s past has been decisive in the musicological career of
Radamés: having lived among *soneros* and learned the intricacies of *son,* its
deep philosophy, has provided him with essential access to the development
of the best-known Cuban musical style in the world, the genre that—as he
himself can attest—has given rise to salsa.

Chief editor for art and music at Letras Cubanas, frequent contributor
to cultural publications in Cuba and other countries of the region, and author
of books such as *Leo Brower, la guitarra en Cuba [Leo Brower: The Guitar in
Cuba]* and *Heitor Villalobos: Una sensibilidad americana [Heitor Villalobos:
An American Sensibility],* in addition to several compilations of texts, today
Radamés Giro is putting the final touches on a truly encyclopedic project
that seems from another era: his *Diccionario enciclopédico de la música en
Cuba [Encyclopedic Dictionary of Music in Cuba],* which surely will revolu-

RADAMÉS GIRO

tionize the study and appreciation of figures, genres, and moments of the lengthy musical history of the greatest of the Antilles.

From the height of his musicological knowledge, I now turn to Radamés to close the circle I've drawn around salsa: his opinions as a devoted scholar, open to the most disparate theories on the salsa phenomenon, come to my aid as a well-reasoned colophon to this conversation with salsa, with its conscience, its creators, its promoters, and—now with Radamés—its scholars.

In the Time of Salsa

LPF: If you'll allow me, I'm going to ask you the question: What is salsa?
RG: As a first, very general definition, I should say that for me salsa is a new synthesis of Cuban *son,* conceived and stylized in a contemporary, up-to-date fashion. That said, if we proceed to a more in-depth analysis, then I'd say that salsa is the result of the natural give-and-take that characterizes Cuban music in its relationship with the music of the Dominican Republic, Venezuela, Puerto Rico, and other countries of the Caribbean. And I say this because in the complex of Cuban *son,* long before the emergence of salsa, there was already a confluence of diverse musical elements from the regions I've mentioned. After all, Cuban *son* didn't appear out of the blue, nor is it the mechanical union of music from Africa and Spain; it is actually the confluence of different styles of Caribbean music that, like Cuban music, have their origins in the music of Africa and Spain, and also—why deny it?—France and Italy. Therefore, salsa, real salsa—the salsa that goes beyond the complacent imitation of the old Cuban repertoire—is the union of all those elements with a new result from the melodic and even the technical point of view. Sixty to seventy percent of its makeup, however, consists of elements from Cuban *son*—and not only from old-time son, but also from the more contemporary variety—and therefore one can argue that, in essence, salsa is a new form of *son.*
LPF: We're talking about a new "mulatto-izing" of *son,* are we not? So, what allows *son* to be able to absorb so many diverse influences without losing its definitive essence?
RG: Perhaps the principal morphological characteristic of *son* is precisely that of being an open music, capable of incorporating different factors into its evolution—and that's precisely why it evolves so much and so quickly. In that regard, its morphology is similar to that of jazz, which is also an open music, with roots similar to those of *son*—European and African—

and which has gone about evolving while still being jazz. Keep in mind, for example, that *son* is even capable of assimilating and transforming other rhythms and genres, like the *guajira,* the bolero, the *guaguancó,* and even jazz itself—as Mario Bauzá did—and of adapting them to its model. Finally, *son* had the privilege of being the first Caribbean rhythm to establish itself fully outside the region: by the 1920s and 1930s, Heriberto Rico and Julio Prado were enjoying great success with Don Azpiazu's orchestra in Paris, and in New York people were also dancing to Azpiazu, to Antonio Machín's quartet, and they were recording los Matamoros. . . . So salsa takes advantage of the receptive character of *son,* and of its very prestige, to thrive in an atmosphere where Cuban rhythms were already well known. Seen in this light, salsa can be considered nothing more than a new stage in the enrichment of *son,* created, as I was saying, in a new, definitively contemporary dimension.

LPF: And how did that enrichment, which would later be known as salsa, begin to come about?

RG: In my opinion, everything began in the 1960s, starting with the contributions of Juan Formell in Cuba and Eddie Palmieri in New York. To them we owe, at the very least, the transformation in tone color, which they worked on with a style and sound and musical vision that were utterly contemporary. Meanwhile, during that same period, the lyrics begin to be worked on with an eye toward renovation, in a very different fashion from the lyrics of the original *son,* from the era of the Sexteto Habanero. In the case of Ignacio Piñeiro, as you well know, the lyrics already have a different elaboration, as is true with Arsenio Rodriguez, who includes elements of African languages in many of his compositions. But the *salseros* go even farther and begin to consider problems that the *soneros* ignored. The *salseros* talk about everyday concerns and social and political conflicts that the *soneros* didn't deal with in that specific way. And this, logically, should be seen in its context: it's not that the *soneros* from the 1930s, 1940s, and 1950s didn't have social concerns, or that they never reflected them in their music, but that for the *salseros,* this preoccupation is part of their style and artistic intention.

On the other hand, the structure in which the *salseros* move no longer corresponds to the formal patterns of *son,* and it's important to mention this because oftentimes they ignored the *verse-refrain, verse-refrain* format in search of more open and innovative forms. Although, in all truth, we must acknowledge once again that Piñeiro himself had broken that mold on more than one occasion, as Arsenio and Benny Moré would later do. But the *salseros* definitively raised the bar, experimented with greater freedom, and brought new musical and intellectual concerns and intentions to Caribbean popular music. And the cradle where this new creature was rocked was the city of New York, that "devil's melting pot" in which the musical references of the entire Caribbean commingled. And that's where the explosion occurred.

LPF: You've analyzed musical and literary elements that characterize salsa with respect to *son,* and you talk about artistic intentions. Am I to understand that you accept salsa as more than a commercial phenomenon?

RG: That famous slogan (which many people in Cuba repeated like a mantra) of considering salsa a commercial product, or reducing the problem to the fact that the term "salsa" is a commercial label, is a false and superficial judgment, in my opinion. First of all, because a commercial name doesn't stick and endure all on its own. In popular music, at least, it doesn't stick because the music is for dancing, for immediate consumption. I'm not about to deny that there are commercial elements in salsa, because this music is also made to sell, but we can't consider these the only defining characteristics of salsa. Even from the Cuban side of the equation you have to go a bit deeper and recognize that salsa expanded the Cuban music that was traditionally made on the island, as well as the music made here from 1959 to the present. Fortunately, while many people were staunchly opposing salsa, the best Cuban musicians, like Adalberto Álvarez or Formell himself, acknowledged the merits of salsa, adapted its innovations, and cultivated it according to their own interests and idiosyncrasies.

But while all this is happening, the river of business keeps running along. What happened—and this is explained very clearly by César Miguel Rondón in his excellent book *El libro de la salsa*—is that salsa produced a boom that took many impresarios by surprise. Suddenly they were selling more salsa than it was possible to produce artistically, and so they had to look for substitutes, the first of which—and herein lies the origin of the anti-salsa posture of many people in Cuba—was the old Cuban *son* from the 1940s and 1950s, now marketed as "salsa." That's when they started looting Cuban music: they revived la Sonora Matancera, they dug up Celia Cruz and opened up the old *son* repertoire, just like that. And that was an essentially commercial phenomenon.

LPF: You started out by mentioning two names that you consider important in this history, and I'd like to go back to them. You were talking about Eddie

Palmieri and Formell. Why do you consider them so key in the creation of what's now known as salsa?

RG: Salsa is a strange phenomenon: it's perhaps the child who has the most parents of all. Arsenio Rodríguez is considered its great prophet, but others say that everything started with Mario Bauzá's Machito and His Afrocubans, while others consider El Benny to be its great precursor. And it's logical that there are so many alleged paternities because they all contributed to the evolution of *son* and took it to the threshold of salsa.

But when referring to Formell and Palmieri, I should remind you that, in the first place, we're talking about two extremely intelligent, well-rounded, and up-to-date musicians. There are three basic reasons for what happened in the 1960s, although I have to emphasize the Formell case most of all, which is much less known than that of Palmieri, in spite of the fact that, in my judgment, he's even more revolutionary in terms of salsa music. In the first place, Formell did, in fact, intentionally set out to change elements of Cuban dance music; in his case it was a conscious effort. For me, he's one of the first musicians to undertake such a task with a specific purpose; in other words, in his case it's not a product of chance or circumstance, not at all. There's a purpose there, and Formell explicitly takes it upon himself to renovate Cuban dance music in terms of tone color. And rather than resort to the traditional *charanga,* he decides that *charanga* can have another sound and begins to consider which instruments he can use for this change. Like Palmieri—who did it first—Formell turns to the trombone, but while Palmieri emphasizes the trombone, Formell goes a bit farther. In what sense? He understands that for the transformation to be real, it has to be carried out through other instrumental factors. That's why he introduces new rhythmic elements with the double bass, or why he decides that the violins can have a different sound, or he conceives that the violin and the flute can form a sound duo in unison. He also proposed that the singers could sing in three voices, that is, no longer in the Aragón orchestra format with three singers in unison. Formell proposes all these modifications with a specific purpose, which is achieved, and that's why I give enormous credit to his work in the development and transformation of the tonal factors of Cuban music. Furthermore, you've got to consider Formell the lyricist: in his work there's always a dialogue with Cuban reality; he never distances himself from what's happening, which is why you have pieces like "La Habana no aguanta más" ["Havana Can't Take It Anymore"], "Que se sepa" ["Let It Be Known"], "No es fácil" [It Ain't Easy"]. And he undertakes that approach to the quotidian with a real flair, without falling into vulgarity or bad taste.

In any case, in my view Formell is one of the greatest Cuban musicians of the last twenty years, and the reason he's stayed on top for so long is not a coincidence, but rather owes to the fact that there's quality and constant innovation in his music.

Palmieri represents another dimension of the phenomenon, and it's interesting that two musicians of this quality began to confront the same questions of renovation virtually simultaneously: Palmieri in 1966 and Formell in 1967. What characterizes Palmieri, however, is not continuity but rather division: he attempts to break, to experiment, to change everything that's changeable, and that's why his music, despite its importance, is not as well known, because often the experiment swallowed up the communication that's indispensable in popular music. But none of that contradicts his being a pioneer in the melodic change that was produced in New York in the 1960s.

LPF: So the second half of the 1960s can be viewed as a moment of change in terms of melody and the very conception of Caribbean dance music?

RG: I think so. All you have to look at is the very fact of a conscious program of change on the part of Formell, Palmieri, and other musicians such as Larry Harlow, who was also searching for other ways of approaching the phenomenon by starting with Arsenio's music. With these explorations, the changes begin to become evident, and la Orquesta Revé, with Formell, is a *charanga* that no longer sounds like Jorrín, Fajardo, Estrellas Cubanas, or Aragón. And the same thing happens in New York with the sound of *son, bomba, plena,* and other types of Caribbean music.

LPF: And isn't there also a change in mentality and cultural projection in the musician?

RG: There's a change in personality in the musician because his environment has also changed, and the musician is aware, consciously or unconsciously, that he can't live outside of those transformations. On the other hand, he realizes that he needs to have a strong technical formation, which up until that moment wasn't essential to what he was doing. He at least needs to know sol-fa and theory, and later on he begins to consider other things in the conceptual order of music itself. Those phenomena make him change and project himself in a different way in a society that has changed politically and economically. I think that at this time a cycle of historical rotation is beginning, which encompasses all aspects of cultural life. And don't forget that this was the decade of The Beatles, when the music world received that enormous impact and people could no longer project music as they did in the 1950s—neither in its dance function nor in its function as a literary or melodic message.

LPF: Another revolution that salsa produced was in the orchestra format: there are no longer ensembles, or *charangas,* or typical orchestras, but rather a mixture of forms. Why did this happen?

RG: Salsa has that virtue: it doesn't conform to any fixed format; it uses any it finds necessary. That's why it's nothing new, because the same thing happened with *son* from time immemorial. Remember that *son* stabilizes at determined moments with determined formats, but these are always breaking down due to two fundamental necessities: the need for musical experimentation and the musician's need to earn his daily bread. When money is tight, if the director can get by with six musicians, he doesn't use seven: subsistence dictates the format. And in New York the same thing happened: at a certain moment the big bands begin to dissolve and smaller groups are formed that are more viable from the point of view of the musician's economic needs at a time of crisis. This apparently has little to do with music, but it does and can sometimes be a determining factor. For example, to survive as big bands during the 1960s, Machito's Afrocubans and Tito Puente's orchestra had to switch to jazz, because necessity dictates. In Cuba, however, it was easy to maintain a band of twenty musicians because they had a fixed salary and didn't depend on getting contracts. That's why music can't be analyzed only from the point of view of the results: you've got to see it in its context, and when talking about formats and the number of instrumentalists, you can never forget the economic factor.

LPF: The last Caribbean country to be conquered by salsa was Cuba. At first, salsa was rejected and denied in Cuba and enjoyed very little diffusion, but later it started to infiltrate the country until reaching the status it now enjoys. How did this penetration come about?

RG: I think that, as in the case of formats, the answer is found on a tangent: the dancers imposed it, quite simply. Just as with The Beatles: officially they were prohibited in Cuba, but behind closed doors the young people danced to them. While the theoreticians and the radio stations denied its existence, the dancers imposed salsa because it responded to new necessities. When Dimensión Latina came to Cuba at the beginning of the 1980s, it merely reaffirmed a phenomenon that had already been accepted by the dancers, who are the ones who decide. And Oscar D'León's performances shortly thereafter were the apotheosis that opened many people's eyes to the importance of salsa for the dancers. Then there were very intelligent Cuban musicians who immediately caught on to the phenomenon and started working it from their perspective, as happened with Adalberto and his Son 14, who, rather than prejudice themselves, took the pulse of the times, saw the positive things in salsa, and took off to find their own path. That's also when the stage of copying and repetition begins, but even imitation is necessary when you're starting something. Today in Cuba, salsa—and I mean salsa in the sense of what I told you at the beginning, as a new vision of *son*—has become a central element in the creation of Cuban musicians.

LPF: Within the salsa universe, there's a genre that has maintained a certain independence: merengue. What relationship—both musicological and commercial—do you see between salsa and merengue?

RG: I'm not surprised by the relationship that's been established between merengue and salsa. I recall that around the mid-1950s, when the Dominican Alberto Beltrán was in Cuba, merengue practically dominated the dance-music scene. Then he recorded with la Sonora Matancera, and soon thereafter you started hearing a group of *merengueros* who created something of a merengue boom in Cuba. And during carnivals at that time, mostly merengue was played, and the Cuban groups had to incorporate it because merengue was essential to get people moving. And remember that this happened in one of the golden ages of Cuban music.

As I was telling you earlier, from the outset, *son* had many elements of other types of Caribbean music, but starting in that era, a fusion between *son* and merengue becomes consolidated, something that didn't happen with other rhythms of popular music in Latin America and the rest of the Caribbean. So when the salsa boom occurred, I never imagined, in spite of these antecedents, that merengue could enter into that realm because of the strength salsa had acquired and because salsa itself barely had merengue in mind during those years before the boom. But later, when merengue penetrated the salsa universe, I realized that it had succeeded because of one fundamental element: merengue is a wonderful dance music and has no great complexities for the dancer. It also has a sort of nervousness, a spring that gets you moving, which is why it wins people over so easily. Furthermore, the merengue that got "exported" to salsa was no longer the merengue from the 1950s, but rather a merengue that has managed to feed off Cuban music and salsa as well, at the same time, and that's why it spoke a language more accessible to the salsa public. But what sealed that penetration once and for all was the presence of an artist who's a remarkable phenomenon in popular Latin American music: Juan Luis Guerra, a man with extraordinary talent as a composer, interpreter, and promoter of an artistic image and conception. It's true that his work had important predecessors, such as Johnny Ventura first and Wilfrido Vargas later, but he transformed merengue into a boom for several reasons. In the first place, he works aspects of merengue that had not been sufficiently exploited, such as its rhythmic variety or its relationship to other types of Caribbean music. In the second place, he achieved a very high quality in his verses, bestowing upon them a content whose message applied to all of Latin America and to the Hispanic community of New York. He himself has admitted that his work has been influenced by the Cuban *nueva trova,* and that's also important: Juan Luis Guerra's merengue is something akin to the quintessence of merengue, its utmost stylization (while never ceasing to be merengue), but definitively transposed into a language and a style that transcend any sort of localism. That also explains his success in several parts of Europe.

LPF: I have a few names here of musicians about whom I'd like you to give me your judgment concerning their place in salsa. Let's start at the top: Celia Cruz.

RG: Well, Celia is one of those singular phenomena of permanence who triumph by singing the same things . . . but with the virtue that what you hear in the background is no longer the same. In the 1970s, her music is no longer that of la Sonora Matancera, in spite of the enormous importance that the "Sonora" sound had in the development of salsa. But Celia triumphed through that quality of *son,* that way of speaking, that type of phrasing, that "creolization" which she never altered, and that grace, which is a natural gift. And I would say, furthermore, that in Celia's artistic personality many factors of Caribbean music came together, and that's why you see her move about like a grand dame in any genre at all, from merengue to *cumbia.* But in order to achieve all of that, she's had to maintain her vocal quality, which is a true gift of nature. After all, as she herself said in an interview, it seems as though God gave her a voice rather than giving her children.

LPF: How about Mario Bauzá and Machito?

RG: They're also an exceptional case, but one that moves in other dimensions. Machito creates his personality with his maracas, which he adds to his very personal style of *son,* which is not that of Abelardo Barroso, nor that of Antonio Machín, who are two great figures of his era. Machito had a tone that, while not being as stellar as Celia's, turned out to be irreplaceable for his way of making *son*. And he enjoyed the good fortune of having as his bandleader none other than Mario Bauzá, a true genius in his way of viewing music and orchestras, and even in his way of directing the show. In addition, Mario managed to fuse jazz and Cuban dance music in an equally brilliant fashion: it was a perfect marriage, as he says, so much so that Cuban music was never the same after Mario. And he achieved that over there, in the cradle of jazz. So, that projection he gives to his group and his music allowed him to succeed, and it's why people today still listen with amazement to what was accomplished by Machito and His Afrocubans, the way they made the musicians and the dancers vibrate with energy. For those two, music was life itself.

LPF: And what about Cachao? What did that half-forgotten figure bequeath to Cuban music and salsa?

RG: He left an entire oeuvre to Cuban music. The *danzones* by Israel Cachao López are a true contribution to the genre. As a double bassist, he created a style that I describe as a monumental tribute to the instrument, such a strong way of playing that I've never seen it in other double bassists, which is why it influenced musicians from Cuba, from the entire Caribbean, and even from the United States. From an artistic point of view, he's a transcendent musician who has not received all the recognition he deserves. I think he's a personality who needs to be rediscovered, made known, and we have to leave a record of what he represents for Cuban popular music. He's been forgotten for too long in Cuba, as has happened with others, people like Mongo Santamaría, Chocolate Armenteros, Chico O'Farril, or el Patato Valdés, who are all institutions of Cuban music. Furthermore, a man like Cachao has been hurt by his excessive modesty. I don't even think he has a grasp of his own greatness.

LPF: There are three more figures whom I've interviewed for this book and about whom I'd like you to give me your judgment: Rubén Blades, Willie Colón, and Papo Lucca. What do you think each of them has accomplished? What have they contributed to salsa?

RG: Rubén Blades, first of all, has handed down lyrics of great quality, which not only have important content but are also works of great beauty. On the other hand, he succeeded as an excellent interpreter, proving beyond a shadow of a doubt that he's a good *sonero* as well as a magnificent *bolero* singer, with a style all his own, capable of succeeding in an arena where Tito Rodríguez had reigned supreme, and that's no mean feat. After working with Willie Colón, during what many consider the best era of both, he had the courage to create his group, Los Seis del Solar, when no one could even imagine that with such a small format he could achieve what he did, and the reason for his success was his strength as an interpreter. Something I admire in Rubén is his audacity: just as he's dared to take on the *guaguancó,* enriching it at times, he's also dared to take on all the genres imposed by the greats of Cuban music: Benny, Arsenio, Cuní. And he always succeeded, because at each moment he was conscious of what he was attempting. He chose those elements from Cuban music that he considered indispensable, and he managed to adapt them to his personality.

But his project is much more complex. There you have the case, for example, of a work like *Maestra Vida,* a true masterpiece with the structure of a sonata, with very concrete tempos with music that corresponds to each movement of the dramatic development, and with a well-told story and an accomplished melody. In addition, it's a compendium of genres and approaches to popular music, with the virtue that you can listen and dance to it, and that is a great accomplishment in and of itself.

Papo Lucca is what you call an out-of-this-world pianist. It's worth mentioning who his progenitors are, because he himself admits it: Lilí Martínez and Peruchín, two giants who also haven't received their due. They are two truly transcendent figures of Cuban piano, and part of that transcendence is right there, in Papo Lucca. And with respect to the possible influences in Papo, it's admirable to see that the salsa musicians have been so respectful of Cuban music as to recognize what they owe to it, admitting its paternity. But Papo is a pianist who's managed to create his own style, that way he has of connecting the notes when he's doing his flourishes and solos, which strikes me as something very beautiful, interesting, and important. His particular way of approaching *son* is not evident in any other salsa pianists, some of whom indulge in facile repetition, even in several Cuban groups. Papo's piano has a very salient role within the ensemble, but *within the ensemble.* I think Papo is also an excellent arranger, in sum, an integral musician. Recently he's done some things with Cheo Feliciano—who's also a distinguished interpreter: he's made *sones* of a remarkable quality that are truly transcendent. Nevertheless, Papo Lucca is not one of the most recognized leaders of salsa, at least at a popular level, and perhaps that's due, as in the case of Cachao López, to the fact that he's a simple man, more interested in making music than in shining like a star.

LPF: And now, Willie Colón. It's been said that he's not a good singer, that as a trombonist he's not a virtuoso, although he is recognized as a good arranger and band director. With those "strengths and weaknesses," however, Willie has been one of the leading figures of salsa for over twenty-five years. What type of a judgment would you offer of this figure?

RG: First of all, in a case like his, that judgment of him as a bad interpreter is relative, so relative that I can affirm that he has the necessary vocal quality to interpret what he does. Look, if you manage to transmit what you've set out to, virtuosity is no longer that important, because in art, projection is fundamental. I think Willie's case is reminiscent in some way of Machito's, who, as I was telling you, founded a style without being an exceptional vocalist, or the case of Silvio Rodríguez himself, who's not considered a good singer, but no one can sing Silvio's things like he does, and that's what matters and, in my judgment, what counts.

That's why Willie, as they say, has played on all the teams and has never batted at the bottom of the order, and has been a presence throughout the entire history of salsa: as a singer, as an instrumentalist, as a composer, and as a bandleader. And I think this is the case because he has the virtue of having never phased himself out; he's always been ahead of the game and has known what's been needed at each moment, without getting caught up in success, formats, or styles. He's sailed with the current, and sometimes against it, but he's always sailed in accord with his indisputable quality and the very studied projection of what he does. And at this point, it's simply not possible to talk about salsa without mentioning Willie Colón: there you have his solo work, or his work with Rubén or Lavoe, and it's all way above the commercial salsa, the made-to-order variety.

LPF: Radamés, to finish for now, let me ask you who's the best *salsero* among the Cuban musicians of today?

RG: Look, right now there are a lot of them, and some are very good. I've already talked quite a bit about Formell. José Luis Cortés, the director of NG la Banda, is a rapidly rising figure, and there are others. But I think that as *salseros* go, Adalberto is a key figure in Cuba, not only because of the quality of his music but also because of the intelligent way he assumed salsa without rejecting it. He started to study what was happening and what was appropriate for his projection, and after a period of trial and error, when he became known for the numbers he wrote for Rumbavana, he took aim again and started looking for his own sound, and he achieved it. Therefore, you've got to consider him not only as an excellent composer, but also as a man who managed to create an "Adalberto sound," just as Benny, Sonora

Matancera, Aragón, Formell, and Papo Lucca all created their own "sound." And let me tell you, that's one of the most difficult things in popular music, to achieve your own sound, what some call your hallmark. And Adalberto's got it, and even though he's a *sonero,* he's also a true *salsero.* . . . That's the enrichment of *son* that I was talking about at the beginning, no? Havana, Cuba, 1993

Conclusion

Ten Reasons and Five Opinions to Believe (or Not) in the Existence of Salsa

"You are my first reason."
—Juan Luis Guerra

One: "Que yo me defiendo como puedo"

Toward the middle of the 1970s, an amusing and dance-happy ghost (a new one) begins to traverse the American continent, from New York to Buenos Aires. Endowed with an uncommon power of penetration, it travels around most diverse corners of the Caribbean conquering all available spaces, sticking in the ears and to the feet of the people, of millions of people. Since the 1940s and 1950s, when half of humanity was captivated by the mambo missile that the Cuban Dámaso Pérez Prado launched at the world from his barracks in Mexico City, and by the cha-cha-cha of the likewise Cuban Enrique Jorrín, no Latin American musical movement had managed to achieve such a degree of acceptance. The decade of the 1960s, dominated by The Beatles and pop, had been the years of a musical retreat for Latin rhythms, which, at a promotional disadvantage, ceded their patrimony to the English-language ballad and to an irreverent brand of rock that tried to acclimate itself without much success. But the new arrival of today, christened with the catchy and delectable appellation of "salsa," came back through the jurisdictions and territories that, from the nineteenth century, had belonged to the Caribbean rhythms and dances: the old *contradanza* and its offspring the *danzón,* the unstoppable *son,* as well as mambo itself and cha-cha-cha.

The arrival and diffusion of that so-called salsa, however, provoked the most diverse reactions and rapidly—as usually happens to us—divided into opposing camps all the interested parties: musicians, promoters, musicologists and even music lovers and dancers. The first of the disputes arose at the most external level: Who labeled this music as "salsa"? What should be called "salsa"? Later, the questions began to go to the heart of the matter: Does salsa exist?

While one crowd argued that salsa was a novel musical phenomenon, fruit of the existence of diverse economic and social conditions in the Caribbean that fostered a new cultural crossbreed—a miscegenation of the already mestizo Cuban *son,* the indisputable model of the movement, with other rhythms from the Caribbean, Brazil, and the United States—salsa's detractors denied outright its possible existence by brandishing the same flag that, nevertheless, had different connotations: for the Cubans it was in essence a looting; for the Latino musicians of New York, it was their rightful patrimony given the indubitable *sonero* origin of the so-called salsa; while in other lands—as in the case of Venezuela—it was considered, for the same reason (its affiliation to Cuban *son* and the predominantly Puerto Rican and Nuyorican participation in the movement), a *foreign* music whose cultivation was very nearly a betrayal of the country's musical tradition. But regardless of the dispute, music called "salsa" continued to be made and sold as "salsa," and what's more important, was being heard and danced to more and more because people sensed there was something new in it. But was there really something new?

FIRST OPINION
Other than something such as giving flavor to the interpretation of a *montuno* (let's recall the immortal Benny Moré) or the greater rhythmic effusion of any Caribbean dance music that's thoroughly Cuban, I am unaware of what form, genre or style is called *salsa.* . . . Now then, if you pin me down by asking what is *salsa* or what it refers to, then I'll respond as follows: salsa is used to denominate an entire gamut of modes and styles of interpreting or *son*-ing included in the complex of Cuban *son.* Cuban *son,* which, by the way, has maintained a constant presence in our country since 1910. . . . I do not see, therefore, that it's necessary to defend in Cuba a movement that, in fact, has been circulating here for close to eighty years.
—Odilio Urfé, Cuban musicologist, interview by José Rivero García, *El Caimán Barbudo* (Havana), March 1979

Two: "Siembra"

It's not coincidental that the man considered by many to be the great "prophet" of salsa is also its most relentless and immovable detractor. For years, one of my most exotic dreams was to be able to speak with him, in New York—to see him, get to know him, hear him speak like the oracle he undoubtedly is. Because Mario Bauzá, that young Cuban musician who established himself in New York in 1930 and became a key figure of jazz—musical director of Chick Webb's band and Cab Calloway's orchestra—the creator of Latin or Afrocuban jazz with the orchestra of his brother-in-law Frank Grillo, "Machito"; the necessary bridge between Caribbean rhythms and the bebop of his disciple Dizzy Gillespie; and the definitive introducer of Cuban music in the big city, has been the most privileged witness of this entire musical history.

Finally, one cold and tense afternoon in November 1992, I had a conversation in La Catedral with Mario Bauzá. There, Mario Bauzá, with the authority of his career and from the height of his eighty-two years, told me his simplest truth about salsa: "Can you bring me some 'salsa' written on a pentagram? No? Well, in music what can't be written doesn't exist."

Nevertheless, he himself is at the very origin of what the others—the advocates—call "salsa." Because when Bauzá, along with his brother-in-law Machito, founded the Afrocubans in 1940 and initiated the decisive experiment of fusing Cuban *son* with American jazz, he began to produce one of the fundamental mutations of a highly transcendent evolution in the field of popular Caribbean music. That "marriage"—really an elopement of equals, the two most popular musical genres of the century—had the virtue of preparing *son* for future combinations. But at the same time, thanks to Bauzá and Machito, a singular and highly significant phenomenon was produced: in New York, people listened and danced to *son* played by Machito and His Afrocubans, and the temple of that consecration was a place called the Palladium that no longer exists today on 53d and Broadway. There, the success of Mario Bauzá's mestizo music opened up for the first time a space in the city to "officialize" the vitality of Latin rhythms: alongside the Afrocubans, Tito Puente (another detractor of salsa) and His Piccadilly Boys, soon to be known as Tito Puente and His Orchestra, played on the Palladium's glamorous stage, as did Tito Rodríguez, the Puerto Rican who with his golden voice would satisfy the sentimental expectations of the Latin communities of New York, as well as Fajardo y sus Estrellas, at the very height of the *charanga* era, when the orchestra of the great Cuban flutist was capable of competing with the untouchable Aragón. In the Palladium, with elegance and good taste, dressed in tuxes and tails, their hair gleaming with brilliantine, those true "mambo kings" planted the seed of a musical taste, and what's more, of a cultural presence of Latin music in New York that had no choice but to give fruit, despite having no new notations on any pentagram.

Three: "Buscando guayabas"

The sustained and fervent presence of Caribbean music in 1950s New York would soon become, however, a sort of idyllic dream of the past. This favorable panorama would radically change with a political event that happened in 1959 and that would have immediate repercussions on a cultural manifestation so apparently far removed from politics as music. The triumph of the Cuban revolution and its later radicalization, together with the response from the United States and the Organization of American States, blockaded all the island's products, one of the most affected of all being its music. The direct and natural flow, continuous until then, breaks down, and the Latin music cultivated in New York thus loses its most influential point of reference. The change in temperature is felt almost immediately: while the commercial firms try to erase from the atmosphere the presence of anything Cuban "from Cuba" and turn their eyes toward a new market—this time the Brazilian one, in the days of bossa nova. The lavish orchestras of yore lose their preeminence and find themselves obligated to become smaller, to confine themselves to small clubs or to completely cross over to the welcoming bosom of jazz—as did Machito and Tito Puente—while Tito Rodríguez takes refuges in the unshakable security of the bolero.

Those rhythms that would periodically win over the public's taste stopped arriving from Cuba, and on the island itself, through a rare paradox, a creative stagnation begins in which the death of some of the greats—such as Benny Moré, the greatest of all—combines with the definitive exile of others—Celia Cruz, Pérez Prado, Israel Cachao López, Fajardo, and Arsenio Rodríguez—and the uncommon rise of an artistic mediocrity that can only be understood as the product of populism and a lack of competition. The road of pop and beat, even for the tastes of the Latino communities of New York and of certain Caribbean barrios, was thus swept clean of debris and left in peace.

However, in New York people keep making music. With reduced formats, without the joy of yesteryear, without the big stages—the Palladium closes in 1964, supposedly because it had lost its liquor license—the Cuban musicians living there continue their work in silence, always on the edge of oblivion (as happened to El Ciego Maravilloso, Arsenio Rodríguez) at the same time that the exodus from the entire Caribbean to the big city was reaching its greatest proportions.

At the beginning of the decade, after a slight revitalization of the Fajardo-style *charangas*—one of which counts among its members a highly significant figure in this history, the Dominican Johnny Pacheco—certain musical styles begin to be cultivated in New York that, in spite of their ephemeral presence, keep alive a spirit, and therefore, the possibility of a resurgence as well. These are the days of Bebo Valdés's *pachanga*, the only rhythm that left Cuba, of the acculturated boogaloo, with its bilingual lyrics as a desperate attempt at survival, of the fleeting watusi, more rock than *son*, patented by Ray Barreto. And little else. . . .

Nevertheless, a new generation of musicians—Latinos and non-Latinos from New York, Puerto Ricans, Dominicans, and, of course, Cubans—began creating, on the margins of the established market and without the brilliant pretensions of their forbearers, a music that was the most logical fruit of desperation (cultural, economic, social), and of resistance to the environment: something that started as a manifestation of the ghetto. And that music, accepting the maternal capacity of *son* to commingle with all things similar, began to represent, for the first time, the character of the Latino barrio of New York and, therefore, of all the barrios of the Caribbean, in which poverty, cultural degradation, marginalization, violence, and life, in sum, could all look quite alike. That was the bud born from that seed.

SECOND OPINION

I think that in those spiritual necessities and the lack of communication beyond the borders of the barrio, we can find the profound psychological and cultural factors that give rise to salsa precisely in the Latino barrios of New York, where it emerges as a manifestation of cultural resistance. After all, if we know we're still not completely accepted by North American culture, why not follow the lead of rock and roll or another type of music? And salsa emerges as something of our own, which is why it's full of politics and stories from the street. It's a music of the city and its melodies are essential urban.

Salsa is like a newspaper, a chronicle of our lives in the big city, and that's why it talks about such topics as crime, drugs, prostitution, pain, uprootedness, and even about our history of exploitation and underdevelopment. We no longer talk about cutting sugarcane or the life of the *campesino*—although that's still possible—but rather about social problems of Latinos living in the modern world and the causes of these problems.

I don't believe that salsa is a rhythm or a genre that can be identified or classified: salsa is an idea, a concept, the result of a way of approaching music from the Latin American cultural perspective.
—Willie Colón

Four: "Ya viene llegando"

Almost twenty years after the birth of the controversy surrounding the possible existence of a music, a musical movement, or a mere commercial product called "salsa," some things, at least, acquired a certain clarity as the passions began to lose their hurricane-force winds. From the 1970s to the present, popular Latin American dance music—which has essentially always been a Caribbean product—has basically followed the path marked by the melodic and stylistic patterns of the "salsa" concept created in New York by a group of Puerto Rican, Cuban, Dominican, and Latino-Nuyorican musicians. Even in Cuba, several of the most influential musicians in the present-day panorama of dance music admit to being, in the final analysis, *"salseros"*: Adalberto Álvarez, Elio Revé, Isaac Delgado. . . .

This music, the most listened and danced to during these two decades, has several unifying characteristics that allow it to differentiate and personalize artistically. The first truth about salsa is that its musical origin is in Cuban *son,* a rhythm which, from Santiago de Cuba to Havana, initiated a journey without limits or borders as it became, by the 1930s or 1940s, the musical model of the entire Caribbean owing to its principal morphological value: *son* is a popular music—not folkloric, and therefore, alive and evolving—capable of renovating itself with the unstoppable incorporation of new melodies and styles able to adapt to a solid basic structure that has remained unalterable since its creation. Such is the process that, indisputably, this genre follows from los Matamoros and Ignacio Piñeiro's Septeto Nacional in the 1920s, to the creation of the *"conjunto"* or dance ensemble by Arsenio Rodríguez in the 1930s, to the glorious revolution of its sound by Benny Moré and la Sonora Matancera, to the modern conceptions of an Adalberto Álvarez.

This *sonero* origin of salsa has two fundamental and logical manifestations: while for one group of creators it served as a model for novel, openly experimental recreation, in which other Caribbean rhythms such as *bomba* and *plena* reinserted themselves—transported to the New York scene by Cortijo y su Combo—Dominican merengue, Colombian *cumbia,* and so forth were for others a classic gold mine to which one could descend time and again, sack on shoulder, to emerge with a few numbers from the ample Cuban repertoire that, once dusted off and updated, were sold as "salsa."

Along with this essential element, so-called salsa music has in its origin an indelible mark that will characterize the best of its production: the new Latino barrio that gives rise to the need for a new type of expression. A product of the barrios—first of New York, later of San Juan and Ponce, of Caracas and Barranquilla, of Santo Domingo, and even of then-marginalized Havana—this musical movement attempts to be, in its authentic and novel manifestations, the reflection of a life that has definitively stopped being peaceful and melancholic, to become violent and torn apart. Musically, the manifestation of this new reality will have as one of its hallmarks the rough and shrill sound of the trombones which, no longer the anonymous members of the brass section in the big bands of the 1950s, will become the protagonists of a melody starting with the record that some consider the first salsa album, *La Perfecta* (1967), by Eddie Palmieri, and will announce the arrival of Willie Colón, eventually winning over all the orchestras of the Caribbean with their car-horn shriek, displacing the melodious and warm saxophone. Lyrically, meanwhile, different things were being said than the sighs for *"el viejo San Juan"* or the bucolic evocations of los Matamoros and Arsenio Rodríguez: people were now saying—as Joe Cuba did during the precursory years—that *"la calle está durísima"* ["the street is really tough"], and the protagonists of the stories were marginal characters, unemployed, uprooted, forgotten, in a long ascendance that has its culmination—still unbeaten—the "conscious salsa" of Rubén Blades and Willie Colón singing to "Pedro Navajas" and to the family of Manuela and Carmelo da Silva in the salsa opera *Maestra Vida,* one of Rubén's most ambitious works.

Obviously salsa could be—it already was—the sung chronicle of a harsh and cutting everyday life.

Five: "Llegó mi niño"

When, on August 21, 1971, the second and most transcendent version of the Fania All Stars makes an appearance at the not quite luxurious Cheetah Club on 52d and Broadway in New York, the salsa era—although it was barely starting to be known as *salsa*—becomes a defined movement. Something had happened in the last years of the previous decade to allow this concert by the stellar musicians of the recently formed Fania label to become a milestone marking the end of a prehistory and the beginning of an era that has continued to the present.

The final years of the decade of the 1960s are those of the definitive gestation of a sound—which some have even called the "New York sound"—and of lyrics that, in a disorganized fashion at that time, would evolve to become a model for musical production and taste for the consumer of this type of music.

Along with the desperate cultivation of those momentary solutions that turned to the melodies of pop and rock, precariously combined with Caribbean rhythms in this era and without the spectacular pretensions of previous years, a modality of *son* begins to be worked on, from the format of the *charanga* to that of the modest *conjunto*, quite removed from the cultural reference of the island and therefore open to the most diverse contaminations. The place where this music is played is the aforementioned Latin barrio—Spanish Harlem and the South Bronx, the so-called Caldera del Diablo [the Devil's Cauldron]—and its practitioners are, in the majority of cases, the offspring of this social and cultural circumstance who try to express the characteristics of a way of life through the artistic manifestation most in tune with their idiosyncrasy: music.

In many cases, these characters have never attended a conservatory, nor have they had an artistic education: in most cases, they lived unaware of the possibility of a market; and, finally, their work is the fruit, almost always, of a spiritual necessity more than of an organized and defined project. The first result of such spontaneity could be no more than a logically spontaneous music, at times badly executed and without many frills, which nevertheless started to break through, little by little, into the necessities of artistic consumption of their Latino compatriots. The most important thing, however, is that this lack of compromise generated something that the future "salsa" would rarely achieve again: freedom to experiment, to search, to try out new things, extremely diverse melodic and lyrical solutions whose final result could be nothing less than a new product: that which at this stage can be considered *la verdadera salsa*, true salsa.

In a parallel fashion, in 1964 a very modest New York record label is born that, with the passing of time, acquires incalculable importance in this story: the Fania label, created by the Dominican musician Johnny Pacheco and the American lawyer Jerry Massuci, which beginning in 1966, started to sign, in addition to Pacheco's *charanga*, a whole range of marginal musicians and groups determined in their desire to create something "new." The names of Larry Harlow, Bobby Valentín, Ray Barreto, and, around 1967, that of seventeen-year-old Willie Colón, began to give the label commercial shape and, more importantly, artistic form. The project, in the able hands of Pacheco and Massuci, started to function as designed, and once the required potential was in place, it was only necessary to launch it commercially. To do so, however, required a name—and Pacheco got it from the ambience: *salsa*—and an image as well: that of the young barrio tough, fundamentally incarnated by the youngster of the company, Willie Colón. Finally, a good launch was needed, and the concert at the Cheetah on August 21 was ideal: several of the label's stars were gathered together along with other musicians from the Latin scene—Pacheco, Colón, Ray Barreto, Bobby Valentín, Yomo Toro, Larry Harlow, and seven other musicians, with the voices of Ismael Miranda, Héctor Lavoe, Pete "El Conde" Rodríguez, Adalberto Santiago, and Bobby Cruz. Thus the great salsa jam session was produced, from which emerged, like a banner, four albums and a movie—*Nuestra cosa latina [Our Latin Thing]*—after which the rest is history.

THIRD OPINION

Salsa never intended to establish itself as a specific rhythm. Quite the contrary: if salsa is to be the music that fully represents the convergence of today's urban barrio, then it must assume the totality of the rhythms that make up that convergence. Salsa, after all, has no nomenclature; it has no reason to have one. Salsa is neither a rhythm nor a mere style for confronting a defined rhythm. Salsa is an open form capable of representing the totality of tendencies that come together in the urban Caribbean circumstance of today; the barrio remains its only definitive characteristic. . . . In this sense, salsa cannot emerge as an utterly new music; that is absurd. The barrio implies an amalgamation of traditions.
—César Miguel Rondón, *El libro de la salsa*

Six: "Échale salsita"

Starting with the transcendent concert at the Cheetah Club, it was no longer possible to deny the existence of a new movement in Caribbean music and, what's more important, it was impossible to halt its advancement throughout the entire region that belonged to it. Like gunpowder, that music christened as "salsa," which in its form looked a lot like old Cuban *son* but was no longer the same thing, neither in its intentions nor its songs, lit up the barrio dance halls of the entire Caribbean—with the exception of Cuba, which was going through a period of indescribable cultural grayness, even in music—and from 1971 to 1975 enjoyed what César Miguel Rondón aptly described as the period of *Salsa de Oro* [Golden Salsa].

These years, in which people start to take notice of the cultural—and commercial—projection of that enterprise which had been born wild, are the stage of the great musical productions created through a truly artistic work of expression and, of course, this is the moment of an expansion that started creating a more homogeneous form for the music that was being made in other latitudes of the Caribbean which join the movement: from Puerto Rico's El Gran Combo and la Sonora Ponceña, now in the hands of Papo Lucca, to the birth of groups like Dimensión Latina in Venezuela, where Oscar D'León would launch his career, or the lone orchestra of Juan Formell's Los Van Van, the only interesting group in the Cuban panorama of the era.

The rise is produced at an exponential rate, and soon the only thing people sing and dance to is "salsa," which sings to the everydayness of the barrio, the street, the city, as happened at the beginning, as well as to the eternal themes of love, music itself, and traditions.

Nevertheless, all that musical vitality was soon unable to satisfy a market that, dominated by Fania during all those years, was now capable of devouring more records than could be made. The dilemma was posed then in commercial terms, in terms of *quantity:* How to satisfy a real demand? An idea then surfaces among the directors of Fania that, to a great extent, has become the "avocado" of discord (there are no apples in the Caribbean) regarding the existence or not of salsa: to turn to the old Cuban *sonero* repertoire, that of Benny Moré, Arsenio, Chapotín, and even of Cachao López himself, alive and performing in New York, or even going back to the old arsenal of los Matamoros and selling it as "salsa."

The reaction of the Cubans (both on and off the island) is then more understandable: How can something new called "salsa" exist if "salsa" is, precisely, "Échale salsita," the old standby of Ignacio Piñeiro's Septeto Nacional and everything that, for decades, was known as Cuban *son?*

Seven: "Cargando su contrabando"

It's difficult for a writer to take a literary product, almost copy it, and make his own "version" without being accused of plagiarism. Painting, film, and theater, in their own way, enjoy the possibility of creating different versions. But if there is one artistic manifestation in which this phenomenon of the remake has become strongly rooted, forming part of its very nature, it is music. From generation to generation, from country to country, from language to language, people have practiced this reinterpretation of the musical and lyrical product created as the formula of two very different approaches to the work of art: to copy it and thus take advantage of the success already achieved in another time or place, or to recreate it and contribute a new aesthetic vision of an original subjected to certain transformations.

In salsa, the art of the remake—in both of its modalities—undoubtedly had one of its sources of subsistence and sales, as well as of inspiration and creation. The second posture is at the very origin of the movement, in its very conception, when, turning to the structure of *son* and even to some of its anthologized pieces, it took advantage of this rhythm to create a new appreciation of the musical product, seen in other cultural and social circumstances. So far, so good.

The possibility of the exact copy, however, in which everything is neatly resolved with the recognition of the authorship of a certain number in the liner notes, was, meanwhile, the commercial lifesaver of salsa and, very soon, the stone that was tied to its neck. The time of this rapid transformation was around 1975, when, in the wake of the commercial boom, salsa transitioned to a phase of exhaustion which would soon provoke a crisis.

The brazen attitude that existed on the part of many musicians—not to mention many producers and impresarios, most of all—toward the use of the remake reached dimensions of a full-scale looting and clearly invalidated the authenticity of many works of "salsa." This is what happened, for example, with a good portion of the repertoire of musicians such as Johnny Pacheco and Larry Harlow, which was extracted from the patrimony of the Cubans, who viewed this appropriation from the island with disapproval while they remained blockaded (or at least marginalized) in their promotion outside the country. Nevertheless, the strategy worked and even appeared novel thanks to a few intelligent arrangements, and it allowed the full-blown resurgence of one of the brightest stars of Cuban *son,* transformed from one day to the next—with the same numbers as before, with her same style—into the Queen of Salsa: Celia Cruz.

The case of Celia is especially significant for determining the validity of salsa. A star in Cuban music since the 1950s, when she became the soloist of Rogelio Martínez's Sonora Matancera, this singer suffered through the same crisis of acceptance as the rest of her compatriots in the New York and Caribbean music worlds in the 1960s. Nevertheless, astutely rescued by Fania for its salsa promotion, Celia Cruz was transformed into the special guest of important orchestras—that of Pacheco himself, or Willie Colón's, among others—and sold as a "salsa" singer. However, it was the same Celia as always—in her style, her projection, and even in her repertoire—just that instead of being a *sonera,* she was now a *salsera.* Without a doubt, behind the greatest female voice that Cuban *son* has ever had, there now moved a commercial structure powerful enough to change territory of her domain from one day to the next, without her crown being touched. This time, the detractors of salsa were correct: Was that "new"? Was that "salsa"? It was neither of the two, and not only in the case of Celia Cruz, but also in a good portion of the record production that appeared at the time.

FOURTH OPINION

Although there are different versions, I think the real people responsible for the acceptance of this term were Jerry Massuci and Johnny Pacheco, when they founded Fania and began to cultivate and promote all the rhythms of the Caribbean under one umbrella. So they grouped them under one label, in one style, which was called salsa. But behind all that, more than anything else, it's a more contemporary treatment of the Caribbean music that originated in Cuba. When the Cubans became a bit marginalized during this evolution, however, I think it was the Puerto Ricans—both those who were living on the island as well as those in New York, such as Willie Colón or Héctor Lavoe—who did the most for this movement's success. Nevertheless, this music has been influenced by every possible genre, and that's why it has elements of jazz and pop, of *bomba* and *plena,* of merengue, and even of Brazilian music. In fact, Frankie Ruiz's first hit, the number that made him, is "La rueda," a Mexican song. So, salsa has been enriched with elements from everywhere, not only from Cuba, and at this stage of the game it's not fair to say that it's simply old Cuban music with contemporary arrangements. Because even if you can't speak of salsa as a genre per se, it's obviously a movement that has transcended all national affiliations to become a musical phenomenon of the entire Caribbean.
—Enrique "Papo" Lucca

Eight: "La vida te da sorpresas"

Formally and conceptually, "salsa" left all the doors open from the beginning. Two of the most important figures of the entire movement, Willie Colón and Eddie Palmieri, can be considered models of a true salsa conception of Caribbean music (a novel one), in spite of the fact that in their works there exist quite different creative patterns. While for many years, for example, Willie Colón remained respectful of the fundamental scheme of *son*—one theme for the soloist and variations for the chorus, repeated until the end, in other words, *son* and *montuno*—and turned with equal emphasis to elements and even complete works of *bomba, plena,* and Brazilian music, maestro Palmieri took the liberty, from the beginning, of obviating the *son/montuno* scheme to make use of—with a freedom closer to the style of jazz—the Caribbean rhythms in which the rhythmic and tonal characteristics were maintained. The works of these two musicians, of course, contributed an air of novelty and in the majority of cases, their lyrics finally proposed a new vision of the environment in which they themselves developed.

The confluence of these two paths, both essentially "salsa-ish" owing to their novelty and validity, would come about, however, in a figure that would prove to be paradigmatic and definitive in determining the possible existence of salsa: Rubén Blades.

Having arrived in New York shortly before the consecration of Fania with its stellar concert in 1971, Rubén tried to penetrate the world of Latin music through a route that was too scandalous for the tastes of the record labels: a sort of protest song—a genre flourishing throughout Latin America at the time—which, in place of the solitary guitar or folkloric instruments, was meant to be played to the rhythm of *son,* fronted by a typical ensemble.

Only the overwhelming talent of the Panamanian singer-songwriter, and the imminent crisis in the salsa repertoire during the days of the looting of *son,* allowed his music, little by little, to be accepted by some of the figures of the milieu—Pete Rodríguez, Ismael Miranda—until Ray Barreto decides to make him the lead singer of his orchestra. The musical revolution proposed by Blades then begins to take shape until becoming one of the most interesting modalities of the movement, the so-called conscious salsa, a variety in which he established his reign alongside the indispensable Willie Colón.

Rubén's oeuvre, from pieces such as "Cipriano Armenteros"—the story of a nineteenth-century Panamanian outlaw—to "Pedro Navajas," "Plástico," or his later album *Contrabando,* is based on two fundamental characteristics: the narrative sense of his lyrics, always charged with messages, histories, reflections, and clear political positions, and the versatility of his music, which, at times supported by the *son* scheme, is equally at ease taking on the forms of the *guaguancó,* the *cumbia,* and even the ballad and the bossa nova. This creative freedom, fruit of the independence that, as has been said, was proposed from the 1960s by musicians such as Willie Colón and Eddie Palmieri, carries the movement to its full maturity just when, as a business, the exploitation of the Cuban repertoire is beginning to exhaust itself. What, then, is the true "salsa?": that of these musicians or that of the remake? Are we to consider equally as salsa "Mata Siguaraya," popularized by Benny Moré in the 1950s and recovered in the 1970s; "Tiburón" by Blades; "Calle Luna, Calle Sol," by Colón; or the quasi-anthropological and sadly ephemeral work with Caribe rhythms by the unforgettable Grupo Folklórico y Experimental Nuevayorquino?

Nine: "Ojalá que llueva café"

As a commercial product, salsa enters the decade of the 1980s in a deep crisis that even ended up toppling the Fania empire. The indiscriminate creation of "stars," orchestras, and records could only be sustained through a standardization of the products, which can work for a time, but not all the time. The support that the dancers and music lovers lent to the movement—when it was considered a novelty to listen once again to those old hits—is definitively exhausted, and only the most gifted of the players in the big business manage to stay afloat. With equal ease, the crisis does away with Celia Cruz and the Venezuelan Oscar D'León, who made part of his career by reviving the old repertoire, style, and even the stage presence of Benny Moré. It affects Pacheco the musician, Pacheco the producer, and the dozens of orchestras he inspired. The jug went to the well one time too many and ended up shattering, opening up the floodgates to release, in all its force, that which theretofore had been excluded: Dominican merengue. Johnny Ventura and Wilfrido Vargas quickly became the stars of the moment, and although they've also been called *"salseros,"* this time the pigeonholing was of no avail.

But other options had to be found and some new voices—not always good ones, by the way—picked up the salsa banner and gave it a last name: *salsa erótica*. This modality, halfway between the bolero and a *son* of lamentations, was exclusively dedicated to singing about love, with a more straightforward proposition than what was customary and from the perspective of a "star" who occupied the entire stage, relegating to the background the richness of the musical execution. For them, at least, the business stayed afloat.

However, true salsa had not lost the fight. One salsa—the simplified version, if it even was salsa—had become exhausted, along with the possibility of accommodating so many people. One style was in crisis: the one that repeated a catchy refrain ad nauseam. A business was in crisis: that of giving *"más salsa que pescao."* What was left, then, to validate salsa, to prove its existence, to save the novel and authentic elements that coexisted with the business and the remake?

An important displacement occurs in the 1980s—and continues to this day—in the world of the most authentic salsa, and it has had much to do with the permanence and definitive consolidation of the movement: the center (New York) lost its preeminence, and the periphery (Caracas, San Juan, Santo Domingo, Barranquilla, Cali, and even poor Havana) jumped into the forefront, contributing voices and figures, propositions and styles that were openly "salsa-ish" and that complemented, without a doubt, the circle that the movement has traced. While in New York, Willie Colón, Blades, Palmieri, and other "vanguards" continued to fight the good fight, in Puerto Rico, for example, groups such as El Gran Combo and la Sonora Ponceña were making a more traditional music that was nevertheless elaborated with modern propositions and that brought with it all the strength of a salsa capable of feeding off all the sounds of the Caribbean. Meanwhile, in Venezuela, the greatest consumer of salsa in the region, the salsa groups were multiplying to the point of dominating the musical landscape of the country.

In Cuba, meanwhile, musicians who had been widely recorded but to little acclaim, such as Juan Formell and Adalberto Álvarez, become the focal point for the dancers of the region thanks to a promotion that allowed them, finally, to transcend the borders of the island with their orchestras and their music. The Cubans—especially Adalberto Álvarez—then begin an intelligent process of approaching the salsa sound and bring to their *son*—the original from before, now so impoverished—the phrasing, aesthetic perspectives, and even the onstage behavior patented by salsa in a process of remodeling—more mulatto-izing—that allowed them to escape the iron grip of the old Cuban tradition.

Another country of the region, Colombia, has been the setting of the most vigorous expansion of salsa in the last ten years. In quintessentially Caribbean cities such as Cartagena and Barranquilla, salsa has acquired an extraordinary strength, while in Cali, closer to the Pacific than to the Caribbean basin, an especially noteworthy figure such as Joe Arroyo, creator of the "joesón," has achieved an important fusion of the black Cali rhythms with the melodic pattern of *son,* thus carrying out an important revitalization within the movement. In addition to Arroyo, groups such as Niche, created and directed by Jairo Varela, or the Guayacán orchestra—a spin-off of the former—have begun, for their part, to synthesize of the country's folkloric music with the habitual salsa models in an experiment whose fruits can be seen in the very acceptance these groups have achieved outside their local ambit—even in the United States and Europe.

At the same time, in a place barely touched by salsa, such as Miami, a Cuban musician who has lived in that city since childhood, Willie Chirino, has opened up a space for himself in this history with an oeuvre that is completely unprejudiced with respect to the diverse musical modalities it employs: from *son*—played as *son,* and played very well, by the way—to merengue, *plena,* and rock, thus creating a music that, in addition to its significant poetic value, once again works the miracle of melding together in one plane all the musical potential of the Caribbean, starting with the national model with which he has identified himself: once again, *son.*

In Santo Domingo, as the last and greatest example, harvesting the fruits of the merengue explosion, the lyrical teachings of new Cuban song, his command of jazz and certain traditional models revitalized by the commercial salsa boom, a figure such as Juan Luis Guerra has managed to transform himself into the most sought-after personality of Caribbean dance music in the last three years, thanks to his "salsa-ish" conception of the influences that are wisely combined in his rhythms—*la bachata,* earlier known as the *bolero-son*—and in his lyrics, which once again sing to the barrio, to the country, to the entire Caribbean, from his *"pueblo enano,"* his "tiny country," with a music that openly takes up his social commitment. Like Rubén Blades or Willie Colón, Juan Luis Guerra has also known that the forces of the market can be a drag on creativity if they are not constantly challenged: his albums are the products of such challenges, in a constant search for novel forms of musical expression and of texts that, each and every time, will communicate new ideas, feelings, and worries.

FIFTH OPINION

I think salsa has had highs and lows. I have great respect for the first generation, which made interesting contributions. I'm talking about Rubén Blades and Willie Colón and their record *Siembra,* which is one of the masterpieces of the movement, as well as Cheo Feliciano, Eddie Palmieri, Papo Lucca with la Sonora Ponceña, and Oscar D'León. I think that was a respectable body of work, where music was always the protagonist of important social and cultural events. Later, due to commercial pressures, there was a tendency in erotic salsa where you couldn't tell who was arranging or who was singing. . . . Fortunately, however, I think now we're getting back to that bold music which is true salsa. And proof that this is happening is that many people who made their fortune from erotic salsa have disappeared. . . . But people still prefer how El Gran Combo plays, how Willie Rosario's orchestra plays; they like to see a *timbal* solo by Tito Puente, a piano solo by Eddie Palmieri, with the musician giving his all and making the most of his talents. And that he's putting salsa on what he's making.

—Adalberto Álvarez

Ten: "Toma chocolate, paga lo que debes"

A definitive verdict? Salsa exists. It exists, as has been said, in a new form of expressing a new reality, in a creative appropriation of the entire musical patrimony of the Caribbean, and, of course, in the work of "different" musicians such as Willie Colón, Eddie Palmieri, Papo Lucca, Rubén Blades, and many others. It exists, finally, in the acceptance and incorporation of a new generation of Cuban musicians of more than ample talent who, after introducing their works, have managed to materialize their presence in the Caribbean ambit. It exists, as Willie Colón affirms, as an idea, a concept, and a perspective.

But it has also existed, in spite of the laments, as a fashion, a big business, capable of rechristening an entire extensive musical tradition with the name of "salsa," as old *sones, bombas,* and *cumbias* have been presented during these years.

Lacking a nomenclature, salsa nevertheless has a literature; without being a new rhythm, salsa has, without a doubt, a different sound; without possessing a unique and all-encompassing formula, salsa has the chameleonic property of transfiguring an entire tradition, and the capacity of uniting it all, acclimating it to a contemporary perspective.

But there are, in the final analysis, more than ten reasons and innumerable opinions to believe or not believe in the existence of salsa, twenty-five years after the fact: it all depends on how credulous or incredulous one happens to be.